D0070353

Being and Loving

Being and Loving

Revised Edition

ALTHEA J. HORNER, PH.D.

JASON ARONSON INC.
Northvale, New Jersey
London

Copyright © 1990, 1986, 1978 by Althea Horner

10 9 8 7 6 5 4 3 2 1

All rights reserved. Printed in the United States of America. No part of this book may be used or reproduced in any manner whatsoever without written permission from Jason Aronson Inc. except in the case of brief quotations in reviews for inclusion in a magazine, newspaper, or broadcast.

Library of Congress Cataloging-in-Publication Data

Horner, Althea J.
    Being and loving / Althea J. Horner.—Rev. ed.
        p.   cm.
    Includes bibliographical references.
    ISBN 0-87668-774-5
    1. Identity (Psychology) 2. Intimacy (Psychology)
3. Developmental psychology. I. Title.
    BF697.H56   1990
158—dc20   90-33413
                                                                CIP

Manufactured in the United States of America. Jason Aronson Inc. offers books and cassettes. For information and catalog write to Jason Aronson Inc., 230 Livingston Street, Northvale, New Jersey 07647.

To My Family

CONTENTS

INTRODUCTION

I HAVE UNDERTAKEN this revision of *Being and Loving* as a new decade is about to begin. The first edition was written in the 1970s, the so-called "Me Decade." This era itself was a precipitate of the social revolutions of the 1960s. The overthrow of institutional constraints held out promises of self-fulfillment and self-realization, promises that all too often failed to materialize. Meanwhile, little of substance came to take the place of values that had been discarded.

In the 1980s, a wave of materialism developed, with the yuppies leading the way. It was a decade of frenzied consumption and the accumulation of debt. The drug scourge, the Black Plague of the modern era, which began as part of the 1960s revolution, today draws on a philosophy of marketable happiness, while people turn to television for a peek at the *Lifestyles of the Rich and Famous*. At the same time, the fads of the "new age," a striving for spirituality, tried to fill the gap left by the rejection of organized religion.

But the stock market crash of 1987 burst the bubble of many who were riding high on a crest of newfound wealth. The individual and social destructiveness of substance abuse can no longer be denied. And the high cost of living has propelled many women into the work force, not for some mythical fulfillment, but to help pay off the mortgage, or to put bread on the table. With the demise of the extended family, child care is increasingly being turned over to day-care facilities, to successions of baby-sitters, or to a nanny, our most recent import from abroad. The mental health professionals of the twenty-first century will be writing about the long-term effects of these changes in the family on today's children.

It is predicted[1] that the 1990s will be seen in restrospect as the halcyon days, when the baby boomers will be wrestling with decisions of where to send their kids to college, and how to balance work and family. It is hypothesized that with their move into middle age, there may be an era of stability and normalcy reminiscent of the 1950s, that the dominant themes of the 1990s will be raising families, quality-of-life concerns, and high productivity at work. More and more, people are likely to work at home or on flexible schedules. Personal, home, and child-rearing services will continue to burgeon. "The key social issues for baby boomers [in the 1990s] will be education, dependent care, aging parents, quality of life, and the environment. . . ." And, it is also speculated, "as many more individuals struggle with such 'fortysomething' issues as physical decline and unsatisfying jobs . . . individual frustrations could add up to a collective midlife crisis" (p. 143).

It is also noted that as generations age, community and family values often become more important. Some predict that the aging boomers will grow more conservative—particularly parents—because of the dangers of AIDS and drug abuse, and the decade is already being dubbed the "no-no '90s."

With such massive changes in the social structure, can we

[1]How the Next Decade Will Differ. *Business Week* (September 25, 1989), p. 142.

find eternal values and verities to sustain us emotionally and spiritually? With all that has taken place over the past three decades, I hear certain unchanging themes in my clinical practice—a struggle to find a solid and valued sense of self, and a yearning for intimacy and commitment. The removal of barriers to sexual expression has not helped in either arena. Women who opted for careers on a path of promised self-realization are confronted with the reality of their biological clock, and some, almost frantically, are seeking to retrieve what was rebelliously discarded. But in so doing, they do not want to return to the era of self-abnegation that characterized the role of women in earlier eras. And their male counterparts are loath to take on the economic burden of present-day living single-handedly. They want partners to help them along. The concept of "we" has been modified to encompass the individualities of partners as well as their common goals and values. Perhaps now, more than ever, there is a socially sanctioned opportunity for both *being* and *loving*, for both identity and intimacy. Role assignment and social sanction ignored the importance of an authentic identity for the individual. They were replaced by a philosophy of "if it feels good, do it!" The antithesis now comes together in a new synthesis, a synthesis that has been too long coming and, unfortunately, even in a favorable social climate, is still not that easy to achieve.

I have used the terms *being* and *loving* in a particular way: to denote the desired end points of a developmental process that begins at the very start of life. Loving does not refer only to the momentary overflowing of good feeling toward someone else. It entails an emotional attachment to another human being, one predicated not only on one's dependency needs, but also on one's valuing and cherishing the other as the real person he or she is. Positive emotional feelings predominate in spite of occasional conflict. It is an attachment that is constant over time and circumstance. Love does not disappear when there is separation. Love does not die when there is anger.

Being refers to that clear and uninterrupted sense of "I am.

I exist. I go on." It is the capacity to experience oneself as a separate, real, and whole human being. The self-perception of the individual who has this capacity involves neither overidealization nor undeserved contempt. There is a realistic acceptance and integration of the many diverse qualities that characterize any real person.

The conflicts and fears that inevitably arise over the earliest years of psychological development and that get in the way of both sense of self and emotional intimacy still make their voices heard. Indeed, the more things change, the more they stay the same. Whatever the impact of social change on the development of today's children, the effects are likely to be felt in these same two areas, those of being and of loving, and will be reflected, for better or worse, in both health and pathology. The barriers to the wished-for experience of the "we" continue, and most likely will continue in the future as well, to plague and frustrate many people. This book addresses those barriers in the hope that confronting them and struggling past them will enable some to achieve a new synthesis: a self able to love, to commit, and to share, and, in the spirit of generativity (Erikson 1952), to pass these capacities on to the next generation.

In this new edition of *Being and Loving* I have integrated newer insights into the development of identity and the capacity for intimacy. These insights draw upon an ever-growing body of clinical and observational data, including the input of the child who is born with a genetically endowed temperament and hard-wired propensities to express its own individuality as well as to seek attachment to its caretaker, although these propensities may, unfortunately, be overridden later on by an environment that does not nurture them. I have also included the developmental impact of abuse, particularly sexual abuse, dark secrets that are increasingly coming into the light of scrutiny.

Being and loving—will they facilitate each other or will

they come to be experienced as mutually exclusive? In the following chapters I will explore their genesis in normal development and the barriers to their expression in adult relationships.

Being and Loving

1

BEING VERSUS LOVING: THE CORE CONFLICT

CAL HAS BEEN married three times and has had numerous affairs. Drawn by a yearning for warmth and closeness, for the approving smile of a woman who really understands him, he enters into each new relationship with all the elation and excitement of falling in love. Her adoration and excitement make him feel wonderful about himself, and he loves her for doing that for him. He appreciates her appreciation, and she, for a time, feels loved in return. But as the relationship progresses and the woman expresses her own needs or wishes, Cal becomes irritated by what he experiences as her demands. He feels burdened and controlled by them and is angry at her failure to meet his own emotional demands without question and with a smile. Eventually, the warmth and intimacy that he sought, and thought he had found, are replaced by annoyance and resentment at a relationship that seems to deprive him of his independence and what he experiences as his right to have what he needs when he needs it. As he sees it, he cannot be himself if he gets too close. He feels in danger of being overpowered by the self of his partner.

Elizabeth has always been proud of her capacity to adapt. As a child, when she moved from city to city because of her father's job, she would look over the new situation at school, size up how she would have to act to fit in, and then easily slide into the social niche she picked out for herself. Later, this capacity to adapt had helped her play the roles laid out for her as the wife of a rising young business executive and had enabled her to accept crises and problems that had come along over the years as part of marriage. Furthermore, she felt most soft and feminine when she was in a yielding mode. Her mother had always said, with some pleasure, what an easy child Elizabeth had been, and her father smiled his approval as well. She never made waves the way her sister did.

But now after years of being a dutiful wife, concerned mother, and active in community improvement projects, her world seemed to be crumbling. One evening Bob told her that he wanted a divorce. He was involved with another woman who was younger, vibrant, and exciting. Faced with the frightening prospect of being alone, and having no idea what she wanted to do with the rest of her life, Elizabeth turned to a women's support group. Most of them were around her age, in their fifties, part of an earlier generation that had accepted the roles that were assigned to them, believing in the "happy ever after" that went with their acceptance. Like Elizabeth, they had begun to struggle with notions of identity and self assertion. But they all worried that those notions would take them on a path of loneliness.

Sara and Leon have been married just over five years. Part of the younger generation, while still planning their marriage, they agreed that Sara would continue to work full time, not for the added income, but for Sara's sake as a person in her own right. She was adamant about not ending up like her mother, who had given up her dreams to raise a family. Now both she and Leon have positions at the managerial level in their professions. Intelligent, attractive, and successful, they would seem to be a perfect match for each other. But their weekends alone are a disaster. When one feels sociable or sexual, the other is too involved in some important project to respond. When one is in a playful mood, the other is depressed. In effect, when one says "Come close," the other says "Go away," and vice versa. They have an unconscious pact not to endanger each other's autonomy and they take turns expressing the wish for closeness and defending against its felt dangers. They each complain of chronic dissatisfaction with the other, but neither is able to break the stalemate, as that would disturb their uneasy homeostasis.

What we see in the cases of Calvin, Elizabeth, and Sara and Leon are examples of one of the fundamental conflicts of human nature: the conflict between being and loving, which is so often expressed, "How can I achieve love and intimacy with another person without losing my own sense of self, my own identity and independence?"

Many, in fact most people, to some extent, attempt to resolve the conflict by sacrificing one to safeguard the other. As in the case of Calvin, some will push away love when it seems to threaten either the existence or the well-being of the self. Others, like Elizabeth, sacrifice their identity or independence in order to preserve an important emotional relationship, while people like Sara and Leon seem unable to move in either direction and remain trapped in their own ambivalence.

None of these solutions is very satisfactory and they are made at a cost that is high in anxiety, loneliness, depression, or frustration and the anger that goes with it. For many of these men and women true love remains elusive.

But what does *love* mean? It certainly has different meanings for different people. It may be used to signify a variety of emotional attachments, or perhaps just a momentary mood state. Some believe the needy possessiveness of another person to be a manifestation of love. Some will say "I love you" to anyone who makes them feel absolutely wonderful about themselves. Others will say "I love you" in the afterglow of good sex with its unique experience of oneness.

In the sense that love is used here, it is not familial love between parents and children or between brothers or sisters. It is used here to signify the newer love of adult life, a love that supersedes those earlier relationships but which also often carries their stamp. A healthy and mature love entails the realization that love is not a threat to the self, to one's sense of who one is, to one's boundaries or one's autonomy, or something to be bargained for and received in exchange for the core of one's personhood. It involves the capacity to give and care for another in a manner that does not entail the sacrifice of one's identity.

When we applaud, we know that our hands are separate. Yet they come together in a common enterprise in such a way that we cannot tell which hand claps and which is clapped. The sound they produce can exist only because of the readiness of each to engage the other without concern for which does which.

This is the nature of true love and intimacy, which can only exist between two people whose sense of their own individual separateness and wholeness is secure enough to enable each to engage the other fully, with no fear of loss of self and without concern for who gives and who receives. There is an ebb and flow of mutuality in which each person is aware of self and, at the same time, sensitive to the self of the other.

Few of us realize this ideal perfectly, for it rests upon foundations laid down in the formative first three years of life. Development is inherently conflictual and it is almost inevitable that some derivative of these early conflicts or developmental dilemmas will surface later in life when the individual moves toward an adult intimate relationship. The more compromised these earliest stages of development, the greater will be the conflict between being and loving.

During the crucial first three years, the primary mothering person must care for and respond to the child in such a way as to facilitate the establishment of the attachment bond, the emotional connection with the principal caretaker that is the basis for the capacity to love. The benevolence of this connection also engenders what Erikson (1952) calls *basic trust*. At the other extreme, if this period is experienced by the infant as frightening and unsafe, a persecutory, paranoid core will form where basic trust should be.

Just as the mother must promote a benevolent attachment, she must be as ready to promote and lovingly support individuation, the child's process of becoming a separate and unique individual. This loving support is the basis for a later security in the belief that "I can be myself without losing love."

But given the imperfectibility of the world and of the men and women who live in it, our parents may have been unable, unwilling, or just too preoccupied with the other demands of their adult life to provide such careful nurturing of our delicate psyches. From the child's side of the equation, there is an ambivalence intrinsic to growing up. For every step forward, something must be given up, and this built-in conflict makes it difficult for even the healthiest of parents at times. Furthermore, we are social beings, and unless we live as hermits on a mountaintop, we must find a way to be in the world without doing damage either to ourselves or to others. The balance between self and other, between the individual and the group, is a difficult one to maintain. The extent to which we succeed in adult life in achieving true love and intimacy and commitment depends to a large degree on how we deal with problems left over from the very earliest years of life.

The fact that most of us as children differed with respect to the vigor and persistence of self-expressive behavior adds further to our adult conflict between being and loving. Persons like Elizabeth who adapted without protest while growing up were likely to have been viewed as "good" children. As adults, however, they may well find themselves struggling with issues of identity. Adults who as children protested and fought for what they wanted were very likely to have been labeled as bad. They may still be paying the price of loss of love or social isolation. Under interpersonal stress, some children cling anxiously, others strike out, and still others withdraw. These innate temperamental differences affect different parents differently, and constitute one aspect of the child's side of the equation in its own development.

Along with the quality of parenting and our innate temperamental predispositions, the demands of the developmental process itself, the nature of the family structure, religion, and wider social and cultural values all contribute both to our healthy development and to our conflict.

Although a stable and interpersonally benevolent family is the ideal setting for the development of both the capacity to be and the capacity to love, some families, headed by parents who themselves have problems and unresolved conflicts with respect to these very issues, develop mechanisms for blocking the emergence of individuality in their members because this individuality is viewed as a threat to the stability and continued existence of the family as a unit.

Consider an adolescent boy whose interests have quite normally moved from the family to the world of peers and who is labeled selfish for wanting to go to a party rather than staying at home for a family barbecue. His father tells him he is spoiling the family's good time. As a result, the boy is beset by guilt that, in turn, inhibits his efforts to graduate out of the family and to make a life of his own as a man. For him, love is won at the sacrifice of autonomy. He will think more than twice before having a family of his own when he grows up. He will leave relationships when he is expected to make a commitment.

Even more subtle and powerful are covert threats of emotional abandonment. Doris is a 32-year-old executive secretary who lives alone and who suffers from periodic bouts of depression.

When she was 13 she was invited for the first time to spend the night at the home of her girl friend. She phoned her mother to tell her this and to say that she would be home the following morning. Her mother replied:

"Who is this?"

"It's Doris."

"I can't hear you. Who is speaking?"

"It's Doris. Your daughter."

"I'm sorry. I still can't hear you."

Discouraged, Doris, who had been practically shouting, mumbled, "Never mind. I'll come home," to which her mother cheerfully replied, "I'll see you in a little while, darling."

This nonrecognition by her mother as soon as Doris attempted to define herself as separate was a threat to the girl's very feelings of existence. So powerful was it that it pulled Doris back within the confines of the family and prevented any further healthy assertion of her self as a separate and autonomous individual. Doris had been subjected to this kind of covert control from the earliest years of her life, so she never developed the sure sense of self that might enable her to oppose her mother in the adolescent years. The rest of the family aided and abetted the system by showing disapproval whenever she questioned her mother's perfection as a parent. Her sense of reality was not confirmed, further undermining her sense of self.

Despite the failure of many families to foster healthy development in their children, the challenge lies in addressing and correcting the failure itself rather than doing away with the family as an institution. The nuclear family is becoming more of the exception than the rule, however, and alternate forms of child rearing may, in many instances, make the development of the capacities to be and to love even more problematic. Certainly, if these two threads of human life are deemed important, the setting up of alternative forms of child care must tend to the necessities of their formation.

For some people, the conflict between being and loving resulting from growth-inhibiting family systems has been intensified by their religious upbringing. Religious teachings concerning moral and ethical obligations necessarily impose upon the self certain constraints with regard to other people and to one's community. Social values, in many cases, have been overthrown in favor of individual values in the past three decades, and not always for the good. In some instances, religious teaching has contributed to the anxiety and guilt associated with experiencing those aspects of self that conflict with the rules and values of one's faith. This has been particularly true of sexuality, and the sexual revolution did its best to throw off those constraints. Whatever their origin, when sexual guilt or anxiety is sufficiently severe, a vital component of the self must be cut off, denied, or repressed— ultimately at the cost of one's sense of wholeness.

Beyond certain problems sometimes generated within the family, wider social attitudes and values aggravate the early developmental conflict between being and loving. This has been particularly true with respect to male and female role expectations. While in some countries this situation still exists to an extreme degree, such as in Japan, there have been significant changes in American society, although these changes are not universal and have not been completely assimilated by many men and women who have grown up during the era of change. Younger individuals seem less bound by these disparities than their older brothers and sisters. The women's movement coincided with the main thrust of the 1960s and 1970s. In giving up the passive compliance demanded by their role as it used to be defined, they have also had to give up the expectation that they would be taken care of. Equality means pitching in with the economic demands the world makes upon the family today. As in growing up, something must be relinquished along with the gains and opportunities of maturity. The net effect of the waning of role definition seems to be more overt struggle going on between men and women with respect to being and loving, with fewer individuals ready to resign their individuality in order to secure an emotional attachment. Perhaps this has something to do with the large numbers of men and women who seem unable to find the mate they say they want to share life with. They are wary of the cost of commitment to themselves individually.

Although men have traditionally held greater social, economic, and political power, both in and out of the family, they have the same basic struggle and conflict with respect to being and loving. Perhaps they have a greater tendency to sacrifice loving for being as an outcome of the struggle of the little boy to escape his dependency on his mother by denying his loving relationship with her. The closeness with her may stand as a threat to his sense of maleness as well as to his need to live up to what is expected of him as a male. What can be worse for a little boy than to be teasingly called a mama's boy? On the other hand, a little girl will preen with pride when she is called daddy's little girl. Although she may turn away from mother in the service of her own individuation, there is no cultural demand that she do so. She may stay closer to mother longer. Mother's wish to keep her little daughter close may result in the child's sense that she may have to give up being—give up individuating—to keep mother's love.

In his sensitive short story "I Don't Need You Any More," Arthur Miller (1967) writes of a little boy who angrily spits these words at his mother in his attempt to extricate himself from the web of her overprotection. He wants desperately to be one of the men.

> And suddenly he remembered: "I don't need you any more!" His own words came back, shrill and red with fury. Why was that so terrible? He didn't need her. He could tie his laces now, he could walk forever without getting tired. . . . She didn't want him, why did he

have to pretend he wanted her? The horror in it escaped him. Still, it
probably was horrible anyway, only he didn't understand why. . . .
How fine it would be to sink into the ocean now, he thought. How she
would plead with his dead, shut-eyed face to say something. [p. 15]

Mr. Miller conveys beautifully the struggle for selfhood and
for manhood in this young boy–child, and shows how, in
anger at his mother's frustration of his wish to be, he denies to
her and to himself his need and love for her.

Men and women who shut themselves off from feelings of
warmth or love in order to protect the integrity of the self
ultimately come to feel deprived of those very experiences. The
experience of deprivation, in turn, generates anger. Pillow
pounding to get the rage out, as is the fashion in some therapy
situations, is an exercise in futility. What is at issue is not the
need to get in touch with the rage, which comes all too
readily, but the avoidance of attachment. The problem is new
here-and-now anger that continues to be generated as a result
of the self-induced deprivation. The death fantasy of Miller's
character is like many a suicidal fantasy of the angry individual
who denies attachment. "I don't need you any more!" is the
final scream of rage.

Whether it was the innate developmental conflict between
being and loving, the demands and expectations of family,
religion, or sex role assignment, the coming together of
diverse forces and pressures that oppose the achievement and
expression of a valued self created the counterforces of the
revolutions of the 1960s and the era of the Me Decade. The
slogan "If it feels good, do it," books such as *Looking Out for
Number One* or others that encouraged the individual to say no,
along with movements such as est that promised personal
power, stranded the readers and seekers in the developmental
position of the 2-year-old who discovers negativism as his or
her first conscious and deliberate vehicle for self assertion.

Rollo May (1969) comments, ". . . autonomy and freedom cannot be the domain of a special part of the organism,

but must be a quality of the total self—the thinking-feeling-choosing-acting organism" (p. 199). This is the essence of identity, of the sense of self that implies an integration of the many different facets of one's personality. When the wish and longing for love and intimacy are denied, there can be no such integration. When identity is inaccessible or when the real self must be kept in a secret psychological sanctuary, there can be no such integration. When living is a series of reactions to others rather than an expression of that which is inherently and intrinsically part of the self, there can be no such integration. Saying no will not be enough to assure us that we can, indeed, be masters of our own fate. The goal is to have the freedom to say yes without losing one's sense of self or one's autonomy, for true intimacy involves both yes and no.

There are certain inevitable restrictions on our spontaneity simply because we are social beings who must live within an organized society. To the extent that we exercise even common courtesy or consideration for others, we are not always being fully spontaneous. We also limit our spontaneity on the basis of the realistic consequences of its expression. One may not think well of the boss, but will choose to inhibit those thoughts in the interest of keeping the job. We do not act upon every wish and impulse. Even so, we hope that we can still *feel* real, remain in touch with our experience and our own identity, and maintain a firm sense of our own psychological boundaries.

Access to the real rather than the reactive self is the sine qua non for being, and without it loving and intimacy are impossible. When only the reactive self participates in a relationship, the real self remains isolated and lonely. The suicide of the man who has everything may sometimes be an expression of that despair.

There are no quick and easy solutions to the dilemma presented by the equally powerful but often antithetical drives for intimacy and identity—for loving and being. Some people deny the yearning for attachment. Others renounce the self. In the best of all possible worlds, each of us would be able to achieve both and to give up neither. Although it offers no simple solutions, this book hopes to enable you to strive, however imperfectly, for ways to resolve your own personal conflict.

The first step in solving the problem of attaining this best of all possible worlds is to define it, to know it, to see where the stumbling places are along the way, to articulate those choices that will have to be made, and to decide what will have to be left behind as well as what is being sought.

Looking back to the very start of life at the developmental path we all have had to follow during the critical, formative years not only sheds light on the origins of the problem as it exists for any one of us today, but also foreshadows what is to come, what we must do to resolve our dilemma, for all the steps toward this best of all possible worlds are originally laid out in the first three or four years of our psychological development. Some lucky individuals make the trip the first time. Some may get stuck in some cul-de-sac along the way, and even as men and women, continue to struggle with the unresolved conflicts. Looking back is a necessary and integral part of moving ahead.

2

WHY LOOK BACK?

UNDERSTANDING HOW CERTAIN aspects of the past have left their mark does not necessarily change the quality of one's life. Explanations such as "I never developed self-confidence because my father was always criticizing me," or "I was afraid to speak by own mind because my mother was so domineering" can be reassuring insofar as they offer a rationale and justification for self-defeating attitudes and behaviors or for anger and righteous indignation. But such partial insights alone do not help. This fact has led some psychotherapists to dismiss the value of insight overall. They may favor techniques of self-discovery that rely upon the experience of the moment. With an emphasis on the here and now, there may even be a prohibition on the search for understanding.

It is certainly true that since the past is memory and the future is hope (or dread), this moment in time is the only one we really ever have. It is also true that the past may be used to avoid looking at the present, to protect ourselves from an awareness of immediate pain or conflict, or from the anxieties inherent in change. Blaming our parents is also more comfortable than facing answers to "what is there about my

character, my psychological makeup—the ways in which I
relate, the assumptions I make about myself and others, the
expectations I hold, the meanings I assign to what I experience, the self-deception I practice—that contributes to the
continuation of my unhappiness?"

To understand our basic personality structure in a way that
will enable real change to take place, we need to know what
formative processes led to that structure, to make sense of it,
to reevaluate our child's perception and understanding with
out adult mind, and to see how the inner world constructed by
that child continues to direct us in the present. Our present
ways of experiencing and defining ourselves in various relationships and circumstances are an outgrowth of our earliest
experiences in the world of humans. What we experience today
takes its meaning from the total context of our lives, not just
from the here and now. Our reactions to events in our lives are
based not only on objective facts but also on the meanings we
give to what we experience.

Suppose you are a woman of 32 who met an attractive man
at a singles club two weeks ago. He said he would call. He
didn't. What meaning do you assign to these objective facts?

Do you think, "I can't trust anyone to follow through on a
promise"?

Do you begin to obsess about what can be wrong with you
that drives people away?

Do you expect people to be exploitative and assume he was
just manipulating you to make himself feel good?

Do you approach things from a practical and realistic
position and assume that he must be just as busy as you are?

Perhaps there is another explanation that comes to your
mind. What is it? Does it fit your characteristic way of
understanding relationships?

Each one of these interpretations can be directly related to
a generalized feeling about the self and others.

Limited understanding of cause and effect, a tendency to
think concretely and egocentrically, and a very limited capac-

ity to understand how others work psychologically make a child prone to distorted conclusions about the self and about others that persist as the core of our basic premises for adult life. To try to change only within the context of the here and now necessitates denial of the existence not only of conclusions of childhood but of the effects of the rational superstructure that was designed to fit and corroborate these conclusions and developed by a person over a lifetime. The here and now manifestations of the conflicts of early childhood are called derivatives, and to work only with derivatives is like looking at a smudge on your nose in a mirror and trying to remove the smudge by polishing your image in the glass. Meaning is embedded in the original experience and needs to be deciphered within that context.

Looking back and reviewing the evidence, as it were, enables an adult to understand how his or her psychological makeup came about and how it had survival value for the helpless child of the past. Children do whatever they can to create conditions of emotional safety and a modicum of self-esteem, although these efforts may be, unfortunately, insufficient to counter a hurtful environment. And even when these efforts worked during childhood, they usually prove to be not only ineffective but detrimental to adult living and relating.

In psychotherapy, adult intellect, strength, and understanding are brought to bear upon meanings constructed before one had language or logic, often with the result that the relationship between present experience and developmental forerunners becomes fairly obvious. This is especially true when the early events took place within the time of conscious memory.

Lisa could not understand why she had been experiencing a wave of anxiety for the past few weeks. Everything was going well in her life and she was looking forward to the free time she would have now that her 5-year-old son would be going to school. She was even considering taking a part-time job. Tomorrow was to be Paul's first day of school and he was looking forward to it. Nevertheless, Lisa kept looking at him, searching for the hidden anxiety she assumed to be there. As she became aware of what was going on in her own head, she realized that her anxiety of the past weeks had been stirred up by her identification with her little boy. It was as though this were to be *her* first day of school, and she experienced herself once again as a little girl who had not wanted to be separated from her mother. She suspected that this had something to do with her procrastination in checking out job opportunities as well. Her present anxiety could be viewed as a feeling memory of the early situation with all of its conflicts and anxiety.

There are similar types of feeling memory that come from the more remote past, from what Margaret Mahler (1975) calls "the bedrock of mental life that does not divulge its content and nature by verbal means—the 'unrememberable and the unforgettable'" (p. 197). More recently, Bollas (1987) has called this experience "the unthought known."

These archaic memory-experiences are often not based upon a single event but are built upon repetitive experiences whose fundamental quality permeated the early years of life. Because they are rooted in a time before there was language and thus before experience could be articulated and remembered as such, they seem to be totally irrational and even "crazy" when relived by persons who know themselves to be rational and competent adults. They may involve not only feelings such as anxiety or foreboding, but even unexplained perceptual shifts. I have known some individuals who, when these early memories were activated, experienced the room as becoming much larger, much as it would have looked when they were very small, perhaps confined behind the bars of a crib.

Ginnie often experienced a vague apprehension that something she enjoyed would be taken away from her. The very fact that the fear was irrational upset her even more. Through therapy she was led to recognize clearly the frustration and despair she had experienced in infancy and childhood when she was not responded to in terms of her own needs and rhythms. Feeding, love, and affection had been given her, but her parents had imposed on her their own timetables and tastes. Often, for example, the nipple had been taken from her mouth while she was still hungry or needing to suck. This pattern in which she had to adapt to her parents' wishes, needs, and rhythms continued throughout Ginnie's growing years. What went on in her interaction with her parents seemed to have little or nothing to do with her own state of being. She and her environment were always out of sync.

When, in therapy, Ginnie's vague apprehension could be related to her earliest experiences of this nature, it became possible to tease it apart from the realities of her adult experience and understand it in terms of its origin. She could understand the belief system that had evolved to explain this fundamental aspect of her unrememberable and unforgettable early experience. Ginnie could have compassion for the little girl she once was and for the child's way of coping by attempting to comply and to please and to see how similar behavior in present-day relationships was based upon old anxieties. She could understand that what seemed to be something irrational in her made great sense in the light of her own history. In the context of her relationship with her therapist, she began to risk not complying and not pleasing and by so doing, began to learn more about who she really was and to bring that self into other relationships as well. As she became more authentically herself, her relationships became more rewarding.

As I wrote earlier, understanding how we got to be the way we are will not automatically make things better. It can provide foundation and direction, but if we are truly to grow and change we must commit ourselves to the process with all its inherent dangers. We must struggle against our own archaic paranoia, our sadism, our drive for vengeance, and our envy, as well as our wish to retreat to the safety of mother's arms. At the same time, we must make an effort to renounce the magic of our fantasied omnipotence and face the fact that we are merely human.

In the next chapter we will look back at the path we have all traveled since birth, particularly that of the first three years of life. This is the period when what Margaret Mahler calls the psychological birth of the human infant takes place. It is during these early years that a healthy and secure sense of self, the capacity to be, is consolidated. At the same time, the ability to relate to others as the real persons they are comes about. No longer are they valued simply because they meet one's need to be noticed or to be taken care of, or one's need for approval or validation. Thus *loving* develops hand in hand with *being*.

3

BECOMING ONE: THE BASIS FOR LOVING

Two souls with but a single thought,
Two hearts that beat as one.
                    Von Munch Bellinghausen

THE POET'S VISION of love as blissful union expresses the romantic dream of countless men and women. Plato wrote of the love between a man and a woman as a "meeting and melting into one another . . . becoming one instead of two. . . ." He explained this experience as an expression of an "ancient need . . . of something else which the soul of either evidently desires but cannot tell, of which [they have] only a dark and doubtful presentiment. . . ." (Symposium, p. 158).

What is this ancient need? What is the almost universal experience that lies at the core of this dark and doubtful presentiment? And why does awareness of a fantasy or wish for emotional union with another human being stir up fear or anger in the hearts of some instead of yearning and anticipation?

Without benefit of modern theories of child development, Plato intuited the early psychological unity of infant and mother which is subsequently lost and forgotten in the course of normal development. He sensed its relationship to the yearning of the adult for love as well. Unfortunately, for some men and women this ancient need presents a threat to

19

hard-won individuality and cannot be allowed into conscious experience.

Selma Fraiberg (1977) notes that the baby has the rudiments of a love language available to him or her. "There is the language of the embrace, the language of the eyes, the language of the smile, vocal communications of pleasure and distress. It is the essential vocabulary of love before we can speak of love" (p. 29). She remarks on the experience of the 18-year-old who falls in love, supposedly for the first time. In his declaration of love he will use such phrases as "When I first looked into your eyes," "When you smiled at me," "When I held you in my arms." Fraiberg notes whimsically, "And naturally, in his exalted state, he will believe that he invented this love song."

We are not born with the capacity to love, only with the potential for it (Bergmann 1971, pp. 15–40). Back at the very start of life, although there is an awareness of what is going on in the immediate surround, there is no recognition of either self or other, no *idea* or mental representation of self or other, and no conflict between being and loving. Life is a series of unconnected bodily and sensory-motor experiences that are yet to be woven into meaningful patterns that then become organized as enduring mental representations of a *me* and a *you*. The infant's colic is an alien force that disrupts its sense of ongoingness even though it comes from within its own body. The sensitive nurturing of the mother, who is in a state of what Winnicott (1975, pp. 300–305) calls "primary maternal preoccupation," is as though it is a part of the self, inasmuch as it supports the infant's experience of its own ongoingness.

By the time the infant is 4 to 5 months of age, however, one notices a special smile and a general state of excitement and pleasure in response to the mother or to the main caretaking person. A special relationship, the *primary attachment bond* (Bowlby 1969, p. 177), has been formed with her, and it is within the context of this relationship that the child will organize his or her segments of experience into patterns, which eventually will include other people and feelings about them. These feelings will include an attitude of basic trust (Erikson 1963) toward the interpersonal world or, under unsatisfactory conditions, one of basic distrust which, in the extreme, may take the form of paranoia. This special relationship or primary attachment bond, thus, plays a very important role in the mental life of the developing infant. It constitutes the foundation of the capacity to love and also marks the point of departure from which the emergence of the self as an entity, understood consciously by the child to be separate from the mother, will soon take place.

THE ATTACHMENT PROCESS AND THE CAPACITY TO LOVE

The attachment process, which entails the participation and contribution of both mother and child, starts on the first day of life. A newborn child can be observed scanning the face of the caretaking adult, finally fixing on his or her eyes. This eye-to-eye contact is the beginning of the ongoing psychological dialogue between mother and child, which will eventuate in that special bond between them. Rene Spitz (1965) refers to this mother–child interaction as mutual cuing.

Many mothers naturally respond to the infant's search for eye contact by returning the baby's look and talking or making cooing sounds, thus reinforcing the child's innate attachment behavior. Other mothers may respond less readily and talk on the phone or read while feeding the baby. When this occurs, even a breast-fed baby can be deprived of the dialogue that builds attachment and, eventually, the capacity to love. On the other hand, many mothers who bottle-feed their babies provide this dialogue. The interpersonal interaction is more important for this aspect of psychological development than is the actual source of the milk.

The inherent nature of attachment-seeking behavior and the consequences of the failure of the environment to support formation of the bond are elucidated by research and clinical evidence from both young animals and human children.

Harry Harlow's (1964, pp. 154–173) experiments in the 1950s and 1960s demonstrated not only that attachment-seeking behavior is innate in the baby rhesus monkey, but that the interaction between mother and infant is essential to the baby's capacity to relate normally to its own species. In Harlow's experiments, a variety of mechanical substitutes for real mothers were provided the baby monkeys. Some were made of wire and mesh, some of terry cloth; some were warm and some were not; some had bottles attached for nursing while others had none.

Although the ability of the artificial mothers to give food via the bottles was obviously essential for the survival of the babies at one level, feeding alone was not enough to calm them when they were under stress. Under these circumstances they would cling to the terry-cloth mothers. At first the preference for the terry-cloth figures as soothers suggested that contact comfort was the essential psychological ingredient rather than being fed. But even with feeding and contact comfort these monkeys did not develop normally. Maternal response and the moment-to-moment interactions of considerable social complexity that go on between a live mother and her infant were found to be the sine qua non for normal development. When these deprived monkeys grew up, their own maternal behaviors were impaired. They were devoid of the capacity to care for or about their own babies. In fact, they were sometimes so abusive of them that the second generation of infants had to be separated from their real mothers for their own protection. Unloved babies could not grow up to be loving mothers. There is reason to believe that the same principle holds for human mothers.

STABILITY OF THE CARETAKING ENVIRONMENT

Observations of human children who had been placed in institutions during the first four years of life have also shed light on the importance of the early attachment bond with respect to the capacity to form lasting relationships. Children who had the opportunity to form an attachment before being placed did better, even though they experienced severe distress at the loss of the relationship, than did children who made no attachments at all. The effects of separation after the attachment bond has formed depend on a number of other factors, such as the quality of the relationship with the attachment figure before separation, and the quality of the environment and availability of new attachment figures after separation (Rutter 1974).

Children reared in institutions are often cared for by many different people. One immediate result of this may be the decrease in visual responsiveness by the second month of life in these institutionalized infants who have been deprived of the maternal reinforcement of eye contact described earlier in this chapter (Fantz 1966). Children raised in institutions are often described as clinging and dependent, and then attention-seeking and indiscriminate in whom they turn to. In other words, they will be friendly to anyone who will respond to them. These characteristics will probably be true in their adult life as well. Subsequent studies of these children suggest that if they *never* form an attachment in the first two or three years of life, it is highly unlikely that they will do so after that time. In general, they will relate to others chiefly to the degree that the other individual meets some immediate need.

Individuals who want to adopt a child who has had this kind of unfortunate beginning should be ready to understand and accept the child's impaired capacity to love. Their motivation should not be based on a fantasy or wish for a child to love *them*. If it is, inherent difficulties may generate not only disappointment but undeserved anger toward the child who does not respond in the manner not only wished for, but expected. Only if these adopting parents appreciate the hurt the child has suffered and its long-range consequences will they succeed in bringing out the best in their son or daughter. The teaching of sound and caring human values can, in part, compensate for the missing emotional piece if these values are inherent to the relationships within that family.

MOTHERING AND ATTACHMENT

In the earliest months of a child's life there must be, on the part of the mother, an intense psychological involvement with her infant if she is to promote formation of the attachment bond. In this period of primary maternal preoccupation (Winnicott 1975), the mother must be in harmony with her baby's rhythms, emotions, and physiological state. She must respond empathetically to what comes from the child, be it a cry or a smile. This focused attention and readiness to respond to the cue of the infant is referred to by Winnicott (1975) as a time-limited attitude. By this he means that it is appropriate only to this stage of the child's development. Although, one hopes, parents will always be willing to understand what and how their child feels, if this preoccupation were to continue beyond its age-appropriateness, they would interfere with later developmental necessities, such as the child's capacity to understand and value the separateness of others and what is important to *them*.

When he or she is about 4 or 5 months old, the baby has formed the primary attachment bond and has reached the stage referred to by some psychologist as that of normal symbiosis (Mahler et al. 1975). At this stage, mother and child are experienced as a single unit. There is no differentiation between *me* and *you*; only the single pattern, *me–you*. This stage of oneness is the basis of what Plato referred to as that ancient need of which we all can have only a dark and doubtful presentiment. Although some theorists disagree with the idea of the oneness of symbiosis on the basis of children's obvious capacity to perceive the difference between what is them and what is not-them, the issue is how the child organizes its experience cognitively and the degree to which its sense of its own ongoingness includes and is relatively dependent upon, being contained within the mother–child matrix.

To understand this concept of psychological symbiosis, consider the analogy of the air you breathe. The air comes to you from the outside, yet it is experienced as part of you once you have breathed it in. Stop breathing for a moment, however, and you will become acutely aware of the reality that the air is *not* a part of you at all, but is something quite separate. You may, with practice, be able to hold your breath longer and longer and make physiological use of the air already in your lungs—but only for a limited time. Sooner or later you must take in more air or you will die.

Just as prolonged absence of new air is likely to induce panic in you, so excessive and prolonged disruption of the connection with mother once the attachment has taken place will induce excessive anxiety in the baby. For at this stage of symbiosis, the mothering-person experience is felt to be part and parcel of the self-experience. When the first is disrupted, so is the second, and the child experiences general disorganization and anxiety. Just as you can hold your breath for a short time, the child can tolerate mother's absence for a short time, but its capacity to sustain itself during her absence is also limited. Too many such disruptions run counter to the healthy buildup of a continuing sense of self and of the capacity to relate to others. The infant does not yet have the mental tools to deal with the disruption and may become overwhelmed by high levels of anxiety, rage, and depression.

If these feelings dominate the child's experience, they become incorporated into his view of himself and the world. As an adult, such an individual may still crave and be almost addictively dependent upon human contact in order to coun-teract the distress felt at the disruption in this early stage and that continues to be felt in later years. Other children with the same history may cope with the distress by becoming absorbed in the self. As adults they may seem to be unusually self-sufficient men or women, but they may have no feelings for others or live as loners.

The persistence of the drive for attachment and the strength of the bond, once it has been formed, are underlined by the fact that parenting does not have to be good for the process to take place. Indeed, children also form bonds to abusive and/or ungratifying mothers, and strongly resist being separated from them. This way of organizing and structuring the bond affects later adult relationships. There will be a tendency to seek out and replicate the unsatisfactory bond, since this is what feels most familiar and what maintains the sense of inner connection with the primary mothering person.

THE UNSATISFACTORY SYMBIOSIS

When an adult seems to cling to an abusive or unrewarding relationship, it may seem evident to everyone else that he or she would be much better off without it. What friends and advisers fail to appreciate is the force of the pull toward just such a situation. If we dig a little deeper we are likely to discover that it is a kind of reenactment of the relationship with the early attachment figures as the individual experienced and interpreted it through the mind of a child. The individual has constructed the reality of today in a manner that is consistent with reality as he or she experienced and understood it long ago. Through an unconscious selection process in establishing intimate relationships, the individual may ferret out qualities in the other person that make him or her a natural for the role of the early attachment figure with all the atten-dant demands, expectations, and reactions that characterized the childhood situation. There may be a grain of truth to the perception of the new individual as a replication of the old, but there may also be considerable falsehood to it as well. In some cases these qualities of the original significant other are projected onto others in a more unrealistic manner with the result that the individual is likely to become involved in frequent conflict with persons who react with anger to being seen inaccurately or inappropriately. In the situation of what is called projective identification, the attitude that is at first projected may actually have the effect of inducing it in the recipient of the projection. In this way, the individual has actively brought about the replication of the original situation. For example, if the new significant other is accused of being cold and ungiving often enough, he or she may well react with coldness and withdrawal, appearing to prove true the original accusation. He or she seems to have become identified with, taken on the character of, the projected bad parent.

There are also situations in which the attachment process does not go well because of seriously inconsistent patterns of caretaking. The child may live in his own home with his own mother but be assigned to the care of constantly changing sitters, maids, or housekeepers. The discontinuity of experience interferes with the organizing process, and the child is in a chronic state of anxiety and anger. The mother's input is diluted, inconsistent, and generally unsatisfactory; but the continuing nature of her input does provide a minimal structure. However, this inner structure is inadequate for future development and may be clung to as an important basis for the child's sense of organization of self.

The implications of the need for a healthy bonding experience become more problematic as we enter the 1990s, with more and more women returning to work shortly after the birth of their child, either out of economic necessity or because of involvement in a career. Parents will need to be aware of their children's developmental requirements and work out caretaking situations that will meet them at least adequately if not optimally.

One woman of 35 with such a history of inconsistent caretaking could not accept the limits of what her mother could realistically give her. To do so would imply recognition that mother was a separate person rather than some still undifferentiated part of herself. She reacted with rage and fear at any suggestion that she diminish the intensity of her relationship with her mother because she was convinced that if she were to do so, she would die psychologically. In other words, she felt that her sense of self was so enmeshed with her image of her mother that extricating herself from the relationship would tear her apart in some way. When others pushed her in that direction, she experienced their efforts as a wish to destroy her.

Sometimes it is difficult for people who are trying to help such an individual to understand why that man or woman becomes so enraged with them. He or she continues to struggle unsuccessfully to master the aborting and distorting of the love process at its inception, hoping to bring about the conditions that would have allowed it to evolve as it should have. Unfortunately, one cannot turn back the clock, and what would have been appropriate for a baby is not appropriate for an adult. Such a person is defeated time and time again, not only by the reality of the situation, but by the deep-seated fear and anger that will not go away.

In addition to the primary attachment bond formed with the mothering person, children normally make secondary bonds with other people in their world, such as the father, siblings, grandparents, or even a regular baby-sitter. While the primary bond serves a vital organizing function, the secondary bonds help the child move away from its mother, to become separate when the time comes. They counteract the excessive closeness that may develop when there is only one attachment. When there are other safe and dependable figures in the child's world, he or she does not feel the need to cling to mother out of anxiety or fear. Furthermore, these other relationships afford children the opportunity to learn more about the world and to develop segments of their personality less likely to be expressed with only one person in their inter-personal world.

However, secondary bonds can work against the formation of the single primary attachment bond if the mother does not have the interest in giving herself to that process. When this is the case, multiple bonds may form, but no one central relationship will be available for the construction of a unified me–you image and for the establishment of a secure sense of the cohesion and ongoingness of the self. This situation may contribute to difficulties in intimate relationships later on.

Melanie tended to be overly sensitive to and upset by changes in other people, whether the changes were of mood or appearance. Any change, she felt, was tantamount to that person's becoming someone else. Somehow the threat of abandonment was associated with these experiences. The known person, in effect, left and was replaced by someone else, even though both were, in actuality, the same person. A common image in her fantasies and dreams was that of a five-headed monster.

In the first two years of life, Melanie had been cared for not only by her mother, but by her grandmother and several aunts, all of whom lived together. The father was not in the home during these years. Although the child was loved, there was an incon-stancy to her day-to-day experience, with different faces, different hands, different styles of talking and handling. The nature of these caretaking experiences interfered with the formation of the primary me–you image of symbiosis. Melanie dealt with the stress of the changing mothers and the unpredictability of experience by withdrawal to a space within herself where she wouldn't have to cope with the anxiety of the five-headed mother figure. As an adult she also used withdrawal to deal with the stress of too much social stimulation, which seemed to pull her in many different directions. But then, although she would feel more unified, she would also feel empty and depressed. That is, in order to be, she had to renounce love.

If Melanie's mother had evidenced that primary maternal preoccupation about which Winnicott (1975) writes, she would have provided the consistent mothering that her baby needed to form the bond that would constitute the basis for the capacity to love without losing herself. Then, the other women who also lived in the home might have been a source of enrichment rather than a cause of fragmentation. As it was, her mother, self-involved and often depressed, left the care of her little girl to whichever of the other women was available at the moment.

In her analysis, Melanie was able to use her relationship with her therapist to bring the five-headed image together and to experience herself and others in a more cohesive fashion.

THE FALSE SELF

Another common problem that may originate during the attachment process and the stage of normal symbiosis is that of the false self (Winnicott 1965). A man or woman who feels real knows not only what he or she feels, but has access to other aspects of experience as well. Such individuals know what they think, what they feel, what they want, and what they perceive. They also know what they can do and are able to pursue goals and aims. Some people do not feel real. They describe themselves as feeling fraudulent, not knowing what they think, feel, want, or believe. They complain of lack of spontaneity, no pleasure in what they do or achieve, no sense of really being alive. Although they may seem to fare in superior style in the world, from their point of view none of it has any meaning for them. Upon close scrutiny, one can see that they live their lives as reactors rather than as initiators;

their entire identity seems to be carved out of a characteristic adaptation to the external world, to the important others of their life as experienced in the formative years. There may be little awareness of the buried true self. Often this true self, to which there is little or no conscious access, is suffused with feelings of despair, rage, or fear, feelings tiny children experienced at the failure of their caretakers to respond empathically and lovingly to their genuineness and spontaneity.

The false self-identity is that of a reactive self—a self who takes its cue from the other—a responder but never an initiator. One can react by complying *with*, by struggling *against*, by performing *for*, by warding *off*, by complaining *about*. Reactive relating in the first years of life is not conducive to the development of the capacity to love, for loving can only be experienced by a real and authentic self. As an adult, such an individual continues to relate to others through the false self as it developed in the early years. The false self actually serves two important functions: it protects the true self from impingement or hurt while, at the same time, it maintains a connection with the mother. Remember, from the dependent child's point of view, any connection may be better than no connection at all.

This situation comes about as the result of the inability or insensitivity of the mother who disregards or overrides the reality of what is going on inside the child itself. When that happens, her caretaking becomes an intrusion, an impingement—even an assault. A bottle stuck in the mouth of a screaming baby whose cries indicate a need for quieting and soothing is an attack upon the baby from his point of view. He may suck for a moment or two, but then will take up his screaming once again. When this kind of interaction is characteristic of his day-to-day experience, the child's developing sense of self and other, the me–you pattern, becomes consolidated around his reaction to these impingements. The pattern becomes reacting me/impinging you. This kind of failure of parenting can take place anywhere along the continuum of the early years of development. The earlier it starts, the greater will be the impairment of identity, of a sense of a true self and its ongoingness. There is a tendency, in later relationships, to recreate the specific pattern of false self relating that was set up early in life. For example, if the mother needed to be superadequate and her child to be small and helpless, as an adult, this person will continue to act helpless in relationships and induce others to take over responsibility and be the superadequate one.

In healthy development the real self, the core self that is rooted in the child's own intrinsic bodily and sensory experience, becomes connected to external reality by virtue of mother's response to that self. When she fails in this function, the real, or true, self is isolated and shut out from the attachment upon which the capacity to love is predicated. The dilemma of this child as an adult may be that the persistence of the yearning for intimacy exists side by side with the fundamental feeling, experience, and belief that one can only be real when one is alone. This was the belief of one woman who was consistently told by both parents that her feelings were either sick, crazy, or wrong. As she would try to erase what she felt, she also erased her sense of self and would become confused and anxious.

Other men and women are even more cut off from their real experiencing self and are not able to recover it even in solitude. For even when they are alone, they continue to react to inner mental shoulds and demands just as they react to the shoulds and demands of others. Even in their fantasies they are reactors rather than originators. When they do form an apparently intimate relationship, it is often ridden with anxiety about doing the wrong thing. Despite periodic experiences of having their needs met, which makes them feel good (reactively!), there can be no enduring love connection as long as there is no real self available to it. And others are valued, not for the persons they are, but for their affirming function.

On the other hand, when the overall quality of mother–child interaction is based upon the mother's empathic response to what is initiated by the infant, the me–you pattern is based upon that which is intrinsic to the self, to the core self.

THE CONFLICT BEGINS

In the second half of the first year of life, the child begins to become aware, consciously and cognitively, that he or she and mother are not one after all. The child is on the way toward recognition that mother is a separate individual. It is at this point of transition, where experiences of "being one" alternate with experiences of "being two," that the conflict between being and loving comes to the fore.

Many adults still vacillate between the two states of experience that characterize this early stage. The pull of the yearning for the blissful union rhapsodized by poets is a threat to their sense of being, to their sense of self or identity. They express fears of disappearing or of being swallowed up. Yet, staying separate confronts them with the anxiety of the loss of sense of connection, and they feel abandoned and depressed. They experience the full force of the conflict between being and loving.

Whatever the ancient need of which Plato wrote, the yearning for that blissful unity that foreshadows the capacity to love, there is another need that opposes it. This is the push toward individuation and the drive for autonomy that, very early in life, come to exist side by side with the pull toward the loved other. The process of separation and individuation (Mahler 1968, p. 222) begins with the recognition that mother and self are, indeed, not one, but two differentiated entities. It is this conscious awareness, the emergence of a cognitive structure in the mind (rather than a sensory-motor wisdom) that constitutes the sense of "I am," that constitutes the capacity to be.

4

BECOMING TWO: THE BASIS FOR BEING

THE SENSE OF one's existence as a separate and real entity is the essence of being. The earliest awareness of a separate and real self comes about with the infant's recognition that he or she and mother are not a single unit after all. With this recognition that they have become two, the self as a conscious, cognitive structure is born (Mahler et al. 1975, p. 53). Remember, this is different from the sensory-motor awareness of the younger infant of what is part of its own body and what is not. Margaret Mahler refers to this emergence from the symbiotic phase as *hatching*. She also notes that the more the mother, as the symbiotic partner, has helped the child to become ready to hatch by providing the kind of caretaking environment that facilitates the child's organization of experience without undue emotional and mental strain, the better equipped the child will be to organize the cognitive structure of self and other.

This gradual differentiation of me from you, as well as of what is inside the self and what is outside it, begins at about the age of 5 months and is the outcome of the infant's biological maturation. A particularly important factor here is the mental development that accompanies the growth of the child's brain and nervous system in general. The child becomes able to tell the difference between one person and another and gradually builds up a storehouse of memories. The more secure the inner mental image of those close to him, the more he will react to someone who does not fit in with the remembered image. At about 8 months of age the child is noted to react with alarm to strangers. Stranger and separation anxiety are common at this phase.

From about 10 months of age until approximately 16 months, the child becomes interested in new abilities that are the outcome of further maturation of the central nervous system, such as locomotion, perception, and the learning process. The child is also increasingly confronted with the awareness of its separateness from mother. Her ready availability when she is needed and the pleasure the child derives from that mastery of new abilities make small separations tolerable for the child. It is developing the ability to be alone. Mahler (1975) calls this phase the practicing period of the overall separation–individuation process—the process of becoming two. With the culmination of the practicing period around the middle of its second year, the toddler appears to be in an elated mood. This accompanies the experiences of standing upright and walking alone. This peak point of the child's belief in his or her own magic omnipotence, Mahler tells us, "is still to a considerable degree derived *from his sense of sharing in his mother's magic powers*" (p. 20). In some cases of disturbed development, when there has been a severe failure of the environment to provide the toddler with adequate emotional support, he or she may hold on to an *illusion* of omnipotence and develop what is referred to as the grandiose self. The adult he or she becomes can deny anxiety and dependency wishes so long as this inflated omnipotent self is in charge. The other is no longer of any emotional consequence. Thus, the capacity for loving will not develop, and the individual's focus will be on the preservation of his or her sense of being. This dynamic takes place for some anorexia patients who cling to the illusion that they need nothing from outside themselves as long as they can be perfect enough. For them, loving was experienced as a danger to the self.

In normal development, the child moves back and forth, first away from the mother, exploring the environment, and then scurrying back to reconnect with her once more. Margaret Mahler calls this scurrying back "emotional refueling." With the ability to crawl and then to walk, the child can move away from mother under his or her own power. Sensory abilities and the capacity to extract meaning from experience leads to that recognition of "I am over here and she is over there."

Many adults, when pushed by well-meaning friends, guidance counselors, therapists, or simply by the demands of life to take on a measure of autonomy, are unable to do so. They have no sense of a separate and cohesive self, no clear feeling of "I am" upon which to build and to venture forth as independent men or women. Such individuals are numbered among the casualties of the encounter group movement so popular in the '60s and '70s, for whom a therapy aimed at facilitating independence made things worse (Roback and Abramowitz 1976).

As one young man still chronically agonized with this dilemma put it: "If I move close I get lost, but if I move away I get lost." That is, if he moved closer to another person, he lost any sense of himself as having a separate identity; he lost the sense of "I am." If he moved away, on the other hand, there was no firm sense of self to sustain him.

This stage of becoming two is not without problems for both mother and child. One of these problems is the separation anxiety that often appears when the infant is 8 or 9 months old, although it has been observed earlier in some babies. At this stage the infant has two simultaneous and conflicting experiences to cope with: the experience of being one within the symbiotic me–you pattern of mental organization, and the experience of being two within the context of the increasing mental differentiation of self from other. With this dawning awareness comes the first conflict between being and loving, since this most primitive loving consists of being one with mother, while the most primitive being consists of being separate from her. At this point, however, there still is not a very clear-cut mental picture of the self as distinct from the image of the mother. Paradoxically, although the growing sense of separateness is necessary for a sense of "I am," for being, separateness is also a threat to it.

As the sense of "I am" solidifies, the drive toward autonomy of the self becomes more intense. But this drive, in turn, creates anxiety as the child becomes more and more aware of the realities of dependence upon his or her parents.

This conflict is especially intense in the second year of life, and it is often difficult for parents to understand why their child suddenly seems to be clinging and dependent at a time when increased mental and physical abilities should be making him just the opposite. One moment he will want to do things for himself; the next he will insist that someone do things for him.

The mother of 2-year-old Douglas told me:

He wants to do everything himself. "Douglas do it" is the catch cry for everything. This includes going to the fridge and getting himself a pickle from the jar, filling his own bottle, and so forth. Some things, like the latter, are simply impossible and my saying no results in a lengthy tantrum. He is *so* miserable, and even when he is screaming and stamping his feet, he's saying "Mummy" and "uppie" between cries (although when I try to cuddle him he fights me). He really doesn't know what he wants. Eventually I calm him down and he has a bottle on my lap.

It is difficult for parents to know how to respond to these conflicting needs. Sometimes the parents' own confusion and frustration interfere with their being able to help their child. They have to promote and encourage autonomy, while providing the security that goes with having dependency needs met, and it is not easy to decide which to do. As much as possible, helpful parents take their cues from their child. When the child is in the midst of the conflict, as was Douglas, there is little one can do other than weather the storm. Helping the child quiet down allows him to regroup his energies rather than being done in by the distress.

We see Douglas's conflict reechoed in the adolescent who battles his or her parents for increasing degrees of independence and self-determination, but who also becomes upset if dependency wishes are not attended to. In *The Wish for Power and the Fear of Having It* (Horner 1989), I have described what I call intrinsic power, a concept that can most succinctly be stated as "I am, I can, and I will." Douglas's wanting to do it himself is a manifestation of the striving for the "I can" as well as for the "I will." All of these facets of intrinsic power contribute to a healthy sense of self, to a secure sense of being.

Sometimes adults, too, experience the same conflict between their dependency needs and their drive for autonomy. On one hand they may seek a relationship that offers the kind of emotional support a mother gives to her young child. On the other hand, their self-esteem rides on their being competent and autonomous adults. This may be especially true when, as a child, he or she was expected to be too grown up too soon. Although a sense of security required ready access to a parent who would lovingly respond to the wish for nurturance, this wish would evoke responses that made the child feel ashamed. Even more subtly, praise for being grown up, for being a big girl or a big boy, implied the opposite, and while performing in the way that brought praise created a sense of pride, the unexpressed wish for nurturance and support automatically evoked feelings of shame. Thus, security and self-esteem came to be mutually exclusive. One could not have both, and a choice had to be made. The especially bright and capable child will often opt for the choice that makes him or her feel proud. Later in life, it is very difficult for this kind of person to ask for help, and seeking professional help from a psychotherapist evokes enough shame to interfere with getting that help.

Fred is in this kind of no-win position. He feels neglected and angry if his dependency needs aren't met by his wife. And he feels resentful if they are met, since this undercuts his feelings of manhood. Just as the parent of the conflicted child finds it difficult to know how to respond to the mixed messages of the little girl or boy, so the adult partner of the man or woman who struggles with this conflict is likely to experience frustration, confusion, and helplessness. No matter how one responds, one will be met with anger or resentment. Since there is greater cultural pressure upon the developing male to renounce dependency yearnings, a common defense is to find a partner who will be the dependent one. The greater that dependency, the less likely is the man to be abandoned. Unfortunately, the flip side of this is that the partner who will never leave because of her dependency starts to feel like a burden, and the repressed passive dependent yearnings of the man leave him feeling frustrated in that department. Because the little boy is not able to grow out of his early conflict gradually, he doesn't get a chance to resolve it. As a grown man he is still caught between his repressed dependency wishes and his need for self-esteem.

Saying no is another way a child attempts to define himself as a separate person. It is a way of saying "I am different and separate from you and I have my own will." Some grown men and women still maintain a predominantly negativistic stance in interpersonal relationships as a way to ensure the boundaries of their self. Their problem is not that they say yes when they want to say no, the compliance that comes out of a fear of asserting one's separateness from the important other, but that they *must* say no even when they want to say yes. They need to preserve and protect the sense of self and its autonomy, and this takes precedence over all other aspects of a relationship, including accepting needed help or wished-for support and affection.

Many young people and the adults they later become develop an entire identity based upon this negativistic stance. They must reject everything that parents are and everything they stand for. When their own wishes and values correspond to those of their parents, they must be denied. As I pointed out to one woman of 30 who was struggling with this issue, "You seem only to be able to define yourself in opposition to your mother. It is as though your identity can be described as 'not mother.'" Her decisions, goals, attitudes, and opinions were determined by her need to oppose being like her mother in any way, thus preserving her sense of a separate self. Unfortunately, this way of being got in the way of her freedom to explore and discover her own nature. As Rollo May (1969) points out, this attitude interferes with the achievement of free will, an aspect of intrinsic power and thus of a fully evolved self: ". . . protesting is partially constructive since it preserves some semblance of will by asserting it negatively. . . . But if will remains protest it stays dependent on that which it is protesting against" (p. 192).

And so in the second year of life the conflict between the two antithetical drives, being and loving, is at its height. The pull toward mother with the need to stay emotionally connected with her is in opposition to the push away from her with its impetus to become a separate individual who can manage the challenges of life by him- or herself. It is a time of separation anxiety and of interpersonal strife that results from the need to oppose mother and all other adults as a way to affirm the self. The early conflict between the impetus toward separateness and the importance of the psychological bond, the uninterrupted sense of connection with mother, is experienced again and again throughout life. The entire life cycle is a more or less successful process of synthesizing the polarities of loving and being into a state of harmonious integration.

HOW PARENTS CAN HELP (OR HINDER)

The demand on the mother and on mother surrogates at this critical developmental crossroads is twofold: first, to continue to support the attachment bond by meeting the emotional needs of the child, and second, to promote and encourage the child's move toward separateness.

As during the initial attachment process, the mother will have to be able to support and nurture without feeling put upon or controlled by the infant's needs, and thus resentful of them. She will also have to possess a strong enough sense of herself as a person so that she will not want her baby to continue to need her in order to provide her with a role to play or to feed her self-esteem. Sometimes the child's attempts to define himself as a separate person stir up in the mother her own early anxiety over separation from her own mother, and she may react by becoming overprotective, blocking the child's moves away from her. If the mother experiences the child's moves toward separation as an abandonment and punishes the child by withdrawing love or attention, the child is likely to experience his own abandonment fears. When this happens, the child is pulled between what are now experienced as mutually exclusive goals. Unable to integrate the drives toward loving and being, he may retreat from developing further in the direction of separateness and autonomy.

Sometimes this scenario is activated as the child moves toward the father. If the mother is jealous of her little daughter's affection for Daddy and becomes emotionally punitive, the little girl may retreat from her first move toward a significant male adult inasmuch as she is still so emotionally dependent upon her mother and her mother's goodwill. In some cases of female bisexuality, because of this block in forward development, developing sexuality can only emerge in the dyadic context of the mother–daughter bond. Only after therapy dealt with the anxiety associated with trying to individuate from the possessive mother, could Natalie feel free to express her wish for a loving and sexual relationship with a man. The little boy who is blocked in this same manner is impeded in his attempt to move toward and identify with his father, and may have disturbances in his gender identity as a result.

Whereas some mothers cannot tolerate the idea of their children growing up and not needing them, others are only too happy to be done with the burden of responsibility. Such a mother may resent the child's demands as intrusions upon her boundaries and autonomy, and withdraw help and support before the child has developed psychologically to the point where this will not be experienced as an abandonment. I have heard a number of men and women openly state that they refuse to grow up because they are convinced that the price of growth is to be on one's own for all time with no right ever to ask or hope for help. They do not realize that a mature and autonomous adult can still say, "Hold me. Warm me. Comfort me." A child who is denied the continuing support he needs may develop pseudoindependence and maturity or, at the other extreme, cling to the unresponsive mother in fear or anger. As an adult he will exhibit the same characteristics as he continues to struggle with the early dilemma.

Some parents fail to realize that their child is becoming a separate and unique individual. When this is the case, we find the parents reacting to the child as though he were an extension of themselves. They may expect him to walk sooner than other babies on the block, to be an A student at school, to be socially popular, or to win the swimming trophy—or whatever—in order to serve their own pride and esteem. Often in this kind of family setup, the gratification of parental approval reinforces the child's readiness to relate in this manner. However, this is not without conflict inasmuch as the child's awareness of what is happening leads to a feeling that the parent is stealing his or her achievements, and the child cannot develop a clear sense of why he does anything. Life goals are contaminated and the individual finds it impossible to get any pleasure or esteem out of his own successes.

A child who is expected to function as an extension of his parents can never develop a fully differentiated sense of self. Often as an adult he or she will establish relationships in which there is a replication of the earlier interpersonal pattern. He or she will communicate to an adult partner, "Stay here. I need you," or, "Go away. Don't bother me," or, "Be my gold star." In the first situation the partners become locked in by virtue of their mutual needs. In the second, a stance of pseudoindependence covers over the long split-off and repressed dependency needs, although the associated anxiety or depression may break through from time to time. And in the third situation, love and approval once again become contingent upon maintaining the partner's pride and and self-esteem.

It is during the stage when the child begins to move away from the mother and into the world at large that the role of the father takes on greater importance. The secondary attachment bond, which the child has made with him (as well as with other regular caretakers), makes the father a source of security that enables the child to increase his distance from mother without becoming unduly anxious. Thus, the relationship with the father is an intermediate link to the wider world beyond family. When there is no father, or when he is harsh or violent or cold and distant, the child's closeness with and dependence on mother is intensified. This makes it more difficult to develop as a person with a self that is separate from hers and more difficult to become independent of her later on when it is appropriate to do so. The same outcome can be expected when the mother actively shuts out the father because of her own needs for exclusivity in her relationship with her child.

New patterns of living, especially those of young women who elect to have and to rear children on their own, certainly raise questions about the long-term effects of such arrangements. In many such cases this mother–child dyad constitutes the entire interpersonal world of mother and child with the result that the mutual dependence for emotional nurturance is intense. Others who elect alternative styles of living provide secondary attachment figures such as aunts and uncles or family friends who can serve the same function as the father in diluting the intensity of the developmental tie between mother and child. With the increasing prevalence of divorce and single mothers, the importance of the relationship with the father is beginning to be taken into account and joint custody is becoming increasingly common.

Still, a child raised by his mother alone in an exclusive, intense relationship will have considerable difficulty in resolving the early dependent tie to her and in taking the necessary steps toward becoming two. Family therapy, the psychological treatment of an entire family together, often has as its goal the loosening of the tie and the structuring of the psychological boundary between mother and child (Minuchin 1974). The interest and cooperation of the father in this enterprise is essential to the process.

The consolidation of the sense of self, the experience and affirmation of one's being, is a long and complicated process that begins with the emergence of the self out of the symbiotic oneness with mother. It continues to be a lifelong concern for most of us.

Optimally, it is a process that allows for the concomitant expression of love and intimacy. But the human experience is rarely optimal, and in the course of our psychological evolution we run head-on into a variety of problems and pitfalls. One of these is the issue of power that comes to the fore in the midst of the emergence of the self and recognition of mother as a separate entity. Children, and the adults they become, must eventually come to terms with what I call the power pivot.

5

THE POWER PIVOT

HELEN IS CAUGHT in a paradoxical bind that inevitably sabotages her relationships. Her self-esteem requires that she perceive herself as perfect, and for her, perfection means being all-powerful. Imperfection is being without power or in someone else's power.

If Helen finds herself attracted to a man who meets her standards and whose apparent power makes him especially desirable, her hopes for an idealized relationship are aroused. But—and here is the rub—if he is also attracted to her and wishes to pursue the relationship, there is a power shift. By virtue of his wanting her, Helen now has power over him. She has the power to say yes or to say no, to make him happy or to upset him. This, as far as she is concerned, renders him imperfect and thus no longer desirable; in fact, she now views him with contempt. At this point, of course, she no longer wants to see him. If, on the other hand, he is essentially indifferent and only throws her an occasional crumb of affection or attention, he remains powerful and therefore perfect. But Helen then has to contend with the hurt of rejection, damage to her self-esteem and, at worst, feelings of humiliation. Now she experiences her own powerlessness and its associated imperfection. She is in a no-win position.

Helen's problems with power and perfection can be traced back to the normal developmental process of becoming two during which these issues emerge. Up to then the child has participated in its mother's power inasmuch as mother has been perceived as an extension of the self. The child wants a cookie on the high shelf. He points and says "cookie." Mother smiles and reaches to get one for him. As the sense of self evolves, however, the child is confronted more and more with the reality of his helplessness and relative inadequacy. There is a shift from the omnipotent part-of-mother self to the power-less self who is a separate entity. Because of the central role this shift plays in the development of personality, it can be viewed as the *power pivot*. The evolution of this shift is characterized by varying degrees of self-centeredness, a period of normal narcissism that, as Heinz Kohut (1971) points out, has important implications for later life. [1]

Resolution of immature narcissism is essential for the capacity to love another person as himself or herself rather than as an object to meet one's narcissistic needs. These needs may range from more severe vulnerability of the structure of the self in which the other is needed to hold that self together, to give it a semblance of cohesion, to a vulnerability to depression where the other is needed to fill up the empty self. The other may also be needed to make the self feel worthwhile. Patho-logical narcissism is a manifestation of something missing in the self, and is not just a selfish attitude. Even the most mature individual feels the need for some kind of reassurance from time to time. However, in healthy interpersonal rela-

---

[1]Dr. Heinz Kohut describes how some people maintain an illusion of their own grandiosity, or else how they may tend, instead, to overidealize and depend upon the other person. When the other fails to live up to the idealization (which he or she must, sooner or later), the individual reacts with anger and contempt and goes back to relying on the overidealized self once again.

tionships, the partners are there for each other at such times in a mutually giving and enhancing way. They can appreciate each other's separateness inasmuch as this separateness is not a threat to the self in some way. Caring and separateness are *not* mutually exclusive.

If the child gets stuck at the power pivot, issues of power become central in later relationships, and love comes to be viewed as a fiction that people talk about but never experience. Situations of helping, giving, or caring take on overtones of demanding and submitting. As in Helen's case, we find the individual rejecting all the pleasures of love out of hand. Healthy resolution of these issues enables the individual to develop the capacity to love a real and fully separate person and to construct a realistic image of him- or herself.

Since the attitudes, expectations, or ways of perceiving the self during the period of early developmental narcissism, particularly those of the power pivot, so strongly influence an adult's self-image and relationships, it is important to consider the specific series of steps that comprise this period. Mahler (1968) refers to this time as the rapprochement phase of the separation–individuation process.

The rapprochement *crisis* is the developmental switch point marking the shift from a sense of omnipotence to a sense of helplessness—from a sense of perfection to a sense of shame. When prior development has not gone well, the conscious awareness of the reality of how very separate the child is, in fact, from mother may be traumatic. If there are deficits in the organization of the self from an earlier developmental failure, these deficits become evident at this time. The child, and the adult he or she becomes, is unable to negotiate age appropriate developmental demands and symptomatic behavior such as anxious clinging develops.

The response of the environment to the child's growth has to allow for the conflicting strivings toward autonomy that exist side by side with the intensely felt dependency needs. The term "rapprochement" suggests the alternating moving away from mother and the returning to her for emotional refueling. Healthy parents do not have a need for the child either to stay dependent and helpless, or to be completely self-reliant. They can shift their way of being with the child, empathically in tune with his or her conflicting impulses and needs, although, as we saw in the case of Douglas's mother, this is often easier said than done.

The narcissism of the rapprochement phase undergoes a step-by-step resolution as children become able to integrate the changes that are taking place within themselves and between themselves and others.

YOU ARE MY RIGHT HAND

When the process of becoming two is barely under way, although physical separateness is obvious to the child, a full awareness of psychological separateness and differentness has yet to be achieved. The child still experiences and expects total power and is very upset when reality intrudes and does not support his illusion. Tantrums are not unusual at this time. Mother is perceived as an extension of the self to be moved and controlled as one would move or control one's own arm or hand. Baby grunts and squeals, pointing to what he wants, and Mama gets it for him. Some children persist in this kind of behavior long after they have language for asking and long after they can get things for themselves. Often adults who relate to others in this way are given to rages or to sullen, angry withdrawals when their omnipotence is threatened. Generally, however, adults in whom the expectation of total power persists express it much more subtly. Others are expected to know what one wants and to provide it without being asked. When that fails to happen, the result may be angry silence or withdrawal. The other person's mind as well as his or her hand is expected to be an extension of one's own wish and will.

If such men or women do go into psychotherapy, they are often unable to make use of it to grow. In the psychotherapy relationship there tends to be a replication, a replay, of the individual's characteristic mode of relating to others. It is a mini-lab in which relational issues can be explored and change can take place. Men or women with this undifferentiated mode of relating are likely to enter therapy primarily to find someone who will make them feel good by endlessly catering to their narcissistic demands for instant warmth, instant love, or total license to do and say whatever they want. Although therapists have to be sensitive to the vulnerabilities that underlie the infantile demands and to be empathically in tune with what the person is experiencing, obviously they cannot do what the person is demanding of them. As supportive and empathic as they may try to be, there are limits inherent in the situation that confront the individual with the therapist's failures to be what he or she wants—an extension of the self and its demands. When he or she discovers that the wished for behavior cannot be coerced from the therapist, there is likely to be an eruption of rage. Despite their understanding of the problem, therapists may have a difficult time in this situation and may be provoked into ending the treatment, thereby proving an expectation that people cannot be trusted or relied upon. Often the individual in question will try to find another therapist and the same scenario will unfold. These men and women do the same thing in their private lives and have a life history of failed relationships, starting with the peer group of childhood on up to their adult years.

YOU ARE A REFLECTION OF ME

As the process of differentiation moves along, the child is confronted with new concerns. After an initial period of elation at the wonderful, newfound power of standing and walking and discovering the world beyond mother's lap, there is a letdown. The child now experiences the anxiety of its relative helplessness and of the possibility of loss of the needed other.

There is still, however, an inability to understand that the other person has feelings, moods, tastes, or any psychological qualities that are different from those of the self. Self and other are assumed to be psychological twins.

The adult who has not been able to move past this stage of the power pivot may be able to get along tolerably well with a "yes, dear"partner, but not with someone who has any shred of individuality and the wish to express it. When the partner fails to agree totally with what one feels, thinks, or wants, he or she is met with a mixture of anger and/or contempt. The partner may be told that he or she is wrong or stupid or crazy as a way to try to coerce agreement by undercutting the other's confidence. There may be a disgusted "You don't understand me!" which may make the partner feel guilty and bad enough to back down. Since the loss of power provokes unbearable anxiety and the loss of perfection provokes unbearable shame, the main defense against this distress is to retreat to the earlier stage of total power and domination of the other.

Some years ago I was doing research on value orientation, using a test that consisted of a number of paragraphs describing different ways to live one's life. A well-educated man to whom I showed the test material absolutely refused to believe that there was such a thing as a value orientation that differed from his own. He did not say, "I don't agree with the others." He adamantly insisted that they *did not exist*.

One young woman explained her distaste for making love with a man on the basis of the physical differences between male and female. Because he was unlike her, she experienced him as some kind of alien creature. She could only relate physically to a body that mirrored her own.

For the man or woman who persists in this way of thinking and relating, the connection with the other person is maintained by sameness and threatened by recognition of difference. This attitude is projected onto children as well as spouses, lovers, or friends. "You and I are alike" may be a valid statement of similarities in taste, style, values, interests, temperament, and so on. This is frequently what is felt and believed when people first meet and quickly "fall in love." But it may be based on a denial of the actual qualities of the spouse or friend and projection of some aspect of one's self onto him or her. In this instance, any expression of the partner's true self is experienced as either rejection or abandonment, or as evidence of gross inferiority (since the self, of course, is perfect). When, on the other hand, the other person accepts the statement of twinship, he or she is "loved" and given much approval.

GIVE ME YOUR POWER

As the child's intellect and capacity to understand develop still further, he or she is ultimately confronted with the harsh reality of the self's lack of power and perfection. At this point, the child turns dependently toward the parents whom he now sees as all-powerful and perfect. They also become models for him and he imitates them and begins to build identifications with them. Perhaps one day he can be like them and so regain the lost power and perfection. In the meantime, he must share in theirs.

The child's own realistic limitations to power can be tolerated if the parents intervene with help and emotional support when it is needed during this period. If, on the other hand, parents are insensitive or unresponsive to the child's need for support, their toddler is likely to experience the anxiety that accompanies feelings of helplessness. He or she may deal with this distress in a number of ways. One is to regress back to the belief in his or her own illusory power. The defense of the grandiose self is brought into play. As an adult, this individual may show an exaggerated self-sufficiency that covers over the repressed dependency needs. Or he or she may seek to protect the self from this anxiety by avoiding stressful situations. The refusal to attempt anything that holds the potential for failure would be such a defense. They tell themselves they could probably do it if they tried, maintaining the illusion of power, but they may also know that they are unwilling to put themselves to the test. There are many men and women who have opted for this solution. They try to avoid failure and the anxiety and shame of reawakened feelings of powerlessness by never trying anything new or different. Thus, they do not have the opportunities to achieve a sense of mastery over difficulty, which would help build a healthy self-esteem.

In addition to turning to the parents for the lost sense of power, the child at this stage of development becomes dependent on them for his or her self-esteem. When the parents support and recognize the child's growing competence with "Good for you! You can do it!" for example, they forge a link between the child's self-esteem and reality. In other words, the child's self-esteem connects with what he or she actually can do rather than with fantasy or delusion. This sense of "I can," or mastery, is part of what I have described as intrinsic power. Parents who overdo praise, however, with the mistaken notion that this is the way to build up the child's self-esteem, often fail to face the reality of the child's limited capabilities and his need for guidance and instruction. They reinforce the child's earlier grandiose beliefs about himself. In the adult, this illusory grandiosity (usually secret) exists side by side with low self-esteem in realistic situations.

Men and women who do not have reality-based self-esteem may continue to need others as a source of good feelings about themselves as well as a source of feelings of power. The other is needed to counteract feelings of shame and helplessness.

We see this attitude in June, who derives her self-esteem vicariously through her husband's business successes. Reverses in her husband's business are likely to provoke in such a woman rage at his failure rather than support during the crisis. For, by the act of failing, he has ceased to be that source of power and perfection upon which she depended.

In *The Wish for Power and the Fear of Having It*, I explore the tendency of women to idealize and eroticize male power. As one woman put it, "To be sexually attracted I have to see a man as powerful—more powerful than me. It's what excites me. I'm not attracted to the nice guy who loves me." Such women are stuck at the stage of idealizing the father in particular, and they get much gratification out of being special to the powerful man. The sense of power supports the safe existence of the self, that is, it supports being. But in these relationships there is no place for loving.

Paradoxically, the individual who operates in this manner wants power over the needed other who is then required to be all powerful and all perfect. This wish for control is often less conscious and less obvious than that of the person who considers the other to be an extension of the self. But it is there nonetheless. June is saying, "I need you to be powerful, to be perfect, and to be completely under my control so I can make sure of my own power, so I will never have to experience feeling weak, frightened, helpless, or humiliated."

The paradox—be all-powerful but submit to my control—creates an unresolvable bind for persons who receive the contradictory messages. They are to submit to being controlled while at the same time playing the part of the all-powerful parent.

Sometimes the power issues of the human personality become institutionalized in the culture and politics of society. The attraction to charismatic and powerful leaders is derived from the wish to share in their perceived power, and thus to feel less helpless or humiliated. It is a phenomenon that is manifest in gangs and in the slavish acceptance of whatever the gang leader proposes.

Another manifestation of power in relationships is what is referred to as an *identification with the aggressor*. In extreme examples of childhood abuse, the child may actually identify with the persecuting adult(s) while, at the same time, repressing his shame-ridden, weak, infantile self. He takes on the personality of those who appear as powerful figures in his little world. Psychoanalyst Harry Guntrip (1969) quotes a patient's fantasy of hurting a child. "Wouldn't I love to make it squirm. I'd break every bone in its vile little body, I'd crush it" (pp. 204–205). The capacity for loving is stamped out in such circumstances, even when it may have started to develop early in the context of the mother–child bond.

Any man or woman who makes the other responsible for his or her self-esteem is caught at this point of the power pivot. Whether it is being paid attention to at a party, being responded to with adequate enthusiasm, or being called every Wednesday—when the other person has the power to bestow or take away self-esteem by his or her behavior, we are endowing that person with the power and perfection that we once lost and still seek to reclaim. But in this failure to fully individuate out of the original symbiotic oneness with mother, the development of the capacity for loving is stopped in its tracks.

THE ROLE OF PARENTS

If, in their child's early and vulnerable years, parents use their real power in a benign and helpful manner, then their power is the basis for the child's sense of security. If, on the other hand, parental power is experienced as against the self, as something that is not only given but also withheld, the child comes to hate and envy that power and will develop techniques of his or her own to control it. Behind such controlling behavior lies insecurity and anxiety. Parents play a dual role in the facilitation of their child's successful negotiation of the power pivot. On one hand, their emotional availability enables the seeds of love from the earlier stage of oneness with mother to grow and to flourish. Because there is a basis for love and trust, which parents continue to enhance by their availability, the child is enabled to forego his need to dominate in order not to lose them. This is the critical point at which power over the other may come to substitute for love, the juncture at which power instead of love may become the dominant theme in an individual's life.

On the other hand, the healthy parent begins to make demands and have expectations that are appropriate for the child's age and his or her ability to meet them. These demands and expectations are an essential nudge, a push out of infantile omnipotence and egocentricity. They enable children to begin to care for their own needs, to control their own behavior and impulses, and to realize that they will be expected to be aware of and respect the needs, feelings, and boundaries of others. Without this nudge children may fail to move toward independent functioning and self-regulation. Sometimes, because of her own need to keep the child dependent, her view of her child as an extension of herself, or erroneous ideas about what constitutes good mothering, a mother may fail to give this necessary push and, in fact, reward and reinforce the child's omnipotence-laden attitudes. If, for example, the mother fails to correct her child's unrealistic illusions of power and perfection and persists in responding to him as though he were the center of the universe, the child will grow up expecting the world to cater to him in the same manner.

There has been a growing incidence of such self-centered orientation in adults as well as their children, and to some extent, it can be attributed to the influence of books on child rearing in recent decades. Parents were made to feel that any frustration they caused their children would lead to neurotic conflict that would supposedly interfere with the child's happiness and creativity. Some private nursery schools were predicated upon that belief. One mother once said to me, "If my child wants to stand on his head in the corner all day, he should be allowed to do so." Letting him do what he wanted was more important than to find out what got in the way of his being able to participate and play with the other children. The idea of the child centered family even influenced home design and architecture. Parents would not dream of taking a vacation without the children. And lest poor Johnny be upset when Billy got a present, Johnny got presents on Billy's birthday and vice versa. Children were never given the opportunity to wait, to go without, or to be out of the spotlight of parental adulation and attention. The concept of meeting the child's needs was grotesquely misapplied, and the omnipotence and grandiosity of many children of that generation were nurtured and reinforced to the point where these traits became central to their personalities later on. Today, self psychologists who are the descendants of Heinz Kohut emphasize the need for empathic mirroring, not only in the treatment of some disorders, but in the upbringing of children. Without in any way questioning this premise, the overapplication of this philosophy runs the danger of reinforcement of infantile narcissism rather than enabling the child (or the adult in treatment) to grow comfortably out of it.

It is also unfortunate that issues of power in human relationships, which have their genesis at the stage of the power pivot, have become politicized. It is unfortunate that the archaic anger toward parental power has been mobilized in women in a manner that defines the man as enemy, precluding the potential for resolution of these issues in a manner that still leaves room for negotiating a new and more mutually gratifying relationship.

When these early developmental issues can be extricated from the reality issues of economics and social status, women will be able to work more effectively in these important arenas. They will be able to mobilize their real competency and will not need to relate to men in the old ways, yet be able to relate as loving equals. This kind of man–woman relationship seems to be evolving, with a new sense of "we." One would hope that an era of consciousness-raising for both men and women will continue to help people sort out love issues from power issues.

When both parties love themselves in the form of healthy self-esteem rather than on the basis of grandiose illusions, and cherish the other as the real and whole person he or she is rather than as someone to meet the needs of a vulnerable self or to enhance the esteem of that self, then power issues will not be there to interfere with loving. Loving partners will be able to give and take, to help and be helped, to take care of and be taken care of on the basis of the exigencies of the moment, with each person comfortable in either role, rather than locked into one or the other by power issues left over from the second and third years of life and the critical stage of the power pivot.

It is only with the eventual renunciation of the fantasy of the idealized self or the idealized other, and with the acceptance of one's realistic competence as opposed to fantasy omnipotence or impotence and one's real nature as some kind of mixture of good and bad as opposed to illusions of either perfection or worthlessness that any of us can go forth as real men or real women to make a loving relationship with another real man or real woman.

Given human limitations, the built-in paradoxes of the developmental processes, and less than optimal life circumstances, growing up is likely to leave each of us with unresolved problems of the psyche still to be dealt with in adult life. One of these is dependency, a state of being in which one continues to experience the other as a powerful parental figure, and which has troublesome consequences of its own.

6

NEEDING AIN'T LOVING

IN THE PREVIOUS chapters we have seen that one of the most important aspects of the developmental stages of the first three years of life is dependency. In the preattachment period, infants depend upon others to care for the basic creature needs essential for life itself. During the stage of symbiosis when the baby's mind is actively organizing the experiences that come to it through its senses, children depend upon their mothers to help establish a sense of order and predictability out of which patterns of thinking evolve. These patterns of self and other, which are interwoven, lay the groundwork of identity and relatedness. With the process of becoming two, the process of separation and individuation, the small child depends on others to support the developing sense of self by validating and affirming it. Then, as the sense of self becomes more secure, the child gradually and in predictable steps grows out of its dependency. However, each of these normal developmental manifestations of dependency often reverberates in adult life. That is, adults may experience similar kinds of emotional needs, although not as overridingly, inasmuch as the adult has developed mental and physical resources not available to the very small child. Nevertheless, from time to time, they will be felt by otherwise self-sufficient men and women.

We are all dependent to some degree. The needs for love, affection, friendship, and support are part of the human condition. Having a partner, playing together, loving together, being available to one another for comforting from time to time can make life less burdensome and contribute to a sense of well-being. But a healthy sense of self allows for many options with respect to life-style, be it with a partner, a family, or as one who elects to live alone. The individual who experiences the lack of a partner as a calamity to be avoided at all costs often has a dependency problem.

Labeling the dependent man or woman as childish, assuming that he or she is afraid of adult responsibility, obscures the concerns that lie below the fear. Indeed, many people who are tormented with this kind of anxiety, and who therefore cling to unsatisfactory relationships, may carry a great deal of responsibility in their lives, particularly in their business or professional lives. They are obviously neither helpless nor inadequate men and women.

While some people renounce relationships and the wish for attachment and intimacy in order to protect and preserve their identities—their right to be themselves—overly dependent individuals may opt for a quite different resolution of the conflict between being and loving. They often surrender their selfhood to protect the relationship, and pay a price in stunted growth, with a perennial struggle against anxiety, depression, and shame.

Exploring some of the various manifestations that problem-ridden dependency may take in adult life, one can see how they relate to the dependencies of early development. For instance, like the child at the stage of becoming one, an individual may need others to assure him that he exists. And like the child who experiences his separateness but feels small and helpless, others may be needed to make the self feel safe and valued. It

will be different for different people, depending on their own
unique developmental history.

I NEED YOU TO CONVINCE ME THAT I
EXIST

Whenever someone Fran saw regularly in her office failed to
acknowledge her with a smile or a hello, she would feel wiped
out, as though she did not exist. Not only would she become
anxious because of the shakiness of her sense of her own
continued existence, of her ongoingness, but she would
become furious at the other person, whom she blamed for her
distress. According to her way of thinking, that individual had
not only the power, but the responsibility for validating her
existence. She felt quite justified in her outrage at the other's
failure to live up to this "responsibility." Sometimes she would
become frightened at the thought that maybe the other person
actively wished that she not exist. Dreams of people trying to
kill her fit in with this persecutory belief.

Whatever the responsibility of the mother to help organize
and then to confirm her small child's sense of self, people in
one's adult world become resentful and justifiably angry at
having this responsibility laid on them. An individual who,
because of unfortunate or unsatisfactory early experiences, is
stuck at this point, is in a quandary. On the one hand, such
people are dependent on others for validation. But on the other
hand, because of unrealistic and inappropriate expectations
and demands, they bring upon themselves anger, censure, and
broken friendships instead. They are caught in a perpetual
vicious cycle of intense need for others and angry disruptions
of relationships, which then intensify their need.

Often people caught in this dilemma withdraw and nurse a
silent rage, which they communicate nonetheless. But sometimes they choose a different interpersonal strategy and

accommodate, adapt, and behave in a placating manner in order to bring about the kind of response needed to alleviate their anxiety about their existence. Paradoxically, in so doing, they give up and lose any sense of their own identity.

Often this need for validation shows itself in little ways and is played out covertly, without conscious recognition of the process. Sally and Jim are at a party. Sally tentatively comments on the play they saw the previous evening, all the while watching Jim's face. As she sees the tightening at the corners of his mouth that signals disapproval, both her voice and spirit fade away. The challenge to her right to have an opinion of her own also challenges her very right to be, and she feels anxious and confused, losing all sense of herself as a viable being. In a dependent relationship, when one relies on the other to confirm, validate, or endorse the self, the self may be sacrificed to the requirements of the relationship and thereby be lost.

I NEED YOU TO TELL ME WHO I AM

Just as some people use others as a kind of mirror to reassure them that they exist, so others use the people upon whom they depend as a mirror to define them, to tell them who they are.

An example of this is the living of one's life and the experiencing of oneself through a given role. This is, by and large, a most common and widespread way of living. Roles, whatever they may be, offer a kind of security and predictability. Yet, by its very nature, role playing and role living can only be at the expense of authentic being and genuine loving.

When one lives his or her life and experiences the self through a role, others are needed because of their function in a cast of characters that is essential to that particular role, be it that of parent, child, the strong one, or the sick one. A child needs a parent if she is to be a child. A strong person needs a weak one, and a sick person needs a caretaking one.

Narcissistic mothers who are insensitive to the needs of their infants may create sons and daughters who from early on learn to adapt to the psychological needs of the mother instead. The children become adept at sensing the mother's needs and lend themselves to roles required by the psychology of the family as a whole. The role of caretaker, of the child being parent to the parent, is not at all unusual. As adults, such children continue to relate through the caretaker role, be it with friends, spouses, or children. They find it difficult if not impossible to relate on any other basis. This way of being is what Winnicott (1965) calls the false self. The false self becomes a definition of who the person is, while the true self remains hidden away and in psychological isolation. Furthermore, such individuals have a way of subtly or not so subtly inducing others to play the role corresponding to their own, thereby enabling and supporting it.

Jonathan was such a child. When he was 9 years old his father died and his mother went into a depression from which she never recovered. As the older child, Jonathan felt responsible for his little sister. Furthermore, he realized he would have to take care of his mother as well, to help her function as a parent so she, in turn, could take care of him. As a way of coping with his anxiety at the possibility of total abandonment, he became parent to his parent.

When I met Jonathan, he was an exhausted and driven man who was caring for a chronically depressed wife and for his children, whom he infantilized and overprotected. He complained a great deal that no one seemed to care at all about how he felt or what he needed.

But Jonathan was unable to let himself be tended to even if someone did want to respond to him in this manner. His self-esteem had become tied up with his being able to play the caretaker role. Giving it up carried the threat of feelings of shame and failure and, furthermore, would have confronted him with his childhood feelings of helplessness—feelings that were now consciously experienced as self-doubt and a sense of unworthiness.

This kind of covert dependency played out through role relating requires a reciprocal stance on the part of the partner. If the wife is the strong one, the husband must be the weak one, at least on the surface of things, and vice versa.

In some marriages the man maintains his role of the strong one by keeping a tight control of the purse strings so that his wife must come to him for money, much as children must go to their parents. Should he lavish gifts on his wife, he still plays the role of parent, albeit an indulgent one. In this sort of marital relationship, wishes or attempts on the part of the wife to work and make money of her own will be negated with a pseudoprotective "I don't want *my* wife to work," or by an active undermining of her confidence in her ability to do so. While the man is defined as the strong one, hiding his dependency (his wife will always be home when he gets there), the woman is defined as the weak one, and she colludes by hiding the strengths that would jeopardize her husband's self-esteem and security. But the wife's dependency needs are operating in this situation as well. She participates in the arrangement because her needs would be endangered by her husband's anger should his not be met.

This sort of arrangement founders when one of the partners wearies of his or her role and begins to press for change. The strong one may grow tired and resentful of the burden. A giving one may come to feel depleted and deprived. The self-esteem of the needy one surfaces in angry protest, and both partners begin to wonder if the dependent attachment, which they have been calling love, is worth the surrender of their authentic being.

The problem of covert dependency has been far less common in women because there have been social rewards for them in taking a dependent stance in life. In fact, a woman would often meet with hostility and ridicule if she showed too much strength—whatever "too much strength" might be. She might be deemed castrating or unfeminine, both of which are sufficiently abhorrent to her to inhibit her assertive or independent behavior.

Even though this situation is becoming less common as wives have to work to help support the family, and more and more, women are entering the business and professional world at upper levels of power and influence, the old issues remain in diluted form. A husband may be uncomfortable if his wife makes more money than he does or if she is in a position of more power.

Some years ago Denise found herself on a hike through the woods with a group of men and women. She had scrambled up a rather steep hill and looked back to see her husband, a large, heavyset man, having difficulty negotiating the climb behind her. She automatically reached out and offered him a hand. He took it and, regaining his footing, reached the top of the hill. It was very soon evident that he was angry at her, feeling she had robbed him of his (precarious) manhood.

A short time later, Denise found herself playing an old game familiar to women, especially to able and competent women. She pretended to need his help when, indeed, she did not, in order to help him regain his self-esteem as well as not to have him angry at her anymore. But by the end of the day, with feelings of dismay and disgust, she had become aware of the enormity of the charade, and of its cost in terms of her own sense of integrity and being. She had needed her husband to help confirm her definition of herself as feminine and lovable, while her husband had needed her to confirm his definition of himself as masculine and competent.

This was one of those turning points when a decision is made that alters for all time the course of one's life. Denise would no longer play the role of the helpless and dependent one in the interest of maintaining someone else's self-esteem. If there were to be a relationship, the other person would have to accept her with all her strengths as well as her weaknesses. It was one of the many decisions and changes that put more and more stress on a marital bond that would eventually give way under it. In essence, she had decided not to sacrifice her being so that she could have loving. One would hope that in such a marital situation, the partner can also make the changes necessary for authentic being and loving so that the established bond need not be severed. Unfortunately, in some cases this is not possible, as it was not in that of Denise.

Just as some role relationships are based on who is strong and who is weak, others are based on who gives and who takes. In healthy, nondependent, mutual relationships, giving and taking are part of the natural flow and rhythm of the relationship. There is no rigid role assignment. Caring unites with sensitivity, and each participant in the relationship can find a way to be in harmony with his or her own being as well as with that of the other. Being is not in conflict with loving.

There are other situations in which changing roles are part of the natural evolution of the family, and the person who needs things to stay the same in order to define the self and give the self an identity finds it difficult if not impossible to negotiate those changes. A woman whose identity is defined by being a mother may suffer a loss of that identity and of purpose when her children grow up and leave home. Or a man whose identity is defined by his work suffers its loss when he must retire. In any instance when one's role is used to define the self, the loss of that role leads to a crisis of identity and esteem for that person.

I NEED YOU TO KEEP ME FROM FEELING LOST

In addition to role playing, other people can be used to serve the function of a center for the organization of one's world, simply by virtue of being there. This derives from the early mother's organizing function for her child. This is first manifest in the me–you image of the stage of being one. Later, as the child becomes more separate, mother, father, and the home become the center of security and familiarity in the child's life.

For a small child, one of the most difficult aspects of loss through death or separation from a parent is the fact that suddenly the world is a different place. Reality itself, and with it the sense of self, has changed. A man whose father had died when he was a young boy felt that part of himself had died with his father. That was the part of himself that he experienced in the context of being with his father. He would never have that experience of himself again as it was part of the context of their relationship. The dependence upon external organizers is one of the reasons why, when the mother must be away (as in the hospital with a new baby), keeping the child's world as normal as possible reduces the severity of the psychological stress. The more strange and alien elements there are in it for him, the more painful and frightening the separation from mother will be, inasmuch as the sense of a familiar and ongoing self is disrupted.

To some extent, abrupt and extensive changes in the life of adults, changes that separate them from those on whom they are dependent, may evoke an uncomfortable separation anxiety. The security of the self is still tied to the physical presence of the other.

At a university far from home, Karen wrote to me. "It's hitting me real hard how alone I am down here, and I'm scared. . . . There is no going back, that I realized tonight also, and I sit here crying as I understand that I am so afraid to go forward, but have no choice." She went on: "I want to call Steve back and beg for the relationship we once had. I want to call up my parents and tell them I'm coming home." And then she said, "I hear you in my mind saying many things to me, 'Don't go out and get hooked up with someone right away. Be alone for awhile.'" She struggled with "trying to convince myself that I am indeed a whole person who can pull through hard times and go through changes and be loved and love again."

The more one has to depend on external persons or situations to help feel securely anchored in life, the more intense the anxiety of separation from the needed others will be. The more one depends on others for his sense of identity, for his self-esteem and self-confidence, and for his security in the world at large, the more he will have to cling to old relationships or to form new ones that serve the same function for him.

I NEED YOU TO MAKE ME PERFECT

Certain kinds of dependent relationships are used to maintain the illusion of a perfect, idealized self that is normally lost during the developmental stage of becoming two. In one instance, the illusion of one's perfection is maintained by assigning a negative aspect of self to a spouse, a child, or even a friend through a mechanism referred to as projective identification. This attribute is projected into the other who then *becomes* a person having this attribute. For instance, some children are depended on to play out negative aspects of their parents' selves so that the latter can feel superadequate. Parents of such children may actually manage to produce a son or daughter who, despite good native intelligence, plays out the stupid and inadequate role. This attitude preserves the attachment to the needed parent inasmuch as this way of being is required by the parent. It also may function more covertly as a way for the child to get even for the humiliation that goes with the role. The child "forgets," makes mistakes, wets the bed, breaks and spills, and gets away with hostile behavior on the basis of the shared myth of his inadequacy. "He can't help it . . . he's just not well coordinated." The parents in this kind of interpersonal setup often overtly deplore the handicap; but at the same time they continue to foster it by endlessly helping, advising, and overall infantilizing the needed partner. If they take the child to a therapist, they actively sabotage any efforts to change the situation. Or they may angrily remove the child from treatment at the first hint that the therapist believes that the parents play an active part in maintaining the child's helplessness.

By now you will recognize this process as one that creates a false self in the child. What we see is that the false self of the child is the outcome of the dependency of the parents who *need* their little girl or boy to be a certain way.

Other examples of the parents' dependency on the child in this particular manner are many. We may find a situation in which the mother can only feel good about herself if she perceives herself as moral and virtuous, particularly with respect to sex. As her daughter nears puberty, the mother's fantasies become activated as she recalls how she felt when her own sexuality first emerged, and she remembers the terrible guilt those new feelings evoked in her. Instead of being able to empathize with her daughter and to help her through this difficult stage, she goes about attacking any appearance of sexuality in her daughter. If the young girl wants to wear a fashionably short skirt, the mother calls her a tramp. If the daughter walks home from school with a boy, the mother calls her a slut. The girl gets to be the carrier of mother's badness, and in her attempts to punish it, mother can continue to feel good about herself. At the same time, she *needs* the daughter to be sexual in order to carry out this scenario, and in many such cases, this attitude actually propels the young girl into acting out the mother's forbidden sexuality through promiscuity.

In another situation a parent who hated his fearful self would push his little son into terrifying situations, and then make fun of the boy when he was afraid and cried. The father could put his own humiliation at being afraid into the boy and attack it there. Needless to say, the child became a very timid and easily frightened person. But at least the father could feel good about himself in one respect: *he* was not afraid.

Because both partners in this kind of relationship lack an integrated self, they cannot function independently of their psychological collaborator. Such relationships, often between grown men and women and their elderly parents as well as between spouses, are intense, enmeshed, and apparently insoluble. The attachment takes precedence over the integrity of the self, over being. The participants label it "love," but it has more to do with mutual interdependency than loving. In fact, it is a kind of psychological enslavement.

Sometimes a partner is needed to function as a supplement, as a replacement for a lost or split-off and valued aspect of the self. The self is felt to be incomplete. The other is experienced as making the self whole once again.

Terry, afraid since early childhood to assert himself in any way lest he meet with his mother's cold and disapproving withdrawal, was powerfully drawn to highly assertive women. He saw them as having the "vitality" that he lacked. His fundamental sense of being alive was buried along with the repressed anger toward his controlling mother, who punished him for asserting himself against her control.

For a time, in his relationships with women, Terry would feel, once again, whole, alive, and vital. He would "fall in love" with the needed partner. In effect what this meant was that he would relate to the woman as an extension of himself in order to participate in her vitality. In time, the boundary between what was himself and what was the woman would get very fuzzy, and eventually he would lose the sense of himself as a separate person. When he struggled to regain this sense of being by withdrawing from what felt like her control, he would be left feeling depleted and powerless once again.

Sometimes a person who is cut off from emotions is attracted to a partner who is very emotional. But the attempt to regain that lost part of self doesn't work, and the very emotionality that attracted him to the other becomes something distasteful.

A person who uses another to complete his or her sense of self is in a state of constant and perilous dependency. The other person may supply what is missing, but he or she can also take it away. The self of the dependent individual must be even further compromised so as not to alienate the essential partner who has been chosen as the bearer of the lost attribute.

I NEED YOU TO MAKE ME FEEL GOOD ABOUT BEING ME

As the child renounces his illusions of power and perfection at the stage of becoming two, he or she depends on the approval of parents to sustain self-esteem. This form of dependency is also exhibited by many adults who are vulnerable to feelings of worthlessness and unlovability. Needing another's approval in order to feel good about themselves, they may try to "psych out" the other person's wishes and behave accordingly, surrendering their own authenticity and spontaneity in the process. Very often the wishes they believe the other to have are really projections of what they might wish in a relationship, which may or may not be true of the partner. Often the partner may feel uncomfortable but not to be aware of what is wrong in the interaction. His or her own spontaneity and authenticity must inevitably be compromised since there is an element of control to this interpersonal mechanism.

Freedom from such extreme concern for pleasing other people is rooted in early experiences with a truly nurturant and accepting world. If positive parental responses are forthcoming only when the child feels, behaves, or thinks as parents deem he *should*, he will be unable to take in their "Good for you!" reactions and make them a part of how he feels about himself. These reactions will have nothing to do with how or who he *really* is. The praise will be for his pretense and not for his real, natural self, which will remain unconfirmed. Although in healthy development the internalization of the standards and values of parents who are loved and respected is central to the development of the conscience and to one's own standards and ideals, the process allows for the development of the child's authentic being. Living up to parental standards may, on the other hand, be based on fear, either of punishment or of losing approval of parents or of new people who have been given parental authority and power. Consequently, one's self-esteem is placed in the hands of others. To protect that self-esteem, one may strive to live up to the requirements of others at the cost of being in harmony with one's authentic self.

Healthy self-esteem means that an individual lives in accordance with the ideals, values, and moral and ethical standards that he himself has formulated as part of the process of psychological maturation. Although these are derived initially from an identification with loved and respected parents, over time they may undergo certain transformations, especially toward the end of adolescence, when learning about the self, others, and the world leads to a new formulation of what life is all about.

A woman I once worked with was chronically anxious about how people would respond to her. She tried to be as good and as perfect as she knew how so that she would be liked by everyone. It wasn't working.

When I asked her what her favorite fruit was, she replied that it was the apricot. I asked her to pretend that she was an apricot—the most beautiful, perfectly ripe, unblemished apricot there ever was. Then I asked her to imagine someone coming along who did not like apricots and what that person's reaction to her would be. She made a sour face.

Then I asked her to pretend she was another apricot—smaller, not so perfect, with a little bite taken out by a bird and a freckle on the other side. I asked her to imagine this time that someone came along who *loved* apricots. She smiled, understanding what I had been trying to tell her about being one's self and being loved.

No matter how hard we may try to please or to be good (whatever that is!), we surely cannot please everyone. This dooms any efforts at self-confirmation through the eyes of other people.

I NEED YOU TO MEASURE ME AGAINST

At the time of the power pivot, the child moves from the illusion of magical control over mother as an extension of the self, to recognition of the separateness and relative inadequacy of the self vis-à-vis a powerful parent. It is not until the child has developed further along and achieved a sense of his or her own realistic competence and image of the self and the other that this "I'm powerful and you are weak," or, "I am weak and you are powerful" dichotomy can be resolved. Since power and self-esteem (versus powerlessness and shame) go together in the early years (Horner 1989), other values that are later accepted as a measure of one's worth may fall into this same sort of mutually exclusive dichotomy when the early struggle remains unresolved. Although the struggle in adult life may seem to be *against* the other, that person is needed to provide the self-defining contrast.

One woman would say of her sister, "She's prettier but I'm smarter." Her feelings about herself, about her attractiveness or lovability or capability, were not firmly anchored in herself but could only be grasped through a comparison with her sister and with others in her life as well. She needed her relationships as a kind of nucleus around which to organize her perception of herself.

Unfortunately, this kind of relating automatically introduces a hostile and competitive element into the basic dependency. In order to feel good about one's self, the other person has to be seen in a bad light. If one is up, the other must be down, and vice versa. We've probably all seen this kind of seesaw relationship and wondered why it continues in view of the degree of competitive hostility. It continues because each would feel lost without the other through whom the self can be compared, perceived, and defined.

HOSTILE DEPENDENCY: THE COMPROMISE THAT DOESN'T WORK

Fighting is one way to stay close and involved, to have one's various dependency needs met, and at the same time to protect the self by asserting its separateness. Dependent clinging and oppositional behavior often go hand in hand.

This mode of relating is normal behavior for the dependent 2-year-old who is trying to establish a degree of autonomy, but it is the cause of serious problems in adult relationships. As a compromise solution to the conflict between being and loving, it just doesn't work. The hostility precludes the gratifications that go with closeness, while the dependency precludes the development of identity and the unfolding of the real self.

Tom was caught on the horns of this dilemma in his relationship with his wife. The need to oppose her in order to feel separate stood as a barrier to anything positive or affectionate that might take place between them. If his wife reached out to him warmly, the closeness that this implied was experienced as a threat to his autonomy. If he responded to her it would feel like he was doing what she wanted—even though at one level it might have also been what he wanted. Closeness with his mother had, indeed, required that he comply with her demands. Now, he would push his wife away, but then he would feel empty, futile, and depressed at having to deny himself the love for which he yearned. He had to say no when he wanted to say yes.

The evolution of the hostile–dependent relationship is exemplified by a boy of 10 who once asked me to teach him to play the piano. I responded to his apparent eagerness to learn and bought a beginner's piano book for him. The first lesson involved learning the letter names of the keys. We began by finding middle C, and then all the other Cs. Lesson after lesson went on, and each time I would start by asking him to find all the Cs. One time he played all the Bs. The next time he played all the Ds. He was intelligent, but he seemed "unable" to master this simple assignment. One day he broke into a big grin and I realized that he had something else in mind than learning to play the piano. I told him to let me know when he had mastered finding where all the Cs were, and then we would go on with our lessons.

It was clear that this little boy was interested, first, in involving me in a helping relationship, and then in thwarting my efforts to help him. A child who develops this kind of self-defeating behavior does not do so out of some perverse pleasure in failing. His defeat of parental-type figures, however, does gratify his need for power over them and makes sure that they do not have any power over him. Most important, he protects the boundaries of his real but inadequately defined and frightened self. He forms dependent attachments like that he has with his mother, and at the same time maintains his separateness and autonomy by opposing and thwarting those with whom he forms these attachments.

At school this kind of child is often identified as an underachiever. He defeats his teachers by being inept or stupid. His inevitable failure wreaks havoc with his self-esteem despite the fact that he feels a sense of secret power and superiority at having defeated the parent figure.

If this chapter has seemed to be a chamber of horrors of love gone sour, they are everyday horrors that many, many men and women agonize over, rage against, or succumb to. Needing is not loving. It reflects the inability to love another person as a whole person in his or her own right and to cherish him or her for being that person. Needing also reflects the thwarting of being, insofar as the self must be surrendered to the requirements of the relationship.

Acting out the patterns of needing unhappily perpetuates the very blocks to being and loving that they were devised to protect the person from or to enable him to compensate for. They paradoxically bring about the death of relationships or the annihilation of individuality.

Resolution of the conflicts of the power pivot and moving beyond dependency bring the individual to a new and more rewarding level of relating. In the recognition and valuing of the real self and the real other lies the potential for mature loving, which ultimately enhances one's capacity to be.

7

THE BEST OF ALL
POSSIBLE WORLDS:
BEING ME AND LOVING
YOU

As THE YOUNG child moves forward out of the stage of the power pivot, ideally he or she achieves a cohesive and realistic sense of self as well as a realistic sense of the other people in his or her world. As an adult there will be an ability to value others on the basis of the individuals they are rather than on the basis of what they can do for the self. Loving the other will be just as important as being loved *by* the other.

At this stage of development—that is, when the child is about 3 years old—he or she becomes better able to tolerate both good and bad feelings about the self as well as toward others. The capacity to tolerate ambivalence will make it possible later on to establish relationships that will endure in the face of disappointment and anger. And finally, at this stage the child consolidates the capacity to nourish, comfort, validate, and confirm him- or herself from inner resources that will enable him or her, as an adult, to be alone or to live alone without being lonely, depressed, or afraid.

Developmental tasks that confront the individual at each of the successive stages throughout life—going off to school, adolescence, becoming an independent adult, middle age, and coming to terms with death—involve the same issues, although in ever more intricate and complex ways. But if the foundation has been well laid in the first three or four years of life, the later challenges can be met with a minimum of distress and a maximum of fulfillment.

BECOMING WHOLE

Intellectual and cognitive maturation combines with satisfactory life experiences to promote a continuing process of integration. This includes the integration of perceiving, thinking, feeling, wishing, and doing—all different aspects of the experiencing self. Recognition and integration of these sometimes conflicting aspects of self are essential to the process of becoming whole. I may feel angry but wish I were not; I may believe a friend is loyal but perceive he is not; I may feel bored but choose not to show it in my behavior. All of these are elements of me, and I must be able to tolerate and resolve the conflicts between them if I am to "be me."

The process of becoming whole also involves the healing of the good me–bad me split along with the good you–bad you split. This is a normal developmental division that originates in the stage of symbiosis when positive experiences are grouped together in the good-me–you image, and negative experiences are grouped together in the bad-me–you image (see Table 7–1). In the first year of life before cognitive abilities make it possible for the baby to understand the basic continuity of self and other, these disparate sets of experience each have their own separate reality. Gradually, in the stage of becoming two, the me is differentiated from the you. Now the split halves of the me image and the you image must be integrated into single, unified images of a whole self and a whole other, either of which is at times good and at other times bad.

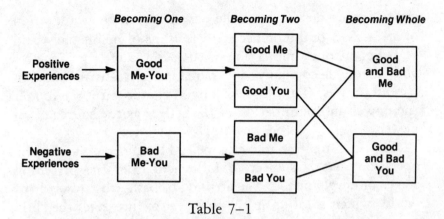

Table 7–1

The continued split of others into either all good or all bad images, and with this, the inability to tolerate ambivalence, is a major factor in the breakdown of relationships. When there is disappointment or anger, the good one becomes bad, and in so doing, the good one ceases to exist in the mind. The emotional connection with the loved other is lost, and what is felt instead is the unmodified hate toward the bad other. This may be accompanied by a depressive reaction to the felt loss of the good other, even though the loss may be purely subjective. That is, the other person may still be there and available, but for all practical purposes, he or she no longer matters.

The untempered hate for the all-bad self can be just as toxic. It can destroy the connection with the valued self and wipe out self-esteem. In the most extreme instances, such rage and hatred may find expression in actual killing, that is, in murder or suicide.

When the final step of integration is successful, the capacity to tolerate an attitude of ambivalence replaces feelings of total, idealized love or total hate. People—including oneself—are experienced neither as devils nor saints, but as the real persons they happen to be. This is a basic requirement for being me and loving you.

The process of becoming whole also entails the healing of

the split that derives from the power pivot. The integration of feelings of omnipotence with feelings of helplessness and of belief in one's perfection with feelings of worthlessness and shame accompany an increasingly realistic view of parent figures. They are no longer viewed either as under the power and domination of the self or as the source of all power.

The final step toward being me and loving you is a complex operation that is subject to influences from the preceding stages of development. The attitude of basic trust toward the world, which is set up in the first year of life, gives the child courage to renounce the illusion of power. With the continued emotional availability of parents during the stage of becoming two, the child's awareness of his or her realistic helplessness and imperfection, with accompanying feelings of anxiety and shame, are counteracted by the parents' support and acceptance. Emotional support of this nature enables the child to relinquish the need for power and the illusion of perfection. It makes it possible for him or her to take the final step away from the power pivot toward authentic being and authentic loving.

It is the same for all of us as adults. It is certainly easier to admit an error (and thus, imperfection) to someone who genuinely cares for us and respects us. It is another matter to do so to someone whose feelings for us are less positive. In the first instance, one can be wrong without feeling shamed. And in such a relationship, I can truly be me and love you.

BEING ALONE WITHOUT BEING LONELY

An individual's capacity to be alone without feeling lonely or depressed is nourished by inner resources that build upon the good me–you image of the stage of symbiosis and culminate in what psychoanalysts refer to as object constancy at around the age of 3.[1] Object constancy refers to the enduring nature of the psychological connection with mother and later, with important people in general when they are gone or when they are not actively meeting one's needs. An emotional connection with a mother who is long dead, with children who are a continent away, with loyal and dear friends we see regularly or only sporadically as busy lives allow, are all manifestations of object constancy. The inner world of ever-present intimacies that continue to nourish and sustain us when we are alone frees us to choose to be alone or to live alone, and to pursue solitary activities that may enrich us even further, such as gardening, painting, or listening to music. A paucity of interests and gratifications outside of intense interpersonal relationships is often characteristic of dependent men and women.

One of the most important early experiences that leads to the capacity to be alone is that of being alone while being *with* mother, the paradox of being alone together. Winnicott (1958) wrote of the importance for the child to experience being alone in the presence of another person. At this time the child plays with the assumption that the person who loves him or her is reliable and available if needed even when the child may not be thinking about that person or attending to her. This is the kind of relating you may have experienced when you and someone you care for have spent an evening reading, each engrossed in your own book but very much sensing the presence of the other. Even though you have temporarily forgotten that the other person is there, there is an awareness that he or she is available at a moment's notice. The child who

[1]Anna Freud (1976) suggests that since the child attains object constancy at about the age of 3, this is the best time to start him in nursery school; ". . . separation from mother is less upsetting, he is ready to reach out to new people and to accept new ventures and adventures." That is, because the inner relationship with the mother is secure in the child's mind, he can be away from her without experiencing undue distress. (See also the appendix chapter and the section for working mothers in this book.)

is beginning to emerge as a separate person has this same sort of experience as he plays with his toys while mother reads, knits, or works about the house. Even though there may be no interaction, there is a sense of being together, a sense of relatedness.

The need for the actual physical presence of the mothering person in order to maintain this experience of relatedness gradually diminishes with the growth of understanding and memory. The child becomes capable of protecting himself from the distress of separation from mother by actively recalling her to mind, by using his store of memories and good feeling to maintain the emotional connection with her. As one analyst put it (Lichtenberg 1975), "The child . . . begins to 'live' a bit less in exclusive response to the outer world; he lives a bit more in his mind" (pp. 453–484).

The capacity to be alone also comes about through the process of learning to do for the self what mother once had to do. An example of this is the kind of caretaking that provides emotional security in the face of stress. If she has done this consistently enough, the child does not become overwhelmed by stress, and her soothing becomes something that he can remember and experience in her absence. When mother isn't available, the young child begins to find ways to do these things for himself. He reaches for his teddy bear or his blanket and comforts and soothes himself with it. This is a very important step in development. He now actively does for himself what he previously passively experienced his mother doing for him (Tolpin 1971). After a time, the young child outgrows his need for the teddy bear or the blanket and develops within himself, at a symbolic level, resources for the kind of comforting that he previously derived from the external supports. It is like having a loving mother within one's self. The self-sufficiency that develops draws its substance from the capacity to love and to treasure what one has been given, however, and not from a denial of the importance of others.

The individual who has not developed these inner psychological resources, the inner good mother, may turn to outside sources of comfort such as food, drugs, alcohol, or casual sexual encounters, all of which he or she will use much as the small child uses a teddy bear when mother isn't available. Developing these inner resources is a problem that such individuals will have to deal with if they look to psychotherapy for help with their problems in living.

When psychotherapy goes well, the therapist may function for a time as a symbolic good mother. At first, patients report such experiences as "I think about you and what you would say to me if you were there." "I carry you around in my pocket and take you out when I need you." Gradually, this inner experience of the good therapist—mother becomes an integral part of the self, and the same patient will report, "I no longer consciously think about you at such times, but seem able to make myself feel better. It seems to happen almost automatically."

BEING ME AND LOVING YOU

Adults who are fortunate enough to have come to this point, whether early in life by virtue of a healthy constitution coupled with good parenting, or later on through direct confrontation of the problems inherent in being and loving, experience freedom and pleasure in their interpersonal relationships. The coming together of two separate individuals into a shared context experienced as the "we" is analogous to Winnicott's (1971) concept of play as taking place in the potential space between the baby and the mother where the child is neither totally within himself and his own inner reality, nor totally outside himself in external reality. He is neither totally separate from the mother nor totally merged with her. She, on the other hand, is able to join in with the

child and play with him in this in-between place. Winnicott
writes:

> In the experience of the more fortunate baby (and small child and
> adolescent and adult) the question of separation in separating does not
> arise, because in the potential space between the baby and the mother
> there appears the creative playing that arises naturally out of the relaxed
> state. [p. 108]

Adults who can experience the "we" do not feel separated
by their individualities inasmuch as each can be sure that the
other is always there and available for participation in a shared
experience, an experience that has the quality of the child's
play with his mother.

Connie and Paul are two such people. They both have strongly
defined tastes, opinions, styles, and interests of their own.
Their friends often assume that there must be power conflicts
between them and that privately one must surely dominate the
other. Yet their life is characterized by an easy and spontaneous
flow, a give-and-take, that allows for the authenticity and
autonomy of each, as well as for the pleasures of sharing in the
manner described by Winnicott as play.

Their home reflects their relationship. Each has space that
is his or her own and that reflects the individuality of their
tastes. Other rooms are a hodgepodge of things they both like
and that fit together. For these rooms they have only one
rule—neither buys anything the other can't at least live with
comfortably. Self-expression is voluntarily limited when it
would constitute an assault on the other. Because both have a
strong sense of their fundamental autonomy, Connie and Paul
are comfortable with their separateness. They do not have to
cling to each other in a compulsive togetherness in order to
experience their ongoing emotional connection. Neither feels
deserted or resentful at the other's wish to have his or her own
time and space.

However, the commitment that each has made to their life together has top priority. Luckily, it is a commitment that allows each the freedom to be as well as to love. For example, each can take pleasure in the other's enthusiasms without feeling that he or she has to be enthusiastic about the same thing, or that his or her own enthusiasms have to be relinquished. Furthermore, since neither has to defend against the domination of the other or to pretend infallibility in order to maintain self-esteem, they can turn to each other with trust when either needs comforting. In Connie and Paul's giving and taking there is a mutuality that is possible simply because it is love, and not power, that connects them.

Paul does not need Connie's adulation or submission to feel good as a person and as a man. Connie does not have to connive to get what she wants and needs. They do not have to manipulate and countermanipulate to get power and dependency strivings gratified. Their relationship is just the opposite of those based on dependency needs and built around role playing according to a predetermined script. Neither is burdened with the responsibility of maintaining the other's self-esteem or sense of self. And unlike those who have to maintain the myth of perfection in their relationship, Connie and Paul can fight and resolve archaic issues of being and loving when these issues become reactivated, as they do for everyone from time to time.

The fact that perfection is a myth that can only be maintained at great cost to the individual, as well as to a relationship, confronts us with the realities of imperfection. In the best of relationships there will be conflict or tension from time to time, which has to be resolved. What is at issue is the nature of the resolution. Does it enhance or interfere with being and/or loving? Coming to terms with the fact that there may be no perfect solution is an essential aspect of constructing a life that allows for both.

8

BEING AND LOVING IN AN IMPERFECT WORLD

You may be experiencing a sense of personal failure as you read this book, recognizing that you have not been able to achieve an ideal integration of being and loving in your life. You may take this as an indication that there is something wrong with you, or with your husband, wife, or lover. You may be finding it just as hard to accept the imperfectibility of relationships as it is to accept your own personal imperfection.

The renunciation of the ideal of a perfect self is a prerequisite for authentic being, while a renunciation of the ideal of a perfect other is a prerequisite for authentic loving. In a parallel way, the reality of the imperfectibility of relationships in terms of being and loving, and the need for repeated conflict resolution, must also be accepted as inevitable and unavoidable. For only with this kind of acceptance can we manage not to overreact to this conflict with bitterness or discouragement, or with anger and blame.

It is not easy to give up our hopes and ideals for a perfectible world—to confront the realities that we do not live happily forever after, that we will not be rewarded or compensated for our suffering, that conflict is inevitable, and that some problems have no good solutions—only less bad ones. [1]

The concept of an ideal resolution of the conflict between being and loving would imply that there is such a perfectible balance in which they can fully coexist at all times. Like most ideals, however, this kind of balance is rarely, if ever, achieved. Even in the happiest of relationships, the conflict rears its head again and again, to be resolved once more. Someone's privacy is not adequately respected. Someone is pressured to go to a movie he or she doesn't want to see. Someone feels misunderstood or inadequately responded to. Someone feels wounded because of a lack of appreciation and acknowledgment. There is a clash of moods. One wants to make love and the other is preoccupied with work problems.

What are your own personal experiences with this kind of conflict? How do you handle these situations? Perhaps you can put disappointment, hurt, or blame aside long enough to consider the ways in which you might be able, realistically, to bring both intimacy and self expression into your life.

Whatever your own unique solution, it will have to be in harmony with the person you are—your temperament and rhythms, your interests and tastes, the demands and responsibilities that you must meet. And it will have to take into consideration the same factors in the lives of people who are important to you. Your solution will have to be tailor-made to your own personal way of life.

Lillian Evans is retired and lives alone. She is well aware of her struggle between being and loving. She has struggled for most

---

[1]Dr. Roy Schafer (1976) describes four basic attitudes toward reality: the comic vision, the romantic vision, the tragic vision, and the ironic vision. He emphasizes the importance of the ironic vision that allows one to confront reality and the imperfections of the world without romanticizing or dramatizing them. It implies a greater detachment and sense of "that's the way it is." This is not a defensive detachment that protects one from the conflicts of being and loving. It is a stance that acknowlegdes that everything cannot always work out well. But sometimes it can. A clear view of reality enables us to know the difference.

of her life to bring them into some kind of workable balance. She knew that the experience of intimacy and deep friendship was terribly important to her. Yet she also realized that she could only fully experience her own identity when she was alone.

Lillian has a strong sense of herself but is basically shy and reluctant to put herself forward. She also tends to lend herself as an empathetic ear for others—her role in her relationship with her father, and one that led her into one of the helping professions. Thus, in many relationships, particularly if she allows herself to feel at all needy or dependent upon the other, she finds herself fading into the background, concerned that if she does not accommodate to the other, she will be let down. A carefully developed self-sufficiency wards off these feelings, although she has learned to turn to others for support when needed. She is no loner. She likes being with people and cares about those within the inner circle of her life. She expresses a need for an even balance of being alone and being with others. Because she knows herself so well, she has been able to live in a way that works for her.

Lillian has been able to reach this solution because of her ability to be alone without being anxious or depressed. A combination of an "inner good mother," with pleasure in the use of her own intellect and talents, makes for contentment and fulfillment when she is by herself. Her solution to her conflict is in harmony with her "shy and noncombative" nature. It entails alternately moving toward people and moving away from them. She has chosen friends who understand this about her and who do not take it personally. They like being with her when she is feeling more sociable and also respect her wish to be by herself. Although she could not bring about an ideal resolution of her dilemma, she did work out one that brought both dimensions—being and loving—into her life. Her capacity to be alone made her unique answer possible.

In some ways, Don is like Lillian. He needs to be alone from time to time to feel fully connected with his own being.

However, he would really hate to live alone. It would feel too much like his days at boarding school where he was sent when his mother died. He was 7 years old, small, and rather timid. He didn't make friends easily because of his shyness, and he experienced terrible homesickness.

He decided quite early that he would marry young and raise a large family. That way he would always be surrounded by people he loved and who loved him. Despite the dependent quality of this arrangement, he loved his wife and fully appreciated the person she was, and he enjoyed the general family give and take in which he genuinely and spontaneously participated.

But at times Don would feel overwhelmed by the hubbub of his home, and would begin to feel increasingly cut off from himself and his own thoughts. Then he would find himself predominantly reacting to the external environment rather than to any sense of what came from within. The clue that alerted him to this shift was an irritability that he couldn't blame on any one person or any particular event. At these times he would feel an intense need to be alone in order to regain his feelings of calm and of being centered within himself.

So Don constructed his private sanctuary. He built a room that was only for him. He designed it, selected the furnishings, and decorated it with mementos accumulated over the years, with things that had private and personal meaning for him. One of these items was a picture of his mother that was framed in an antique silver frame that had belonged to his grandmother. No one else was allowed into his sanctuary except by invitation. He might leave it to have a cup of coffee with his wife, and then go back to immerse himself in his stamp collection, happy as a clam and feeling warm and content in the close proximity to those he loved.

Don used space and seclusion as a way of maintaining his sense of connection with his own being. The loving attachment was always present, and he could move out toward expression of it when he was ready once again to participate in the general we-ness of the family. His solution was possible because his wife Lucy was extremely self-reliant and never at a loss for interests of her own. She didn't feel rejected or abandoned because of Don's need to be alone. She also knew that if she really needed to be with him for any reason, he would respond out of his caring for her and would not feel intruded or impinged upon. They both had a capacity for give and take.

We might accurately predict that Don would face a crisis if he were to lose his family, particularly his wife. But the strong pull toward people and his pleasure in participating in group activities would probably motivate him to fill up his world once again. Even now he talks about opening up his home to foreign students when his children grow up and move away.

For other couples, the resolution of the conflict between being and loving doesn't go so smoothly. And yet, with an atmosphere of basic goodwill, they can negotiate a solution that is at least okay, if not ideal.

Tim worked under considerable pressure in his law office. He felt the need to unwind at the end of the day. For him this meant regaling his wife Pamela at great length with the details of his day. She often felt this as a demand that she become an ear on legs, and sometimes felt as though she herself were invisible. She was just as tired as Tim and would have liked to be on the receiving end rather than giving. End-of-day crises were frequent—angry explosions and accusations of nonlove and noncare. It became clear that something had to be done when their conflict began to escalate and spread to other aspects of their lives. There were more and more fights about who should yield to whom.

Finally they decided that they had better negotiate if their relationship were to survive. They began with an agreement that each was to be allotted ten minutes of wind-down and complaint time when they got home from work, and then the subject would be dropped. They would then fix dinner together.

Despite the apparently oversimplistic nature of their solution, it comprised a definitive statement that the being of each was important to the relationship and that unless they attended to that principle, loving didn't have much of a chance. Negotiating and taking turns became a useful device for maintaining an optimum balance between being and loving for Tim and Paula.

Psychotherapy with couples often focuses on the ways in which each of the partners relates to the other as a quasi-parent figure. When these wishes become activated at the same time, neither can hear the needs of the other and both feel the needs of the other as intolerable demands and feel emotionally abandoned. It is tantamount to two needy and demanding children fighting for mothering, and there is no mother available to respond to either of them. Tim wanted Paula to comfort and soothe him, and Paula wanted Tim to comfort and soothe her. The specific nature of a couple's respective dependencies, left over from their own early development, will determine the nature and quality of what is wanted from the other and the nature of reaction to an experienced failure of caring. In this situation, the being of the partner is forgotten, and the anger evoked by the failure of the partner to respond in the wished for way stands in the way of loving.

There are many different ways to live a life. The full life is one in which there is a place for both being me and loving you. Sometimes the people involved can achieve an optimum balance for themselves as did Don and Lucy, and eventually, Tim and Paula. Sometimes an individual finds his or her own balance in a single life, as Lillian did.

But sometimes there is an imbalance, which the individual or individuals seem unable to remedy by themselves. The imbalance may be the consequence of significant problems left over from the first three years of life. Chronic anger in response to feeling one's selfhood or identity being wiped out, or loneliness because of an absence of loving connections, may interfere with the achieving of a tolerable balance between the two experiences. This may be the time to consider looking for professional help. Now that divorce has become relatively respectable and laws have made it much easier, many couples take this route rather than trying to work out the mutual dilemmas that have them both trapped in an unsatisfactory situation.

Sometimes help may entail coming to terms with the unhappy reality that there can be no resolution to the conflict within the established relationship. In an imperfect world, some problems have no solution. If either Tim or Paula had been unwilling or unable to negotiate and to compromise, their relationship could not have survived except in the form of two people perennially battling to be seen and heard. Sometimes a person feels unable to negotiate because of problems left over from the power pivot. For them, negotiation is tantamount to defeat, and defeat means humiliation. The partner will surely be hated for that.

Giving up unrealistic hope is necessary before real hope can enter our lives. That is, when we come to recognize what is realistically attainable, we can work toward that goal with some real hope of success.

Coming to terms with personal imperfection is a prerequisite for a good enough resolution of the conflict between being and loving. The protagonists of the great tragedies were doomed by their one tragic flaw. Othello was a man who had everything—power, wealth, honor, and the love of a beautiful woman. Iago exploited Othello's tragic flaw, his jealousy, and so brought about his downfall. For Caesar it was ambition, "a grievous fault, and grievously hath Caesar answered it" (Shakespeare, *Julius Caesar*). Sometimes we view the failure of the other to understand us and love us perfectly as his or her tragic flaw.

I have listened to people who agonized over the task of accepting the imperfection of their parents. To do so would mean giving up hope for perfect love and perfect understanding. Yet not until they could take that step would they experience their own love for that parent. The anger of frustration constitutes too great a barrier to the good feelings.

Many years ago, finally giving up the ghost of that struggle myself, I turned to my mother and said, "I don't think you will ever really understand me." She answered with tears in her eyes, "I don't think I ever will." With the mutual acknowledgment and acceptance of the realistic limits of what we could share, I was able to put down my cudgel and to take a good look at this little old lady across from me. I could forgive her for her imperfections, and I could see and appreciate her for who she was and for what she had really given me. Only much later, and with some sadness, did I realize that I had also failed to understand her.

What are your hopes and expectations in reading this book? Do you anticipate that it will provide the solution to your conflict between being and loving, that it will provide a ready-made answer to the question, "How can I be in a close relationship with another human being without losing myself? How can I have intimacy and still preserve my identity?"

And how do you react to the reality that there is no such simple answer? Are you able to accept the fact that you will most likely have to continue to struggle with the inevitable conflict between being and loving, and that your resolution, whatever it may be, will entail some cost, some renunciation, and will stir up anxiety, guilt, remorse, or grief from time to time? And with the articulation of the dilemma, its realities, and the built-in impossibility of an *ideal* resolution, are you able to begin to struggle toward one that will work for you?

9

HOW IS IT WITH YOU?

THE PAST CHAPTERS have described the early developmental factors that contribute to the conflict between being and loving (or between emotional autonomy and emotional dependency). The conflict is intrinsic to the process of growth and cannot be prevented, even by the best of parenting. We all come to our adult lives with some of its derivatives.

This chapter turns to you and invites you to examine your own experience with respect to your sense of self, your identity, and your feelings about intimacy. It asks questions that I hope will enable you to assess where you are with issues of being and loving and to define the nature of your conflict if you do, indeed, experience one. The chapter will offer suggestions that may enhance your ability to take steps toward a better resolution of this conflict. Whether this process is one we undertake by ourselves or with the assistance of a psychotherapist, the issues will be the same.

WHAT YOU CAN DO FOR YOURSELF: TAKING INVENTORY

One of the things you can do for yourself to start the process of self understanding is to take inventory, to clarify where you stand with respect to being and loving. What are your vulnerabilities? How do you protect yourself? What price do you pay for this protection?

What about attachments? Have you tried to solve your conflict between being and loving by denying the wish for intimacy? Do you want to integrate this experience into your life? Which of the following come closest to your experience of emotional attachments?

1. I have no attachments and do not know what it is to have one.

2. I form attachments to animals but not to people. Animals are safer. They make no demands on me to be other than who I am.

3. I form attachments to people on the basis of what I want them to be. For a while they seem to be the ideal parents or family I never had but always wanted. But inevitably they disappoint me; they fail to live up to my ideal, so it is no longer safe to rely on them. That's when I transfer them from my list of people who are all good to my list of those who are all bad. For some reason, I have a very short list of people who are all good and a very long list of those who have let me down.

4. I form attachments but break them off at the first sign of anger in me or in the other person. I cannot be angry and still maintain the feeling of connection with someone else. When I lose the feeling of connection I feel depressed.

5. I make attachments but break them off when I experience pressure not to be me. Even though this may not actually be the case, this is what it felt like with my parents and I expect the same from others. I may possibly see these

demands even when they are not actually there. I would rather terminate the relationship than assert myself within it. I am afraid of the consequences of such self-assertion.

6. I make attachments, but they are based on my own particular dependency needs, and sooner or later I come to resent the other person because she or he has become too important to me and then I end up feeling as though I am in that person's power. Such people may not actually be trying to exert control over me, but it feels as though they are because what they say or do determines how I feel about myself. They also have the power to say yes or no to what I want from them, and I don't want anyone to have that kind of power over me.

7. I make attachments through my false self. As a result, these attachments do not feel real. They are not with my true self. No matter how well things seem to go between me and someone else, I have a secret fear that the other person will abandon me if he or she finds out what I am really like, or if I express what is really going on inside me. No matter how well the relationship goes, I feel alone and as though I have nothing because the real me is not participating in the interaction.

8. I make attachments, but before long the only thing that seems to matter is who has power over whom. When this happens, I find little pleasure or love in the relationship.

9. _____

(Maybe you can add your own scenario here.)

Notice that *how you experience* an interpersonal relationship may not be indicative of what the other person wishes or intends. Everybody has his or her own subjective view of reality. Sometimes one's present view is so highly colored by experiences early in life, there is no chance to learn that there are other ways to relate and people who are able to relate in a more authentic manner.

You may want to try to take more risks in moving toward

people. Perhaps awareness of the source and nature of the distress or displeasure you feel in intimate relationships will enable you to cope with these feelings.

The struggle to maintain an attachment goes hand in hand with the struggle to remain connected with your real self. Here are some guidelines for assessing problems that you may have in maintaining this connection.

1. I don't really have a sense of myself. I don't have that gut level conviction that I am, that I exist, that I go on being. I don't know what I feel most of the time. I'm used to letting others tell me what and who I am, and what I should or shouldn't do. Sometimes I become confused because I receive so many contradictory directives. I gave up therapy because I couldn't tell whether the things my therapist said about me were actually so or not, and I only felt more confused.

2. I do have a sense of me, but feel I have to keep an emotional distance between myself and others in order to preserve it. Attachments are a threat to my sense of identity and to my autonomy, so I avoid them.

3. My real self is a secret self—sometimes even from me. I have constructed an image that I present to the world, to people close to me as well as those who are more distant. Others look at me and think I have it made. But I know it's all an illusion and sometimes I feel alone and frightened.

4. I cover my real self and present the kind of image I know will get attention of some kind, perhaps sympathy if not love. I hate having to play the "sickie" (or the helpless one) even though it does get me what I want. I have no respect for myself, and I resent the others who respond to me as the cripple I tell them I am—even though I set it up this way.

5. I push my real self aside. I am afraid of making others angry with me by not being what I think they want me to

be, because I am so dependent on them. I feel as though I am in their control and resent them because of this.

6. I only feel like my real self when I am angry and stand in opposition to someone else. I need to fight in order to feel separate. Sometimes this means I have to say no to something I really want. Sometimes this means I have to defeat people who are trying to help me.

7. _____

(Maybe you can add your own scenario here, too.)

HOW TO FIND YOUR SELF

A rather natural question to ask at this point would be, "How do I go about getting in touch with the real me? If I knew how, I would."

Sometimes confronting the real self may evoke feelings of guilt, shame, or anxiety. It may mean confronting aspects of one's self that one may wish to disown. Some people cannot tolerate not living up to an ideal image of themselves, such as someone who is always good or moral or right. To confront the dark side would disrupt the sense of the self who is valued and loved, and this might feel unbearable. If we look inside ourselves we might find feelings that also seem unbearable and that we fear might overwhelm us, make us unable to go on about our life. Buried feelings of depression or despair that built up very early in life, because of an inability to establish a safe relationship with the primary caretaker, may be fought off by being very busy and by developing good coping skills that evoke a false sense of well-being. There is a wish never to feel the helplessness or despair again, yet they go hand in hand with getting in touch with the real self. These potential dangers stand as a barrier to the process of self-discovery. Coming to grips with the nature of these dangers—real or imagined—sometimes has to come first, before the individual can feel safe enough to pursue the discovery process. This is often an important aspect of psychotherapy. Having a companion makes the exploration less frightening. But if you want to go ahead on your own, here are a few techniques you may find helpful.

I AM A PERSON WHO _____

If you were to describe yourself, what would you say? Where would you begin? A useful technique is to draw up a list of statements, all starting with the phrase, "I am a person who _____ ." If you have difficulty getting started with this task, try beginning with simple statements such as "I am a person who likes chocolate ice cream." Gradually the self-defining will go into deeper and possibly more painful areas. This task is especially useful for people who are used to letting others define them. The capacity to be honest and to relinquish, at least momentarily, the image of the idealized self will determine the effectiveness of this exercise. Being in touch with yourself and having full access to your own inner resources requires awareness of and owning all aspects of yourself, including those you don't like very much. Only with this process can one achieve a sense of unification and integration. It is a process that takes place more slowly and over a longer period of time in psychotherapy. Sitting down and making a complete list is not always so easy.

OWNING THE DISOWNED

Splitting other people into either all good or all bad makes it impossible to maintain attachments, since all real relationships inevitably have both positive and negative moments. As long as the other person is a constructed ideal or essentially a fantasy, whatever the connection we have with him or her will be neither a valid nor an enduring one.

In the same way, the need to split off and repress or deny aspects of ourself that would threaten our self-esteem, makes it impossible to have a firm connection with the real self. Harry Stack Sullivan (1956) used the term not-me to denote dissociated aspects of the personality, to aspects of the self that have been disowned. He said that in this situation "an important system of the personality is effectively barred from any disturbing influence on personal awareness for a period of years and perhaps for a lifetime" (p. 167).

Denying or repressing feelings and attitudes that we are afraid will get out of control or are afraid will alienate others or will damage our self-esteem in some way, is one way to handle the reality that we are *all* a mixture of good and bad, however we may define these qualities. The quality "bad" implies something different for different people. For some individuals, bad is

1. Being angry
2. Being a show-off
3. Having imperfect judgment
4. Being sexual
5. Having wishes of one's own
6. Showing or feeling tenderness (equated with weakness)
7. Being emotional (also equated with weakness)
8. Being ambitious
9. _____ (add your own)

Women are more likely to disown their ambition and assertiveness because these qualities have for so long been characterized as unfeminine. On the other hand, I have met some young women in recent years who are ashamed of their wish to marry and stay home and raise a family because wanting to "develop my own potential" (have a career) and being assertive were values embraced by women in the social revolution of the 1960 and '70s.

Men, on the other hand, are more likely to disown their

tenderness and emotionality because these qualities have been characterized as unmanly.

Social values and stereotypes are one source of disintegrating pressure. That is, they are the basis for disowning aspects of the self in a manner that interferes with the establishment of an integrated self. Parents may unwittingly interfere with the process of integration of all aspects of self in the early years. A parent may say to a child who is misbehaving, "You're not being yourself today!" The goal of the mother or father may be to maneuver the child into behaving in a more acceptable manner. The message that approved-of behavior is that of the real self while disapproved-of behavior is not that of the real self contributes to feelings of confusion in the child and to a defensive splitting off of different aspects of his or her personality.

A similar kind of dis-integrating pressure is reported by men and women who begin to grow and change as the result either of psychotherapy or of their own spontaneous maturation. "What's the matter with you? You're not being yourself today." This is especially likely to be a reaction to new angry or assertive behavior. The failure to validate the individual's experience of himself is very controlling, and is often enough to coerce a return to old and familiar patterns of interaction. It is not always easy to rediscover and own and integrate the many facets of one's own personality.

Are you surprised at some of the statements you have made about the person you are? Have you found this exercise more difficult than you had anticipated? How did you react to statements you did not like or approve of?

DISCOVERING YOUR EXPERIENCING SELF

The experiencing self is not the same as *what* one experiences. It is the sense of the self who is having the experience.

The capacity to focus on the experiencing self is vital to the process of trying to discover and connect with the self.[1]

When somebody tells me, "I only feel confused," I may ask him to focus on the self who is having the experience of being confused, rather than on the confusion itself. People often become so focused on the experience that they lose touch with the experiencer, that is, the self. By staying centered on the self who is having the experience of confusion, it is sometimes possible to understand what caused the confusion in the first place, such as being defined by a parent in a manner that did not match the child's experience of him- or herself.

In the case of anxiety, one may become so overwhelmed by the feelings that he or she loses sight of the self who is feeling. This adds to the distress. The feelings of disorientation or the confusion caused by lack of groundedness generates even more anxiety, the anxiety of potential annihilation. Then, in an attempt to push away the unpleasant experience—to get rid of the anxiety in this instance—the individual further loses touch with the self.

An experience will not be so frightening, nor will one feel so helpless in the face of it, if one does not lose touch with the self who is doing the experiencing. It is important to be able to say, "Whether I am afraid, or sad, or confused, I still have a firm sense of my own continuity, my own continuing existence, at the center of these difficult moments."

We can get in closer touch with our real self through the body, through our conscious thoughts, and through our dreams.

[1]Rollo May (1973) writes: "The self is not merely the sum of the various 'roles' one plays—it is the capacity by which one *knows* he plays these roles; it is the center from which one sees and is aware of these so-called different 'sides' of himself" (p. 91).

YOUR BODILY SELF

The infant's first awareness of self is the awareness of the physical self—of the body and the sensations from within it as well as from the skin and the sense organs.

If you sometimes feel your sense of self slipping away under certain kinds of stress, you can reconnect with it through the medium of your bodily self. You can try to become aware of your breathing, of the feeling of your feet on the floor, or of your rear end where it is in contact with the chair. By focusing your awareness on your bodily self, you can reestablish the location of your identity within the boundaries of your own skin.

I have suggested that people start this exercise by focusing on their own belly button, the first indicator of separateness from mother and thus the first definition of one as an individual. One young woman who was struggling against the loss of contact with her self in the context of pressure from other people, misheard me to say that she should focus on the umbilical cord. This misunderstanding was a manifestation of her inability at that moment either to perceive or to accept her own separateness.

A second step of the belly-button exercise is to focus on parts of the body at increasing distances from the navel and, with each one, to experience the connection between that part of the body and the belly button. For instance, I might say, "Now feel your knee. Feel just above it. Feel higher. Feel all the way to your belly button. Now back to your knee. Now experience the connection between them." Ultimately the aim of the exercise is to feel real at a bodily level, facilitating the integration of all parts of the self into a cohesive and united whole.

In recent years there has been an increasing concern with staying in good physical condition. People run every day, or begin their day with a visit to the gym where they work out doing aerobic exercises or swimming laps at the pool. One might hazard a guess that along with the physical benefits of such a regimen come psychological benefits that accrue as the result of a greater body awareness, and thus self-centering, that accompanies feeling better physically. One young woman who experienced the annihilation terrors that went with emotional abandonment when she balked at adapting to the wishes of her boyfriend, knew she could regain her sense of self and of emotional calm if she went to a dance class.

It is because of this connection between our body and our sense of self that changes in the body (as during puberty or again in later life) can be disruptive to our sense of an ongoing and stable self. In healthy development, a stable mental representation of the self does not rely so heavily upon the bodily self, and the individual can assimilate bodily changes into the self with relative equanimity. That is, the psychological self becomes relatively autonomous of the physical self. However, at critical moments, recourse to the original physical foundation of self may be valuable in regaining access to the psychological self.

LISTENING TO YOUR SELF

You can get more closely in touch with your self by listening to what is going on in your head as well as in your body. Listening to your voice and your conscious thoughts is one way to do this. Listening to the messages from your dreams is another.

Turning an ear—literally—to our own voice and our own words can be done by speaking into a tape recorder and then listening to what we have recorded. We can also do this by writing a letter to ourselves and then reading it with the same care and attention we would give to a letter from someone else.

Talking to one's self has often been equated with being a little bit crazy, but it can be a very valuable technique for discovering what is going on in our own head. Our tone of voice, the emotional connection to the words as we speak them, and the emergence of thoughts and ideas we may have been unaware of, reveal to us aspects of ourselves that may be giving us difficulty. Sometimes it is difficult to grasp and articulate the thoughts and fantasies that float around in our head. Putting them into words can be revealing. And by putting them into words we gain a significant measure of control and mastery of our own psychological processes. Gestalt therapists make extensive use of such techniques, "giving a voice" to tears, a sudden headache, or clenched teeth. Listening to the messages from within the self, which are expressed in a wide variety of ways, by translating them into words puts one in closer touch with one's self and facilitates the integration of conflicting aspects of the self.

Paying attention to our dreams is another way to listen to our own voice.[2] In dreams we speak in symbols and metaphors, so that the language of our dreams may need some translation before we can understand what we are, in effect, trying to say to ourselves. It is because our dreams are such a valuable clue to what is going on in our own insides that many therapists make translating them such an important part of therapy.

Dreams can be approached in a number of ways. Basic to them all is the recognition that abstract ideas must be expressed in visual symbols, and the assumption that the dream is a kind of metaphor, a symbolic expression of a wish or fear or conflict—some aspect of one's own self and one's own life. Even though other people are actors in our dreams, we are the ones who tell them what to say and what to do. We wrote the script. Their words come from our own heads. One man

[2]Everyone dreams, but not everyone remembers his or her dreams, or even the fact that they did dream. Dr. David Foulkes (1966) reports research findings about dream recallers as compared to nonrecallers. Those who remembered their dreams were found to be less conformist, less self-controlled, and less defensive. Forgetting of dreams or denial of dreaming, then, is related to the *extensive* use of repression as a defense.

told his therapist, "I dreamed that some guy was bad-mouthing you, but I defended you." He thought his therapist would appreciate his support. Then he had to acknowledge that the critical words he assigned to the other guy were actually negative thoughts he had been having about his therapist but was afraid to even think, no less say.

Sometimes the dream can be understood as representing some denied and repressed aspect of self which is nonetheless the basis for troublesome feelings even though there is no conscious awareness of it. One very competent and independent woman often dreamed about lost kittens. The kittens in her dream represented the frightened-child part of herself that had been pushed away very early in life in response to her parents' wishes that she be a big girl. Mother, especially, needed her to be more independent than could be expected for her age when the new baby arrived and mother was overwhelmed by the demands of the new and colicky child. Seemingly irrational bouts of depression or anxiety could not be understood until they could be connected with the lost-child part of herself.

Sometimes a dream can be understood as a statement about one's life. Another woman would frequently dream about houses—houses with many, many rooms, all of them filled with lovely surprises and treasures, but with no people in them. She yearned to share her own inner treasure with someone, but was coming to realize it could not be with the cold and aloof man to whom she was married.

Sometimes dreams represent wishes. One man dreamed of flying high above a distant city. His dream told his wish, which was not yet fully conscious, to be free of the unhappy life he was in and to make a new one for himself.

And sometimes dreams depict our dreads and anxieties, such as the frequent dreams one woman had of tornadoes and tidal waves and hurricanes and earthquakes. In these dreams she would be rushing about frantically trying to protect her children from falling walls or trees. These dreams expressed her intense anxiety over the threatening collapse of her world (and her marriage), and the extent to which she feared its destructive potential for her children. And at still another level, it once again expressed the anxiety she had felt as a child over the imminent collapse of her parents' marriage. At the deepest level of all, there was a fear of the destructive potential of her own anger at both her parents and her husband that was deeply repressed. Her nightmares predated her conscious awareness of these feelings in the present by several years, and until they could be admitted into that awareness, she experienced only nameless anxiety.

Another young woman, at the adult edge of adolescence, often dreamed about bridges, and in these dreams she would be terrified of crossing them. In one dream she sat at a dining table with her family at one end of the bridge. She was struggling with the developmental task of her age—the loosening of the dependent tie with her family. When she came to understand the nature of her anxiety, she was once again able to resume her schooling and the move toward the independence it represented. A young man at the same developmental crisis dreamed he was at a fork in the road and was afraid he would take the wrong path. His parents actively blocked any steps toward emotional independence and he was unable to resolve his crisis as favorably as did the young woman who had more family support for her healthy individuation.

To understand your own dreams, think of them as metaphors, as symbols of some aspect of you, and some aspect of your life now and in the past. You may appear in one dream in several disguises, each of them representing one aspect that may be in conflict with one of the others. For instance, you may appear as both adult and child in one dream. You may be present in the dream as a neutral observer standing to one side as well.

Sometimes people we hardly know or people from our distant past come into our dreams and we wonder what on earth they are doing there. You can discover how you have used someone as a symbol by letting yourself focus on what this person brings to mind. For instance, one man dreamed about a girl who was in his class in grammar school. His association to her was that she was the littlest kid in the class. From there he went on to think about his own littlest kid, his youngest child, and then himself as the youngest child in the family in which he grew up. As he explored the dream further, he could understand that it was saying something about the feelings he had had (and obviously still did have, although unconsciously) about being the youngest and the smallest. He came to understand some reactions he was having at work in his present life, particularly his frustration and anger at not having his ideas listened to just as he had not been listened to and taken seriously in family discussions at the dinner table.

Dreams often take up elements of something that has happened in reality the day before the dream—what is referred to as the day residue—and those events are used as props. They get woven into the issues of one's life as it is in the present and often as how it was experienced growing up. Present-day situations and relationships stir up feelings from old situations and relationships, particularly when these feelings are still heavily loaded with guilt, anxiety, anger, or conflict. The technique of making associations to the elements of the dream, as the man in the example above did, helps us understand our own symbolism and unlock the secret of the dream.

Your dreams are a key to your inner psychological world, and paying attention to them and coming to understand them will bring you into closer touch with yourself. Some people make lifelong use of their dreams as part of an ongoing process of self-understanding.

PUTTING IT ALL TOGETHER

The life of any individual has its own internal organization and consistency. What may appear irrational comes to make sense when it is viewed within the context of one's entire life, particularly one's earliest years.

In this chapter your attention has been directed toward different aspects of yourself, including your attitudes and behaviors with respect to emotional attachments, as well as the depth and quality of your connection with the real human being you are.

Putting these bits and pieces together in the context of your own history may promote a further integration that may, in turn, enable you to come closer to a resolution of your conflict between being and loving.

This task can be approached through the device of writing your autobiography in as great detail as you are able. Check with your family for information that you either do not know or that you have long forgotten. As you begin to reconstruct the story of how you got to be the person you are today, try to tie the present to the past, to discover the connecting links. You may see how you unconsciously reenact the past in present-day situations, or how what happened in the past has colored your perceptions of today.

Although this exercise may promote insight, insight per se is not the primary goal. The writing should serve an organizing and integrating function, promoting your sense of personal wholeness and integrity.

You may come to see how issues of being a separate and autonomous person have always been foremost, in conflict with your needs and wish to be close and loving with others. You may become aware how feelings from the power pivot of the second year of life never really did quiet down, and that you have struggled with feelings of inadequacy and shame ever since then, and have defended yourself against them by retreating to illusions of your own omnipotence and perfection. If this was the case, how did it affect your relationships within your family, with the kids at school, when you started to date, when you got your first job? And now?

The more clearly you delineate yourself as a real, live,

multidimensional human being, the better you will be able to perceive others in the same way. And this is, after all, the most important step in the development of the capacity for authentic being and authentic loving.

WHEN TO SEEK HELP

Check your own experiencing at this moment. Do you have a sense of having a handle on the issues that may trouble you? Do you have a sense of knowing what to do now that you have defined the problem? Or do you feel overwhelmed and discouraged? Do you think you need help in clarifying your problems? A reliable support in the face of debilitating anxiety or depression? Do you feel yourself only getting in deeper and deeper, unable to resolve your dilemma? If this is the case, then you might consider psychotherapy, seeking the assistance of someone with expertise in dealing with problems of being and loving.

Whether the major problem is one of making and maintaining psychological attachments, or of experiencing and maintaining one's sense of self, the integration of both these facets of human experience is the way to the best of all possible worlds, to "being me" and "loving you."

10

CAN THERAPY HELP?

By NOW YOU have read about the genesis of being and loving in the life of the individual and how one's adult experience continues to be affected by the inevitable conflict between them.

You may have concluded that your own feelings of anxiety, depression, or chronic anger are related to this conflict. And you may have decided that you would like to talk to someone about it. Nevertheless, you may also, quite understandably, have some reservations about taking this step.

WHY WITH A THERAPIST?

Psychotherapy provides a unique setting and ambience. It provides a context specifically geared toward change and growth. It provides the support of a to-be-counted-on relationship with someone who is interested in you, whose own needs and conflicts are, in successful therapy, put aside in the therapeutic relationship. Therapy provides objective confrontation and an opportunity to explore and examine your inter-

115

personal issues, particularly those having to do with the conflict between being and loving. The milieu of the therapeutic situation is a mini-laboratory in which what goes on with you in your interpersonal relationships can be highlighted and understood, with the goal of changing patterns that do not work.

The process of change and growth is difficult, and for the most part it comes about not only as the result of introspection and self-understanding, but also as the result of struggling with what we experience in our interactions with others. Just as the child develops the capacities to be and to love *within the context of a relationship*, specifically with the mothering person of the earliest years, so too one needs others with whom to interact in a special way in order to promote growth and development later in life. This is the experiential component of the growth process, whether in therapy or not, and a relationship-as-context-for-growth is one of the major contributions of the therapeutic relationship. Many psychoanalysts have concluded that successful therapy is related to an ongoing focus on the interpersonal process. Friedman (1984) tells us that "The forces that determine the outcome of the treatment relationship are inevitably interpersonal" (p. 172).

It is usually harder to make changes within old and established relationships. They tend to pull us back into old patterns unless the other people involved understand what is happening and are able to participate in the process and to make the kind of complementary shifts that change entails. Sometimes this will happen almost automatically if others do not have a psychological need for the person to stay the same. However, some marriages may be disrupted when only one partner grows and changes. In this situation, if both partners do not work together, the force of the pull and tug may increase until the relationship becomes unworkable. The one who is changing tries to pull his or her partner into a new way of defining the relationship, into new ways of interacting that will allow for individuality and autonomy as well as closeness and reliability, and in a manner that the self-esteem of both is not undermined. The other person, however, may try to maintain the status quo, to pull the one who is trying to change back to the way things used to be. Conjoint marital therapy tries to help both partners to grow together by focusing on the interpersonal processes within the marriage.

The same principle applies with respect to an individual vis-à-vis parents. From the start, some parents are able to make the shifts that are necessary to accommodate the growth of a son or daughter. They do not exploit their child in the service of their own conscious or unconscious needs but support him or her throughout the stages of development from infancy to childhood, from childhood to adolescence, and from adolescence on into adulthood. They provide an atmosphere of safety and respect for the child such that the child becomes an individual who feels secure within himself or herself and who has a healthy self-esteem.

Other parents, however, exert psychological pressures to prevent the individuation of their child in early life, and later, if the child begins to change as the result of psychological treatment. These parents try to keep things as they were. For instance, they may withdraw love or become openly hostile when the young person begins to make noises about moving out of the parental home. There may be subtle and not so subtle actions such as telling the young person who has moved out and who stops by to visit that, since he doesn't live there any more, he may not go to the refrigerator for a snack as he used to. The threat of emotional abandonment may, in some cases, be enough to keep the son or daughter in line, and they pay the price of stopped development. When parents actively try to sabotage the young person's growth, he or she has to make the painful choice between being and loving. In successful treatment one hopes the person will be able to work out an adult relationship with parents as a result of coming to accept the real people they are, along with all their limitations as well as their strengths. In some unfortunate situations, parents may be so undermining as to make this impossible and the individual has to face the loss of letting them go. The support of a therapist can make this pain bearable.

Many people are able to change and grow without therapy, as the outcome of other kinds of growth-supporting interpersonal experiences along with a growing understanding and wisdom about the human condition. But for others, a do-it-yourself approach may be difficult because it lacks the support and reliability of a to-be-counted-on relationship to sustain them through the more difficult times. People in the world at large have needs, motives, plans, and ways of being on their own, and realistically they cannot always be counted on to lend themselves to the service of the extended self-examination and self-discovery that goes with the process of change. They cannot always be expected to bear the burden of the ups and downs of one's feelings, of the preoccupation with one's self and psyche, or of the need for patience and forbearance as one tries and retries new attitudes and behaviors. Therapists endeavor to lend themselves to this process as fully as possible, for that is the defined goal of the relationship.

In addition, the human psyche is devilishly clever at the art of self-deception, and the need for a reliable, consistent, honest, nonhostile, and reasonably objective confrontation is an essential component of the change process. This is the function of the therapist, as he or she facilitates the emergence and definition of the self within the context of a trusting and nonexploitative relationship. The patient is helped to become aware of unconscious feelings and wishes and to develop an understanding of them and how they direct behavior, as well as to face conflict and find a resolution of that conflict.

BUT ON THE OTHER HAND . . .

Whatever their motivation to undertake therapy, many people are also reluctant to do so. The source of the reluctance is often closely related to issues of being and loving, such as self-esteem (shame at "needing" therapy), power (fear of being controlled by the therapist), or the fear of loss through change. Some people who have characteristically sacrificed self and identity in order to preserve closeness are concerned that taking the time and spending the money for therapy is too self-indulgent, too selfish. Coming to terms with the reluctance to engage in the therapeutic process is often not only the first, but the most important step in the process, since the core conflict is often embedded in the nature of the reluctance.

The very fact of needing to see a therapist is experienced by some individuals as a failure to live up to their idealized image of themselves as totally capable of solving their own problems. Thus, it constitutes a humiliation. There is potential for further humiliation as a consequence of being seen in a less-than-perfect light by someone else. Who knows what might be revealed in the course of therapy? And crying, of course, is to be avoided at all costs. Big girls (and boys) don't cry. It is interesting to see how this kind of issue is revealed in dreams. One woman dreamed of going through a waterfall without getting wet—of going through therapy without crying. Another dreamed of a frozen tidal wave—the frozen tears she was afraid would overwhelm her.

Others come to the therapy situation already angry at being in a one-down power position. After all, they come to the therapist, and not vice versa. The therapist must be paid.[1] The

---

[1]The fact that the therapist is paid a set amount is actually relieving for some people, for then they will not have to pay in psychological terms as they did with parents (by being obedient and mindful of the parents' emotional needs).

Another important psychological impact of payment is that it keeps unconscious wishes for a relationship with the therapist, which might go beyond the limits of the professional relationship, from taking over. The money is a reminder of the realities of the situation. The wishes can become conscious and worked with in a way that will enable the person to make a fuller life outside of treatment.

therapist is in control of the time—when the session starts, when it ends, and how long it lasts. The patient or client tells the therapist about him- or herself, but the therapist does not reciprocate. It is a reality that therapy is an inherently unequal situation, in spite of the therapist's regard for the patient as a respected equal in life. What is important is that there is an exploration of the impact of the inequality inasmuch as it will be relevant to other relationships that feel unequal. The reluctance to get into such a position to start with may be enough to deter some people from getting help for their problems of being and loving.

The fear of loss through change relates to both loss of self and loss of important others. People are often concerned that if they change, they will not be themselves anymore, as though changing would make them into someone else. The change that results from therapy, in fact, aims at helping the individual become *more fully* himself, more integrated, and more authentic. Nevertheless, this might still entail a loss of the *familiar* self, and this may be anxiety provoking. Bonime (1989) tells us that anxiety stems from "danger to, or disruption of, the subjective, familiar sense of me that one has while functioning" (p. 27).

Some people mistakenly believe that giving up their dependent ties to family means that one can no longer have anything to do with them. There may well be good and healthy aspects of old relationships that need not be thrown away in a desperate attempt to make oneself emotionally independent of them. For it is the *inner relationship*, how we experience it psychologically, that is the crucial one—whether or not one is tied and bound emotionally in the various ways that have been described in this book, if not in actual time and space. In fact, this inner relationship that is based upon experiences from childhood, tends to shape new interpersonal relationships so they end up being similar to old ones. We see examples of this when people who were abused as children find new situations where being abused is replicated. The *inner* tie is where change has to take place before real life can change. Changing the inner world can lead to feelings of loss of the emotional connection with parents.

Sometimes the fear of the loss of important others is well justified. This would be true when a spouse or parents cannot tolerate the growth and change of the individual, and the relationship is actually terminated. This real danger can be a powerful deterrent to plunging into the therapy process.

Therapy can also be perceived as a threat to an idealized image of the family. Like other idealized images, it is maintained at the cost of coming to terms with reality. Behind this fear lies the danger that if the family were to be viewed realistically, it might be lost. That is, the individual would not be able to fit within it anymore.

In other situations, telling family secrets constitutes a betrayal, and the guilt about this possibility is enough to keep a person from seeking professional help.

If you feel that therapy could help you with your conflict between being and loving but you are reluctant to get involved in the process, be sure to talk about that reluctance if you do consult someone. Any therapist should be willing to respect your concerns and explore them further with you. Perhaps this exploration will help you decide to commit yourself to the process in spite of your anxieties.

Once one has overcome the initial reluctance sufficiently to make that first call, the question arises, "Whom do I call?"

CHOOSING A THERAPIST

Most patients or clients find their way to a therapist via direct referral. Either a former patient, a family physician, another therapist, or someone familiar with the therapist's work will say, "I think this is someone who can help you." Since there is some degree of preliminary matching of patient to therapist with a personal referral, these arrangements are more likely to work than picking a name out of a book. The referral is also a recommendation that is based on past performance.

The therapist's credentials are also a consideration. What is this person's training? Is he or she licensed or certified within the field—psychiatry, psychology, social work, or pastoral counseling? This means that the person has passed a rigorous examination in that field. If not licensed, does he or she work for an accredited agency or clinic? Some indication that this person is accepted as competent by others in the field affords some degree of assurance.

Beyond this, there are a number of different kinds of therapy—different theoretical orientations, different techniques, different therapist styles and values—each of which has its own specific impact on the person looking for help. The age and sex of the therapist are often important in this regard.

THERAPEUTIC GOALS AND STYLES

For the most part, the goal of psychotherapy, regardless of school or techniques that may be employed, is essentially a humanistic one. That is, it aims toward a secure and authentic sense of self and self worth. One can be a behaviorist whose goal is to unlearn maladaptive and self-defeating behavior patterns, a Freudian analyst with a focus on resolving unconscious conflict, or a Gestalt therapist who strives for the integrity and wholeness of the person, and still pursue humanistic goals. Rollo May (1965) wrote of existential psychology, ". . . the term demarcates an *attitude*, an approach to human beings, rather than a special school or group . . . it is not a system of therapy but an attitude toward therapy" (p. 19). He points out that every therapist is existential insofar as he or she is a good therapist and is able to grasp the patient in his or her own reality. There is no one theoretical school that has a monopoly on this approach.

Whatever the therapist's particular style and technique of working, it may have both a positive and negative impact on the patient. Someone might say, "I wish you would talk more. I feel you leave it all up to me." What is important is that the therapist not be defensive and be willing to consider such a statement as an integral part of the process, exploring the nature of his or her impact on the individual. What meaning does the patient attribute to the therapist's style? Does the fact that the therapist leaves what is to be talked about up to the patient make the person feel as he did with uninvolved and distant parents? Does he feel untaken care of? Someone else might like this style, experiencing it as an opportunity for autonomy. A therapist who does not explore these kinds of feelings, who says, in effect, "take it or leave it," is not likely to be able to help the patient come to terms with his mixed feelings about other relationships either.

This does not mean that the therapist should change the way of working just to make you feel better. This might even be antitherapeutic, depriving you of the necessity and opportunity of coming to grips with your reactions. It's the talking about them that is at issue. Sometimes a therapist can be too nice, and that will not be useful if you are to grow. The patient who wanted the therapist to talk more might use this as a way to avoid the responsibility for what is brought up. He or she relates in a passive and compliant manner, following the lead of the therapist. This is the very issue that is probably at the heart of his interpersonal problems and conflicts. Exploring the wish for the therapist to take the lead opens the door to exploring the individual's way of being in the world.

One of the differences between therapists is the extent to which they may reveal their own feelings and reactions. Many therapists realize that they must pay attention to their own reactions, for in addition to telling something about themselves, these reactions often help the therapist know what is going on in the patient. That is, their own reactions may be a basis for empathic understanding of the other. Whether or not these reactions are revealed to the patient will depend on whether the therapist feels that such openness would be hurtful or helpful to the process. They must draw on their clinical judgment to make this decision. Some clinicians write about this sometimes difficult aspect of the treatment situation (Tansey and Burke 1989).

Analytically oriented therapists attempt to maintain an attitude of neutrality, believing that this facilitates the emergence of the kinds of feelings and attitudes that people carry about with them in their heads, and that it facilitates the emergence and growth of the individual's unique and spontaneous self. This neutrality is not the same as indifference, however, although the two are sometimes confused. The analytic therapist lends him- or herself to the growth of the individual much as the early good-enough mother lends herself to the growth of the child. Many analysts believe that self-revelation by the therapist takes away the atmosphere of neutrality and, thus, of safety.

Other therapists work quite differently, bringing their own feelings and reactions in as an integral aspect of the working relationship. They believe that it is important to function as a model for openness. Some people can make good use of this style of working. Others, however, react to it by giving over direction of themselves to the therapist much as they did originally with parents. The more one knows about the therapist, the easier it is to adapt. The adapting individual will conform to what seems to please and interest the therapist. Sacrificing being in the interest of loving will be acted out in therapy just as everywhere else. Sometimes apparent growth (such as improving one's appearance, going to school, or working for a job promotion) may be little more than a manifestation of adaptation to the goals toward which the therapist is offering encouragement. The goal itself remains irrelevant and achieving it has little impact on the individual one way or the other; pleasing the therapist (parent) is still at the heart of the process. Sometimes the therapist's honest reaction will be experienced as praise or punishment for the individual who relates in this manner.

In choosing a therapist for yourself, it would be helpful for you to do some preliminary assessment of your own reaction tendencies. Which one of these approaches do you think would be most helpful for you with respect to promoting growth? It might *not* be the one that would necessarily make you feel better. Feeling comfortable or gratified in a therapy session is not necessarily productive. What is important is that there is a feeling of safety and of being understood. The patient or client must take the responsibility for bringing up discomfort in the interaction so that it can be examined, explored, and worked through. A good-enough therapist should be able to do this.

INSIGHT OR UNDERSTANDING

Different therapists also disagree on the relative importance of insight or understanding vis-à-vis having an emotionally charged growth promoting experience. Such disagreements obscure the nature of growth and change. Understanding without an experience that touches one emotionally as well, is sterile. But the experience without understanding cannot be fully integrated and made part of the self. Many people defend against the anxiety of conflict by separating feeling from thinking, emotions from cognition. They will not be helped to integrate these two aspects of self if feeling and thinking are permitted to remain split off from each other in the therapy process.

Human beings are creatures who seek to find sense and meaning in their experience. We all try to find reasons or explanations for what happens to us in our lives. There are two aspects to meaning: one is philosophical and the other is cognitive. Jean Piaget (1936) studied cognitive development in children. Children often attribute cognitive meaning that is based on their limited understanding of cause and effect and on their limited understanding of what makes people tick. They tend to have an egocentric view of the world and are prone to believing that they cause events over which they really have no control. When we think we understand what something means, it enables us to gain some degree of control or, at least, the illusion of control. There is a cognitive component to what we experience at a feeling level, even though these thoughts or beliefs may be unconscious. Our unconscious belief systems, the meanings we ascribed to interpersonal experiences during our early years, continue to direct our interpersonal behavior, our wishes and our fears, and the strategies we may have developed over time to make ourselves feel safe and worthwhile. A person may be afraid to get too close to others because he believes that others want to control him. By gaining access to both meaning and experience, to both cognition and emotion, these patterns can be explored and eventually modified in a way that will enable the individual to feel safe in interpersonal relationships.

Because of the importance of integrating the cognitive and emotional aspects of our lives, it is important that therapy, whatever its orientation, enable this integration.

GROUP THERAPY?

If you think you are the kind of person who might hide behind words, or who might get caught up in trying to please your therapist, even covertly, group therapy may be the treatment of choice for you. Your behavior will be more open to the scrutiny of your peers, and you are not likely to get away with being teacher's pet in a group. Problems that stem from sibling rivalry, for example, may not show up in individual therapy where one is an "only child," and where an illusion of specialness may be held on to secretly.

The here-and-now social interaction of a therapy group often exposes the ways in which people inject unresolved conflicts from their families into present-day social situations. Some of these would remain hidden in one-to-one therapy unless the individual saw fit to bring them up.

Some people say they want group therapy so they can get feedback from others in the group. They may convert the input of the others in the group to more directives as to how and who they should be. Group therapy may not be of help to an individual who tends to be other-directed unless this stance is examined as part of the process.

A group therapist has to be sure that there is an atmosphere of safety and trust in the group and not allow members simply to act out their wishes or feelings on the others. If someone wants to be the center of attention all the time and manages to bring this about by coming to the group every week with a new crisis, it will be up to the group therapist to deal with this in a way that helps both the individual and the group. Some groups become bogged down because of the member who always wants center stage. As with individual therapy, the therapist has a responsibility to pay attention to and work with interpersonal processes that interfere with the ability to have fulfilling relationships.

As with other factors in choosing the kind of therapy and therapist, the question of whether group will hinder or facilitate your growth is the prime consideration. Sometimes individual and group therapy are combined for a given individual. Assigning a person to a therapy group, however, is usually the decision of the therapist. That is, the therapist may recommend individual treatment, perhaps for an interim period, even if you believe that group therapy would be best. If this is the case, the therapist should explain the basis for the decision. This often highlights problems that need to be resolved in individual treatment first.

MALE OR FEMALE?

Whatever problems one has with respect to being and loving, they will emerge with either a male or a female therapist. The male therapist can be related to as though he were mother, and the female therapist can be related to as though she were father. Some people have a fantasy that a woman will provide warmth and love, whereas a man will be cold and intellectual. These are gross stereotypes that have nothing to do with what happens in psychotherapy. Inevitably, they will have to be dealt with as the fantasies they are. Unfavorable stereotypes may interfere with the person's sense of him- or herself as a valuable person. What is important from the therapist's side of the equation is that if the therapist is a woman, she be informed of the particular developmental challenges that confront boys, and if the therapist is a man, he be informed of the particular developmental challenges that confront girls. Issues of gender and gender identity are related to these tasks.

By and large it does not matter what the therapist's gender is—except:

When an individual has *excessive* fear or anger toward either men or women, it is best to start with a therapist of the other sex. The presence of such strong feelings may interfere with the establishment of the basic trust that is necessary for the process to succeed.

One young woman came into my office for the first time and had an immediate strong negative reaction to me because I wore my hair and dressed in the style of her mother. It is hoped that such feelings can be worked with and overcome, as these kinds of overgeneralizations and distortions of reality (for, after all, I wasn't actually her mother) interfere in the outside world as well. However, in this instance, the initial negative feelings were so strong that it made no sense to try to work together. It would have been impossible to build up a trusting relationship. Since her negative feelings applied to other women as well, it made sense for her to see a male therapist. Strong attitudes of contempt for either gender also do not bode well for treatment with a therapist of that sex.

The opposite situation is also a contraindication for a therapist of a specific gender—that is, when the individual relates automatically in too cozy and comfortable a manner with either one or the other. Too many built-in positive feelings can be just as much of a deterrent to progress in therapy as too many built-in negative feelings. The relationship becomes too precious, and anything that might interfere with the positive atmosphere is screened out and not talked about.

Once you have overcome your original ambivalence about embarking on the therapy journey, you will make the first call and set up an appointment. People generally tend to be anxious at the start, wondering what they are "supposed to do." Dealing with the fact that there are no supposed-tos (other than to come at the specified hour, do one's best to be honest, and pay the bill) is one of the first tasks of therapy. It is most useful to discuss your fears and reluctances at the very start so they can be worked with and resolved. Often the nature of the reluctance is itself the central problem of the individual's life. This is particularly so when it relates to the conflict between being and loving.

PROBLEMS OF BEING AND LOVING IN THERAPY

Inevitably the conflict between attachment and individuation, between dependence and autonomy, between loving and being, will come to light in the therapy relationship itself. Resolution of the conflict in this special setting, then, becomes the nitty-gritty of the work of therapy.

If you have difficulty making and maintaining attachments, this will come up as an issue with your therapist, but at least it can be openly talked about and dealt with here. One young woman struggled with the belief that if she let herself be at all involved with me, I would take her over and make her into what I wanted her to be. She avoided attachments in general as a way to protect her boundaries and her sense of self.

If you tend to break off your feelings of connection every time your therapist makes you angry by not responding the way you want, if you pull the plug, this too can be identified and talked about and you can, with his or her help, work to maintain the feeling of connection right on through the anger.

If you sense yourself pulling out when you hear an interpretation as pressure not to be you, as criticism and withdrawal of caring, this too can be talked about and clarified. You can become aware of misinterpretations you are prone to making in the communication process. Just because your father did not want you to have a mind of your own does not imply that everyone else has the same attitude, although you may have a tendency to attribute that meaning to others' behavior.

You will discover that you and the other person (in this case, your therapist) can be *different* and still be connected. You don't have to be the kind of person the therapist is. The therapist doesn't have to agree with you on everything in order to guarantee that you will still go on existing. You can be angry with each other and neither of you will die.

Or you may become aware of how power issues generate so much resentment in you that you cannot permit yourself to be the recipient of help rather than the giver. To let the other person matter seems to give him or her too much power over you. If you want something, the therapist has the power to say yes or no, as did the powerful mother of early childhood. You may find yourself needing to defeat your therapist in order to maintain your self-esteem, recognizing that the same thing happens in outside relationships. You can talk about your dilemma and, with your therapist's support, untie the knot that binds you.

If you tend to be compliant with what you believe the other person wants or needs from you, this attitude and behavior will also emerge in your relationship with your therapist. As this pattern becomes clarified within the therapy situation, your feelings and beliefs can be explored in a way that gives you the courage to take the risk of being more real.

You may come to realize that you have set your therapist up as the fount of all power and knowledge, and try to get him or her to give you the magic answer. Coming to terms with this fantasy and with the fact that the only secret is that there is no secret, and giving up the search for an all-powerful rescuer in your life will go hand in hand.

One of the most important tasks in therapy is often that of learning to tolerate ambivalence rather than making the other person either all good or all bad. This entails completing the task of healing the split at the end of the power pivot stage of development. This will be carried over to other relationships in which the other can finally be experienced as a single individual toward whom one sometimes feels angry and sometimes loving.

Throughout therapy, the process of self-discovery will continue to facilitate the integration of the self into a unified whole with a healthy, reality-oriented self-esteem replacing unworkable illusions of perfection.

The list of problems deriving from the developmental stages of the first three years of life could go on and on. Perhaps you have been able to identify some of these in your own life or in the lives of people you know. How they are resolved will determine the quality of our life, be it alone or with another, be it imprisoned in the citadel of the self or secure enough to move toward a loving attachment. The struggle to bring being into harmony with loving, to maintain the sense of our own identity and integrity and, at the same time, to appreciate the wholeness of another person whom we love is a struggle that begins in the nursery and is usually with us throughout our lifetime. Sometimes its resolution begins in the therapist's consultation room. We hope that a synthesis of the two will not be beyond anyone's hope or expectation, in spite of impediments to it left over from the early years of life.

APPENDIX

NOT FOR PARENTS ONLY

THIS APPENDIX IS for the reader who is a parent or planning to be one. It is quite obvious that a child does not develop in a vacuum and that something quite special is required of you if that development is to go well—particularly with respect to being and loving.[1] It is also quite obvious that you are a person too, and that you will have to deal with the demands of parenthood as they affect your own state of being and loving. Winnicott (1965) reassures us that the child requires only "good-enough" mothering.

Occasional lapses of good-enough parenting can be weathered by the child as long as they are not a manifestation of a parental attitude that, over time, will prove detrimental to the

[1]Erik Erikson (1963) refers to the quality of "generativity" as a developmental task of adult life. Generativity is primarily the concern for establishing and guiding the next generation. It also refers to creativity in other spheres of activity.

child's emotional well-being, and as long as these lapses do not constitute traumatic abuse. Abuse can be psychological as well as physical.

The disruption of an established sense of self is one of the major destructive effects of sexual abuse in childhood. Bonime (1989) writes of the self that:

> It is a complex affective-sensate-cognitive phenomenon experienced in the course of functioning. Sense of self is ineffable and private. It is a subliminal feeling of being a particular person in an experience, a vague sense of me involved, actively or passively, alive and somehow being in relation to others. [p. 28]

Dr. Bonime notes the relational aspects of the sense of self. Of this sense of self he adds:

> It continually exists for one in the course of living and functioning. The course of functioning takes place whether an individual is accompanied or isolated in an interpersonal milieu. Even hermits live in an interpersonal milieu. They require the exclusion of others to be hermits. This separation from people is determined by particular feelings of self in reaction to people. [p. 28]

He notes how a change of behavior of a close and familiar other can change the established sense of self. When a trusted parent molests a child, or turns abusive in some other way, there is also a disruption of the established sense of the adult caretaking world and of the self in relation to it.

Ulman and Brothers (1988) tell us that there are certain fundamental and necessary beliefs about the self in relation to others that help the child organize his or her sense of self. The trauma of incest shatters these organizing fantasies and with them the self is shattered as well.

One young woman recalled how she felt after she was molested by the father she adored. "After that nothing was the same . . . I couldn't think. I didn't want to know anything.

I began to focus on external things. It was like everything was blown apart, like a personal earthquake. Nothing could mean anything. I was brain dead. . . . It took away every shred of belief that he cared about me. It makes me sick and crazy to think I wanted to be his special girl. . . . I'd rather be crazy than have it be true." Later in her life, loving would evoke an intolerable threat to her being. Her annihilation anxiety was not the result of a developmental failure very early in life. It was the result of the psychological and physical abuse she experienced in her childhood years.

STAGES OF PARENTING

Parenting includes nurturance, protection, teaching, and fostering independence in all mammals (Kaufman 1970, pp. 3–55). Human parents also inculcate values and norms and provide training in certain specific kinds of behavior. They serve as models for adult roles, which the child uses to form his concept of himself and his place in society. And, it is hoped, they also foster in him appropriate self-regard (Handel 1970, pp. 87–105).

Each stage of your child's development, which was described earlier in this book, will call upon a specific and corresponding attitude on your part. Your growth and change as a parent will parallel that of your child as a person. Throughout this process your attitudes and behavior will affect him, and his attitudes and behavior will affect you and the quality of your parenting.[2]

Because of the interactive nature of the parent–child relationship, we can see that a child is not a passive lump of clay to be molded by the parent. He is an active participant in

[2]Rene Spitz (1965) writes of "mutual cuing," the process of reciprocal influence that characterizes mother–child interaction in the first year of life. The concept of mutual cuing can be applied to later stages of development as well.

his own developmental process. Different kinds of children call forth different kinds of responses. A boisterous, active child is more likely to evoke limit-setting responses. An orderly, self-reliant child is more likely to evoke autonomy-promoting responses. A timid child is more likely to evoke caretaking responses. Yet all three have the same basic requirement for healthy emotional development. This is that each goes through the process of attachment to symbiosis, and through the process of separation and individuation. As a parent, you will want to keep these principles in mind, even as you respond to the temperamental needs of your child.

Stella Chess and Alexander Thomas (1987) have studied the relationship between an infant's innate temperament and subsequent development. They describe (1) the difficult child, (2) the easy child, and (3) the slow-to-warm-up child, and how to handle each most effectively. They have conducted a thirty-year study that traces the development of a large group of children from early infancy to adult life. Their conclusions are that

1. Infants are born with a biological endowment that immediately enables them to enter into a social relationship with their parents and to begin actively learning about the world around them.
2. Babies are different from the start. One way in which they are different is innate temperament. The child's temperament influences his or her responses to the parent's caregiving. From the start the relationship is a two-way street; each continually influences the other.
3. There are many different ways to be a good parent. Just as children have their individual characteristics, so do parents. What is crucial for healthy development is a goodness of fit—a good match between the parents' attitudes and expectations and the child's temperament and other characteristics.

When there is not an automatic goodness of fit, caring parents will have to make conscious efforts to tailor their parenting to the specific needs of their child, at least to the degree that their parenting style is not experienced by the child as impinging, assaultive, or abandoning.

When a child is going through the attachment process and moving toward becoming one with mother, you (if you are the mother) will be under maximal pressure to put your own wishes, moods, feelings, and needs aside to tend to your baby. The mother's readiness to do this is called "primary maternal preoccupation," by Winnicott (1975). He describes this very special state.

> It gradually develops and becomes a state of heightened sensitivity during, and especially towards the end of, the pregnancy. It lasts for a few weeks after the birth of the child. It is not easily remembered by mothers once they have recovered from it. [pp. 300–305]

Winnicott tells us that this state

> provides a setting for the infant's constitution to begin to make itself evident. . . . Maternal failures [at this time] produce phases of reaction to impingement and these reactions interrupt the 'going on being' of the infant. An excess of this reacting produces not frustration but a *threat of annihilation* . . . a very real primitive anxiety. [pp. 300–305]

This is the time when your goal will be to meet your infant's needs, to foster the attachment process, and to create an atmosphere of trust and minimal tension, one that enables your baby's "going on being."

If you are the father, your support is needed to help your wife through this period so that she, herself, does not become emotionally depleted. It may be a tough time for you, as you are likely to be mostly on the giving end. You will be confronted with the reality that you no longer have your wife all to yourself, but have to share her and her love with another person. If you are still angry at your mother for bringing home a baby brother or sister before you were ready to give up her undivided attention, the demands of this stage of your son or daughter's life may be especially difficult for you. If never before, it will be evident now that the honeymoon is over!

Before long your child will begin to move toward defining himself as separate from you (the mother) in many little ways, such as wanting to hold his own bottle or spoon. Now the balance begins to shift a little. You are still needed as in the earlier months, but now you must begin to support and encourage these moves toward independence. It is no longer appropriate for you to try to match your rhythm so perfectly to that of your child. You begin to make small demands: he has to wait a little for his dinner. He is no longer on demand feeding as in those earlier weeks and months. Chances are he has already moved toward a regular schedule himself. At any rate, he now hears no-no from you more frequently. As your baby comes to realize that he cannot control you by his will, he becomes more and more aware that you and he are separate. As long as these frustrations are in minimal and tolerable doses, they facilitate his emotional and cognitive development. If frustration is excessive and more than the child can tolerate without becoming overwhelmed by negative feelings, his security in his relationship with others and the cohesion of his sense of self will be compromised.

Father now becomes increasingly important. As you have played with your baby and helped with the caretaking, he has also formed a bond with you. You become most important now in the process of becoming two. You are a source of security and trust that enables him to move farther away from mother without becoming overwhelmed by separation anxiety.

Throughout the process of becoming two, which includes the power pivot, your child will experience conflict between his dependency needs and his autonomy needs. Dependency needs are related to loving in that both move one toward the other, whereas autonomy needs are related to being, in that both emphasize separateness. Their conflicts are also parallel. You will be called upon to support both of the conflicting needs—which can be tricky if not impossible at any given moment. Then you have to decide which is more critical. If your child is upset or distraught over some difficulty, clearly he needs comfort and support. If he is trying to build his blocks into a tower, clearly he needs encouragement without interference.

In any event, the balance continues to shift gradually, with you, the parents, doing less and less for your child as he is able to do more and more for himself. Helpful parents have the emotional flexibility to make these shifts. They are not locked into either one stance or the other because of their own particular psychological needs. They do not need their child to stay dependent nor to become prematurely self-sufficient.

It will also be up to both fathers and mothers to set the kinds of limits that will mitigate the normal narcissism of the very small child. Others are people who count too. "No, you can't have the doll. The doll belongs to Susie." This step is essential to the capacity to love, for loving entails valuing others as real persons. The self-centered individual who relates to others in terms of how they fit in with his need system cannot truly love. Although others may respond to us as adults out of caring and concern—and it is hoped they will—we are not entitled to stake emotional claims on others, for they are also people who matter in their own right. In healthy relationships, caring and concern are mutually and freely given.

Your child's shift out of infantile narcissism requires a further shift from you. Now, not only are you not responding to his every demand, but you are making demands on him. Many modern parents are appropriately concerned with the individuality of their child. However, in the earliest years it is equally important to provide guidance and control. Inadequate structuring of the child's environment may lead to a less secure inner self-structure. In such circumstances, individuality, paradoxically cannot be well developed (Benedek 1970, pp. 109–135). The psychological well-being of the child requires parents who are secure in their educational role as well as in their loving and supporting role.

As with the balance between dependency and autonomy, there must be a balance between demands for renunciation of infantile narcissism and adequate meeting of the child's needs for self-esteem and self-expression. If he feels valued and validated by you (and thus, eventually able to value and validate himself), he will be able to give up being kingpin of the household. He won't have to hold on to infantile illusions of omnipotence. Growth-facilitating parents are able to keep sight of the needs that the child is in the process of outgrowing at the same time as they are anticipating and moving toward the child's next developmental challenges.

Whatever the objective demands of parenthood, those that relate to the expected developmental requirements of the child, parenting has its unique and subjective effects on every mother and father.

PARENTS ARE PEOPLE TOO

We bring to marriage and parenthood the personality that was built up over our own early years (Benedek 1970, p. 110). This includes how we interacted with our own parents and other important people in our world. There is a tendency to identify our child, at least unconsciously, with our parents and to make certain assumptions and to adopt certain attitudes on the basis of this identification. This is why there is often a similarity between the quality of parent–child relationships from one generation to the next (Benedek 1970, p. xxi).

Marcia had to be totally tuned in to her mother's needs. If she did not cater to her mother's self-centered demands, she would be punished by her emotional withdrawal. When she had her own daughter, she felt she had to cater to the little girl's self-centered demands in the same way, a stance that led to the child's becoming increasingly self-centered and demanding, just like the grandmother.

The experience of parenthood can actually be a growth-promoting one. Our own early conflicts tend to be reactivated in our relationship with our child. This gives us a chance to confront these conflicts with the mental and psychological equipment of the adult and thus, to resolve them. Many parents with several children will report that they are aware of how much more mature they were in their parenting of the later children. The firstborn often has the dubious honor of being the one with whom the conflict is worked out. Not all parents grow in this way, however, but continue to play out the conflict in a repetitive manner, just as they did as children vis-à-vis their own parents.

Just as you have an impact on the developing self of your child, so he or she has an impact on you. This impact may generate stress if and when it touches upon vulnerable aspects of your own self, especially those that may relate to your conflict between being and loving. For instance, your sense of being may be placed in jeopardy when your boundaries and autonomy are suspended in order to meet the demands of parenting your newborn infant. And you may lose touch with your loving feelings for your child when your anger gets the upper hand. If so, you are like many other parents.

If you are the mother of a new baby, there may be times when you feel as though your boundaries and your sense of separateness become blurred by the extent to which you give yourself to tending the needs of your infant. Even your sleeping and eating rhythms are set aside in favor of rocking a fretful child or for the 2:00 A.M. feeding.

There may be times when both mother and father react with frustration and anger to the limits placed on their autonomy by the responsibilities of parenthood. No more spur-of-the-moment weekend camping trips. No more easy, "Let's eat out and go to a show." Even if you can afford and can get a sitter, the spontaneity is lost. And that goes for middle-of-the-afternoon lovemaking as well.

Sometimes you may get a sense that power issues have come to the fore as you and your toddler clash over who will control whom. There may be something cute about a defiant 2-year-old, hands on hips, standing toe to toe with the parent who is insisting that it is time to get dressed to make a doctor's appointment. But there is nothing cute or fun about the reality of the power struggle that is in process. Your feelings of powerlessness may frustrate and infuriate you.

It would be unusual if any or all of these feelings were not stirred up, at least a bit, in any parent. We all remain vulnerable to the conflicts inherent in being and loving, even though we may think we have finally resolved them. But, it is what you *do* with these feelings that really matters—whether or not you can get a handle on them and put them in their proper perspective. After all, this 20-month-old baby is *not* your mother or father, even though the feelings in you may date back to your struggle with them. This is a moment of potential growth for you—for the working through and resolution of the original problem. For one thing, you can now see things from your parent's point of view. You can understand how difficult it was for them and you can see that you played an active role in the battles that were fought. It is another step in your seeing your own parents as real people and in accepting them as having done the best they could. Old resentments can give way under the influence of empathy, understanding, and forgiveness.

Some parents, instead, try to defend themselves against their child in old ways, such as by withdrawing emotionally or by being overly compliant and indulgent. Unfortunately,

these solutions generate problems of their own. The withdrawing parent, in effect, abandons the child. The compliant and
overly gratifying parent reinforces the infantile narcissism.
Your own conflicts around being and loving may come to
interfere with your capacity to parent your child in a way that
will facilitate his or her development.

In addition to boundaries, autonomy, and power, issues of
self-esteem may be raised in response to the child's impact on
you. The behavior of our children can function as a mirror of
ourselves. We may or may not like what we see. In their play
and in their behavior they imitate both our positive and our
negative aspects (Benedek 1970, p. 127). We feel good when
we see the positive. We may feel angry and embarrassed when
we see the negative. However, healthy and nondefensive
parents can use the latter as helpful feedback, as a clue to how
the child experiences us in interaction with him and to the
nature of the inner psychological world that is being built up
in his mind. If parents are able to use the child's behavior as
information about the nature of their relationship as the child
experiences it, it is important that they not overemphasize the
positive or be overwhelmed by the negative aspects of the self
as they are exposed through the child's behavior. That is, our
self-image and self-esteem should be secure enough to with-
stand such experiences. Parents who punish their children for
behavior that they themselves have modeled not only do the
child an injustice, but lose out on an opportunity for improving the relationship and for their own personal growth and
maturation. One young mother was very angry at her little boy
for hitting her and screaming at her when she did something
he didn't like. It occurred to her that this was how he
experienced her scolding and spanking, and she decided that
her approach to discipline wasn't working as she had hoped. As
she thought about it, she realized that she disciplined largely
on the basis of her own mood, rather than consistently and in
a way that was directly related to the child's behavior. As she
was able to come to grips with what was going on within

herself, she was able to change her way of handling her small son. Before long, his offensive behavior disappeared.

It is not only important to understand your child and his developmental needs. It is equally important that you know and understand yourself so that you will be able to keep separate what has to do with you and what has to do with him. For how you react to what comes from him will, in turn, affect him and how he is with you. The interaction continues to be one of mutual and reciprocal impact and response. You might find it useful to look back as well, and to consider the impact you had on your parents and how this influenced the nature of your relationship. You were no more a lump of clay in their hands than your child is in yours.

RECIPROCITY—FOR BETTER OR FOR WORSE

How can the parent's conflict between being and loving affect a child's capacity to achieve these goals? There are many ways—some blatant and some subtle. Many have been described in this book.

The givens of children are:

1. Their innate, constitutional endowments such as temperament, intelligence, and physical makeup.
2. Their innate goal-seeking behavior in general and attachment-seeking in particular.
3. The mental activity and organization of experience into patterns to which meaning is eventually assigned with the development of language. (One is the pattern called self. Another is the pattern of the mothering person. These patterns are first organized before there is language and are carried forth into adult life to affect how we experience ourselves and others.)
4. Those functions that develop out of the biological

maturation of the organism itself, such as walking, talking, thinking, perception, sexuality, and various inborn talents. (These functions develop within the context of the mothering environment. The quality of that environment determines whether they are associated with conflict and anxiety, or whether they are free of conflict and anxiety and can thus expand to their fullest and be enjoyed to their fullest.)

Whereas the capacity to love comes out of the attachment, being comes out of the integration of the many other innate and learned aspects of experience into the separated and individuated self. These are significantly affected by the quality of the attachment bond and the nature of the relationship with the mothering person or persons, and later, with the father as well. When these maturing capacities are valued by parents, when parents do not enviously resent them, and when parents do not have to take credit for them to make themselves feel better, the child can feel a sense of his own individuality and feel good about it.

As a parent, you may want to take a look at how the person you are is affected by these given aspects of your child and how the person you are, in turn, affects or has affected these various aspects of your child's unfolding as a person (see Table A-1).

You may recognize that some of the areas of your interaction with your child have not been exactly hospitable to either his growth as a person or to your own. Change in this respect can be difficult in that the system of how your family operates as an integrated whole tends to perpetuate the problems. This is why family therapy is often recommended as an approach to this resolution.

Problems of being and loving *within* each parent as they interact with problems of being and loving *within* each child can be looked at even as they are taking place. These interactions are both verbal and nonverbal, and the nature of the communication process is central to family therapy work. One man described how both his parents would never speak

TABLE A–1

PARENTS

CHILD	Ability to empathize and respond to what comes from the child (*your capacity to love*)	Capacity to tolerate your child's separateness (*your capacity to be and for autonomy*)	Readiness to respect, respond to, and encourage your child's unique talents and abilities (*your ability to relate to others as real and separate persons*)	Your ability to be a teaching parent and not feel guilty at setting limits and making appropriate demands (*your sense of self and self-esteem*)
Attachment-seeking behavior	Capacity to love			
Drive toward being separate	Capacity to be	Capacity to be		
Drive for autonomy	Capacity to be without conflict	Capacity to be without conflict	Self-esteem	Mitigation of normal narcissism of childhood and promotion of concern for others
Unique temperament and abilities		Self-expression, pleasure in achieving, and self-esteem	Self-expression, pleasure in achieving, self-esteem	

OUTCOME FOR THE CHILD

their own mind. His mother would say, "Your father thinks that . . ." and his father would say, "Your mother thinks that. . . ." They never really took ownership of their own feelings or thoughts. This kind of family is referred to as enmeshed.

This is when someone from outside the family system can be helpful in changing these patterns so that the family can continue to grow as individuals. And as the negative aspects of the attachment bond can be resolved, family members can be freer to love one another in a nonhostile and nondependent manner. In effect, both being and loving will be enhanced.

You may want to attempt a few needed changes on your own. If your child or children are young enough, you may be able to turn the unhealthy relating around and get things moving in a more growth-promoting manner. If your children are older, this may not be so easy. I have observed many times that even as parents tried to change, children would pull them back into the old ways of relating. For instance, if the parents tried to be less controlling, the child might provoke control in a variety of ways, such as using the new freedom to get even, to act out pent-up anger, or by pretending to be inadequate and deliberately failing to carry out his part of the bargain. See if you can describe the interaction between you and your child under each of the following headings.

IS PERFECT PARENTING POSSIBLE?

The wish to be perfect and the tendency toward idealization of relationships becomes evident in the context of the family. The self-esteem of the parents can get caught up in the need to be the perfect mother or father, and to have the perfect child to show to the world as proof of it. To be a perfect parent and to have a perfect child is to be a perfect self. But, as in all settings, perfection can only be an illusion that is maintained at the cost of denying reality.

The realities of the developmental process, with its inherent and inevitable conflict of the child between being and loving, as well as the parallel and related conflict between dependency and autonomy, automatically creates conflict between parent and child. There is no way any parent can avoid doing the "wrong" thing (at least in the eyes of the child); there is no way to avoid being the "bad" one, no way to prevent disappointment and anger in the child, and no way to avoid completely some hurt to the child. In short, there is no way that one can be a perfect parent. Some self psychologists who view all psychopathology as the outcome of maternal failures of empathy, as the mother's failure to be a selfobject, place an unnecessary burden of guilt on parents as there is an unstated implication that perfect mothering is, indeed, possible. They deny the existence of conflict that is unavoidable and inherent in the developmental process itself, and essentially blame the mother for the individual's problems.

If a parent sides with the dependency, the aspect of the child that strives for autonomy will feel infantilized, controlled, and angry. If the parent sides with the autonomy, the aspect of the child that wants to be taken care of will feel abandoned, anxious, and angry. The intrapsychic conflict of the child becomes externalized and is played out with the parent. It is sometimes less anxiety provoking to fight with others than to confront one's own internal ambivalencies. This kind of no-win parent–child situation can be observed with grown-up sons and daughters as well. Many men and women I have worked with are caught on the horns of this dilemma, and they cannot free themselves from the frustration and anger that go with it. Eventually they must come to terms with the fact that it is they and not their parents who must take the ultimate responsibility for their being and loving, as well as for their conflicting dependency and autonomy wishes. As long as the power is attributed to parental figures, they cannot move past this conflict. It is a dilemma that every parent will be caught up in, no matter what he or she says or does. This struggle will be especially intensified during the young person's adolescence.

Since perfection is impossible, what can be a reasonable and realistic goal for parents? How much can they ask of themselves?

PARENTING IN AN IMPERFECT WORLD

Having accepted the inherent imperfection in any parent—child relationship, one might hope at least to aim toward doing the most good and the least harm. But how can one know what course of action will meet even these requirements?

When in doubt, I find a useful rule of thumb to respond in a way that enables the child to function at the highest possible level *at the moment*, or that moves him gently forward. That is, he is not pushed beyond where he is able to be, but neither is he encouraged to regress.

It may be that easing the distress that is overwhelming him would accomplish this goal. He is not asked to be a "little soldier." He is given the comfort he needs to enable him to regroup and move forward again. Responding to the dependency needs is indicated. At another time, it may be that encouraging the child to attempt some independent action is indicated. As long as he knows he has your support behind him and as long as he does not become overly anxious, this will tend to be growth promoting, even though he may be irritated at you for not doing it for him.

Expressing loving feelings may make sense at a time when it clearly enhances the relationship and creates the good experience that eventually will become the child's inner source of nurturance. At another time, expressing one's displeasure will serve to mitigate the self-centeredness and enhance his awareness of others as important too.

Sometimes you will guess wrong and have to deal with the consequences. Fortunately, children are very resilient and are able to tolerate many parental failures without being unduly damaged. Winnicott's term "good-enough mothering" can be expanded to "good-enough parenting." If parenting is good enough, the impetus to growth within the child makes its own contribution. In general, promoting growth goes hand in hand with providing a safe resting place. If a child returns period-ically to the haven of the lap, there is no need to be concerned about his dependency so long as he continues his excursions beyond the orbit of the parents with a modicum of success and manageable anxiety. Responding to his love, coupled with validation and support of his autonomous and separate self, will enhance his resolution of the conflict between being and loving. Knowing that he can experience both with you fosters the integration of the disparate aspects of his self. Later on with others, as he can now in his relationship with you, he will be able to "be me and love you."

THE WORKING MOTHER

There was a time when only poor women had to leave their children at home to go to work. With the social changes of the women's movement in the 1960s and 1970s, having a career outside the home took on importance as an aspect of these changes. As more and more women would like to regain the option of staying home with their young children during their formative years, economic pressures have taken away that alternative as an option for many of them. Two salaries are needed to maintain a standard of living both partners grew up with. Downward mobility has become a very real threat. And many women who chose the career path now find themselves in their thirties, not wanting to lose their chance to have a family, but very reluctant to give up the professional and economic advances they have achieved.

It is not my intent to make the woman who has to work or who chooses to work feel guilty, but to help her understand her own tremendous importance as a mother and thus how to go about arranging to have her baby's developmental needs met adequately. This concern has entered the workplace, and we begin to hear about arrangements such as job sharing, a situation in which two women each work half time in the same job slot, maintaining the thrust of their professional development, but also giving sufficient time to their very young children to enhance their early development. Some couples are able to share the major caretaking, with fathers doing more mothering than they have in the past.

There are two issues to be considered by the working mother. The first and foremost is the fostering of the primary attachment bond with the mother herself. The second is the provision of the substitute caretaker, the mother surrogate.

The distinct psychological advantage of having the mother as the primary attachment figure is that she is most likely to be around for the duration of the growing years. This very continuity makes the psychological tasks of emotional development more readily managed by the child. Discontinuity, whether from day to day or year to year, disrupts the smooth flow of the developing self in relation to a stable other. This may disrupt the child's sense of his own ongoingness. It also may confront the child with the sometimes insurmountable task of having to deal with separation and loss (Bowlby 1969).

I have known a number of individuals who made a primary attachment with a nursemaid who was dismissed from the family employ when the child was around 3 years old. Some of them continued to yearn for that which was lost to them. The nursemaid tended to be remembered as an idealized mother figure while the real mothers were experienced as cold deprivers of what had been so important to these children. One woman felt that an important part of herself was gone forever.

Even more damaging is a situation in which there is a repeated changeover of caretakers. I have worked with several people whose early years were insecure and unpredictable with respect to their care, and they finally stopped attaching at all, withdrawing into themselves emotionally, to experience this deadness and emptiness as adults.

If you are a working mother, you can foster the development of the primary attachment with you by means of the quality of your interaction with your little girl or boy when you are at home, although the quantity of time will still be important. The start and end of each day can be special times for being with your small child. Feeding, bathing, playing, tucking him into his crib at night, and singing his favorite songs can help create a special and unique interpersonal ambience that can enable you to be away for a good part of the day and, at the same time, foster this important developmental process. Your emotional presence will be a reliable part of his expectable environment. You will have to arrange your life to make this possible, but as an investment in your child's life, it is one that will pay off.

Arranging for substitute caretaking for your child should be undertaken with the care it deserves. Responsible mothers generally look into the reliability, cleanliness, and kindness of a sitter or of teachers at a day care nursery. The factors of continuity and stability may not be considered as carefully. Employment agencies offering household live-in help have proliferated. The word nanny has become increasingly common among working professionals. Unfortunately, very few of them come even close to Mary Poppins. These strangers, who come and go so easily, make up your child's human world while you are away. Finding someone to take your place while you are away is a difficult and worrisome task. More and more young mothers are trying to work out ways in which they can be at home during these critical early years, at least for a major part if not all of the time. Others choose a carefully selected nursery school because of the stability and predictability it offers, preferring this to the uncertainty of changing strangers at home.

A predictable and familiar world facilitates the process of organization of the self, of attachment to a loved and loving other, and of assimilating new experiences into a growing, integrated view of the self and the world. Disruptions of the child's life—and this includes discontinuous and unstable substitute mothering arrangements—may have their counterpart in the disruption of these processes.

Douglas's mother is a teacher. He stays at a community nursery school while she is at work. He is an especially bright and responsive child. In her journal, his mother described him as happy to go to school, loving his teacher, and as being friendly and cooperative with the other children. At home he was affectionate, lively, and developing emotionally as one might anticipate for his age.

When Douglas was almost 2 years old, his mother put him into a different nursery during the summer when his regular one was closed. He began to scream every day when she left him there, started to hit the other children, and became tense, wild, and uncooperative at home, often striking out at his mother. He also developed a sleep problem. When it became evident that he could not cope with the disruptive stress of the new situation, his mother kept him at home, and he soon resumed his previous healthy course of development. He was able to return to the familiar nursery and teacher once again in the fall, with little more than some initial clinging.

Children are particularly vulnerable to the effects of disruptions of their world in the first three years of life. The working mother, cognizant of her child's developmental needs, can foster the attachment bond and arrange not only for good but stable substitute caretaking. She can create for her child an interpersonal world that will facilitate the capacities for both being and loving.

REFERENCES

Benedek, T. (1970). The family as a psychologic field. In *Parenthood: Its Psychology and Psychopathology*, ed. E. J. Anthony and T. Benedek, pp. 109–135. Boston: Little, Brown.

Bergmann, M. S. (1971). Psychoanalytic observations on the capacity to love. In *Separation–Individuation: Essays in Honor of Margaret S. Mahler*, ed. J. McDevitt and C. Settlage, pp. 15–40. New York: International Universities Press.

Bollas, C. (1987). *The Shadow of the Object: Psychoanalysis of the Unthought Known*. New York: Columbia University Press.

Bonime, W. (1989). *Collaborative Psychoanalysis*. Rutherford, NJ: Fairleigh Dickinson University Press.

Bowlby, J. (1969). *Attachment and Loss*, vol. 1. New York: Basic Books.

Chess, S., and Thomas, A. (1987). *Know Your Child*. New York: Basic Books.

Erikson, E. (1950). *Childhood and Society*. New York: Norton.

———(1963). *Childhood and Society* (2nd ed.). New York: Norton.

Fantz, R. L. (1966). The crucial early influence: mother love or environmental stimulation? *American Journal of Orthopsychiatry* 36:330–331.

Foulkes, D. (1966). *The Psychology of Sleep*. New York: Scribners.

Fraiberg, S. (1977). *Every Child's Birthright: In Defense of Mothering.* New York: Basic Books.

Freud, A. (1976). The concept of developmental lines. In *The Process of Child Development*, ed. P. Neubauer, pp. 25–45. New York: Jason Aronson.

Friedman, L. (1984). Picture of treatment by Gill and Schafer. *Psychoanalytic Quarterly* 53:167–207.

Guntrip, H. (1969). *Schizoid Phenomena, Object Relations and the Self.* New York: International Universities Press.

Handel, G. (1970). Sociological aspects of parenthood. In *Parenthood: Its Psychology and Psychopathology*, ed. E. J. Anthony and T. Benedek, pp. 87–105. Boston: Little, Brown.

Harlow, H. (1964). Early social deprivation and later behavior in the monkey. In *Unfinished Tasks in the Behavioral Sciences*, ed. A. Abrams, H. J. Garner, and J. E. P. Toman, pp. 154–173. Baltimore: Williams and Wilkins.

Horner, A. (1989). *The Wish for Power and the Fear of Having It.* Northvale, NJ: Jason Aronson.

Kaufman, C. (1970). Biologic considerations of parenthood. In *Parenthood: Its Psychology and Psychopathology*, ed. E. J. Anthony and T. Benedek, pp. 3–55. Boston: Little, Brown.

Kohut, H. (1971). *The Analysis of the Self.* New York: International Universities Press.

Lichtenberg, J. D. (1975). The development of the sense of self. *Journal of the American Psychoanalytic Association* 23:453–484.

Mahler, M. S. (1968). *On Human Symbiosis and the Vicissitudes of Individuation.* New York: International Universities Press.

Mahler, M. S., Pine, F., and Bergman, A. (1975). *The Psychological Birth of the Human Infant.* New York: Basic Books.

May, R. (1965). The emergence of existential psychology. In *Existential Psychology*, p. 19. New York: Random House.

——(1969). *Love and Will.* New York: Norton.

——(1973). *Man's Search for Himself.* New York: Dell.

Miller, A. (1967). *I Don't Need You Any More.* New York: Viking.

Minuchin, S. (1974). *Families and Family Therapy*. Cambridge, MA: Harvard University Press.

Piaget, J. (1936). *The Origins of Intelligence in Children*. New York: International Universities Press, 1952.

Plato (1952). *Symposium. Great Books of the Western World*, vol. 7, p. 158. Chicago: Encyclopaedia Britannica.

Roback, H. B., and Abramowitz, S. J. (1976). Deterioration effects in encounter groups. *American Psychologist* 31:247–255.

Rutter, M. (1974). *The Qualities of Mothering: Maternal Deprivation Reassessed*. New York: Jason Aronson.

Schafer, R. (1976). *A New Language for Psychoanalysis*. New Haven, CT: Yale University Press.

Spitz, R. (1965). *The First Year of Life*. New York: International Universities Press.

Sullivan, H. S. (1956). *Clinical Studies in Psychiatry*. New York: Norton.

Tansey, M., and Burke, W. (1989). *Understanding Countertransference: From Projective Identification to Empathy*. Hillsdale, NJ: The Analytic Press.

Tolpin, M. (1971). On the beginnings of a cohesive self. In *The Psychoanalytic Study of the Child* 26:316–352. New York: Quadrangle Books.

Ulman, R. B., and Brothers, D. (1988). *The Shattered Self*. Hillsdale, NJ: The Analytic Press.

Winnicott, D. W. (1958). The capacity to be alone. In *The Maturational Processes and the Facilitating Environment*, p. 152. London: Hogarth Press and the Institution of Psycho-Analysis, 1965.

——— (1965). *The Maturational Processes and the Facilitating Environment*. New York: International Universities Press.

——— (1971). *Playing and Reality*. London: Tavistock.

——— (1975). Primary maternal preoccupation. In *Through Paediatrics to Psycho-Analysis*, pp. 300–305. New York: Basic Books.

INDEX

and dependency/autonomy conflict, 138–139

goodness of fit, 136–137

guidance and control, providing, 139–140

individuation, support for, 138

and limit-setting, 139

primary maternal preoccupation, 137

Perfect other, ideal of, 89

Perfect parenting, as illusion, 148–149

Perfect self, illusion of, 70–73

projective identification, 70–72

and psychological enslavement, 72

use of other to achieve, 72–73

Piaget, J., 126

Power pivot, 47–59, 138

and culture, 55

grandiose self, 53–54

identification with aggressor, 55–56

identification, by child with parent, 53

narcissism and, 48–50

and omnipotence, threat to, 50

other as extension of self, 50–51

other as reflection of self, 52–53

parental power, sharing, 53–54

parental role and, 56–59

psychotherapy and, 51

rapprochement crisis, 49

self-esteem, dependence on parents for, 54

Primary attachment bond, 20–21

and basic trust/distrust, 21

and capacity to love, foundation of, 21

and institutionally raised children, 23–24

Primary maternal preoccupation, 20, 24, 30, 137

Projective identification, 70–72

Pseudoindependence, 43

Psychotherapy, 51, 85, 94, 113, 115, 132

being and loving in, 129–131

conjoint marital, 117

couple, 94

developing inner resources in, 85

goals and styles in, 122–125

group, 126–128

inequality of patient-therapist relationship, 119–120

inner relationships and, 121

insight/emotional experience, integration of, 125–126

relationship-as-context in, 116–118

reluctance to undertake, 118–121

fear of being controlled, 119–120

fear of humiliation, 119

fear of loss of others, 120–121

fear of loss of self, 120

fear of loss through change, 119, 120–121

therapist, 85, 118, 121–122, 128–129

choosing, 121–122

function of, 85, 118

sex of, 128–129

and undifferentiated response modes, 51

uniqueness of setting, 115–116

when to seek, 113

Rapprochement crisis, in separation-individuation process, 49

Rapprochement phase, in separation-individuation process, 49

Mad as the Dickens

Books by Toni L.P. Kelner

DOWN HOME MURDER

DEAD RINGER

TROUBLE LOOKING FOR A PLACE TO HAPPEN

COUNTRY COMES TO TOWN

TIGHT AS A TICK

DEATH OF A DAMN YANKEE

MAD AS THE DICKENS

Published by Kensington Publishing Corporation

A Laura Fleming Mystery

Mad as the Dickens

Dickens

Toni L.P. Kelner

KENSINGTON BOOKS
http://www.kensingtonbooks.com

KENSINGTON BOOKS are published by

Kensington Publishing Corp.
850 Third Avenue
New York, NY 10022

Copyright © 2001 by Toni L.P. Kelner

All rights reserved. No part of this book may be reproduced in any form or by any means without the prior written consent of the Publisher, excepting brief quotes used in reviews.

All Kensington titles, imprints and distributed lines are available at special quantity discounts for bulk purchases for sales promotion, premiums, fund-raising, educational or institutional use.

Special book excerpts or customized printings can also be created to fit specific needs. For details, write or phone the office of the Kensington Special Sales Manager: Kensington Publishing Corp., 850 Third Avenue, New York, NY 10022, Attn. Special Sales Department. Phone: 1-800-221-2647.

Kensington and the K logo Reg. U.S. Pat. & TM Off.

Library of Congress Card Catalogue Number: 2001091007
ISBN 1-57566-838-6

First Printing: October 2001
10 9 8 7 6 5 4 3 2 1

Printed in the United States of America

To my mother-in-law,
Judith Ward Kelner,
who has always honored Christmas in her heart
and tries to keep it all year!

ACKNOWLEDGMENTS

I want to thank:

My husband, Stephen P. Kelner, Jr., for providing his usual unfailing support, and for coming up with the title.

Fellow EMWA members Leo Du Lac, David Housewright, D. P. Lyle, MD., Steve Perry, and Mary V. Welk for answering my questions about blood spatters, natural gas poisoning, and moonshining.

Erik Abbott for assistance with theater lore.

Elizabeth Shaw for proofreading the manuscript in record time.

My daughters, Magdalene and Valerie, for not tearing the house down while I was busy writing.

Barbara Ikeda, Joan Rafferty, Joanmichelle Rafferty, Ivie Skids, and Victoria Walker, for keeping Maggie and Valerie happily occupied.

Chapter One

"Stop, stop, STOP!" Richard paced back and forth in front of the stage, running his fingers through his hair hard enough to pull it out. "What are you people doing? Have any of you even read the play?"

The actors on stage looked at one another as if trying to decide who he was talking to.

"Don't look at each other. I'm the director!" Richard said, jabbing himself in the chest. "Look at me when I'm talking."

Their heads obediently turned toward him.

"I've been involved in theater for over twenty years, and this is the worst rehearsal I have ever seen. I've been to first readings that were more convincing than this so-called performance. It's less than a week until opening night; now is the time to polish blocking, to add nuances to your interpretations of characters. You people don't even know your lines yet."

I saw Seth Murdstone, the man playing Scrooge, trying to hide his copy of the script.

Richard went on. "*A Christmas Carol* is one of the most popular plays of all time. It's been performed in every variation possible, from traditional to musical to the Muppets. Yet somehow, you people have missed the entire point of the play!"

Richard stopped pacing to glare at them. "It can't be done—it just cannot be done." Then he stormed out the door. The cast just watched him go, as if a tornado had blown by.

Even my cousin Vasti, who could throw a mean tantrum herself, was speechless for nearly thirty seconds. Then she wailed, "Laurie Anne, you've got to do something!"

"He'll calm down in a minute," I said, trying to sound as if I believed it, but I'd never known Richard to act that way before. At least, I hadn't before this trip to Byerly. Since then, I'd seen several other explosions from him, each worse than the last.

I was the pregnant one; I was supposed to be the one with raging hormones. But ever since Vasti had called to talk Richard into taking over the production, he'd become as temperamental as John Huston and an Arabian stallion put together.

Vasti was still looking at me entreatingly, so I said, "I'll go talk to him." Then I levered myself out of the chair, once again surprised at how hard it was to maneuver while five months pregnant.

Seth came over and offered me a hand. "I'm sorry, Laurie Anne, I know I'm the reason Richard is so bent out of shape. I'm trying, I really am, but Scrooge has so many lines to learn. I'll keep at it; don't you worry."

"It's nothing to do with you, Seth," I said, which was at the very least a white lie. "Richard's just tired."

"Be sure and tell him how sorry I am," he said as I headed for the door.

I felt bad for him. No matter how hard Seth tried to act as nasty as Scrooge was written, he just didn't have it in him. When he said, "Bah, humbug," it sounded as if he were joking.

I couldn't imagine why Vasti had given him the part. Scrooge is usually portrayed as a skinny fellow, old and pinched-looking. Seth, on the other hand, was a well-built man with a full head of snow-white hair, and was always smiling and laughing. He was as old as Scrooge was supposed to be, but he sure didn't look it.

Had I been back in Boston, where Richard and I lived, I wouldn't have dreamed of going outside in December without a coat on, and I would probably have grabbed gloves, a hat, and a scarf, too. But after so many Massachusetts winters, North Carolina winters seem almost springlike. Besides which, being pregnant kept me warm, even in Boston. So it was a relief to leave the stuffy recreation center building for the brisk, sunny day waiting outside.

My usually mild-mannered husband was standing not far from the door, his hands jammed in his pockets as he kicked at the red clay dirt and muttered to himself.

"Hey," I said.

He didn't answer.

"Hello?"

There was still no answer.

"Richard, I think I'm in labor."

That got his attention. He turned white as a sheet and started toward me.

"Just kidding," I said.

He stopped short and thumped his chest, presumably to make sure his heart was still beating. "Laura, please don't joke about that."

"Sorry," I said, struggling to keep a smile off my face. "I had to get your attention somehow."

"You got it, all right."

"So do you want to go home now, or should we stay through Christmas?"

"What do you mean?" he said.

"We can either spend the rest of the holidays here relaxing, or fly back to Boston and spend Christmas alone the way we planned in the first place. You just said that there was no way you could whip the cast into shape in time. So why beat your head against a brick wall? Give it up now and let Vasti worry about it."

"That wouldn't be exactly kind to Vasti, would it?" he said hesitantly.

"Who cares?" I said. "She didn't tell you the whole story, or you'd never have agreed to come. You were supposed to have two weeks to rehearse, not just one. Besides, you can't stage a decent production with this cast—they're hopeless. I mean, Seth Murdstone is as nice a man as you'd ever want to meet, but he's a terrible actor."

"I know," Richard said. "I hate losing my temper at him, but I think he got that accent from listening to Dick Van Dyke in *Mary Poppins*."

"What about the others? None of them can act."

"That's not true. Bob Cratchit keeps getting better, and Mrs. Cratchit is already wonderful. The Spirits of Christmas aren't too bad, and even though Scrooge's nephew needs work, I could coax it out of him."

"I suppose you could," I said, "but there's no way you can get it done by Friday night."

"Maybe I could," he said speculatively. "If we lose the phony British accents so we get a little authenticity . . . We'd have to rehearse morning, noon, and night, but maybe . . ."

"In less than a week?"

"Look, Laura," he said heatedly, "I've waited my whole life to direct. Do you really think I'd give up my only chance because the cast needs a little work?"

"A *little* work?"

"Okay, a lot of work. I can do it. They can do it. We can do it." He strode purposefully toward the door, then turned back. "I thought you were a programmer, not a psychologist."

I grinned. "I'm practicing for when the baby throws his or her first tantrum."

"Was I that bad?"

"Oh, yeah."

He looked at the door. "Do you think they'll take me back?"

"Of course. They'd be scared not to."

He looked sheepish. "I suppose I should get a grip on my temper."

"Does that mean that we're staying?"

"That's what it means," he said. "I'm going to give the people in Byerly a show they'll never forget!" He started back inside, his shoulders squared like a drill sergeant determined to whip a platoon of raw recruits into shape.

Chapter
Two

I sat down on the low brick wall at the entrance to the recreation center to enjoy the fresh air a little longer, rubbing my tummy automatically. I'd always wondered why pregnant women do that all the time, and I still didn't know, but I'd given up trying to stop myself. I did know why pregnant women speak to their unborn babies, or at least I'd read theories about how it would turn them into genuises. But I did it as instinctively as I rubbed my tummy.

"Don't worry, baby," I said. "Your daddy isn't usually so volatile." I was hoping the baby would inherit Richard's usual temperament, and maybe those deep-brown eyes. I didn't care if he was short like me or tall like Richard, but I did want a child who loved books as much as we did. Richard had voted for light-brown hair like mine, admittedly easier to control than his own, and it would be a lot easier to keep the little one in shoes if his toes weren't as long as Richard's. Maybe I'd be able to see something of my parents in the baby's face, and I really wanted him or her to share my grandfather's musical talent and Aunt Nora's gift for cooking.

Then I started thinking about all the other traits the baby could get from my family: Aunt Maggie's orneriness or Aunt Ruby Lee's sweetness, Vasti's piercing voice or Willis's usual silence, Linwood's mean streak or Earl's gentleness. And that was just my side of the family! "Baby," I said, "with this gene pool, there's no telling how you'll turn out. But your mama and daddy are going to love you no matter what."

Eventually I went back inside, just in case Richard had exploded again. Though things seemed to be running smoothly, Vasti still looked nervous, so I said, "I think he's going to be all right now."

"I sure hope so," said Vasti. "Who'd have known Richard could be so much trouble?"

"It's your fault that he's so aggravated. You told us we had two weeks until opening night, and then you moved it up a week."

"I had to. The recreation center is already booked for that other night. We're just lucky I talked that group into rehearsing somewhere else."

"What about the theater at the high school?" I knew they had a decent one there. I'd bought candy bars and magazine subscriptions from younger cousins to help pay for it.

"It's already booked, too," Vasti said.

"The middle school? Or even the elementary school?"

"Holiday pageants." She indignantly added, "How was I supposed to know that everybody in Byerly was putting on a show this year?"

"Why didn't you set something up sooner?" Lack of planning wasn't one of Vasti's problems. Usually she had each minute of her day planned, and if I gave her a chance, she'd plan most of mine, too.

"I do have a new baby, you know," she said. "I'm breast-feeding, and Bitsy isn't even sleeping through the night yet. Just wait until your baby is born and see how much you manage to get done!"

"All right," I said, relenting. "Richard will do his best. But why didn't you tell us about all the practical jokes?"

"I didn't think it was worth mentioning," she said unconvincingly. "There are always mix-ups when you've got this many people around."

"Not like this! I've already lost track of the mix-ups that have happened just in the two days we've been here." I used my fingers to count off. "The thermostat has gone haywire so we're either freezing or sweating, and the fire alarm has gone off twice. Then somebody tied most of the ropes backstage in knots that took us an hour to untie, and all the lightbulbs for the stage went out. Not to mention the fact that every single roll of toilet paper in the building disappeared overnight." Since my doctor had ordered me to drink lots of water, that last one was the worst as far as I was concerned. Even I was tired of the tricks, despite the fact that I'd attended MIT, where the pursuit of practical jokes was almost a religion.

"I've tried to find out who it is, but nobody will own up to it," she said. "I thought the Norton kids were doing it, but Junior questioned them herself and she swears it wasn't them."

Vasti had cast some of my friend Junior Norton's nieces and nephews as the Cratchit children. Though Junior was a devoted aunt, I knew she'd be the first to admit it if they'd been causing trouble.

She continued, "I was hoping that once Richard got here and things calmed down, the pranks would stop."

"I hope you don't think Richard is going to track down the joker," I warned. "He's got his hands full already. That's another thing—why didn't you warn him about how badly things were going? It's no wonder your other director quit." I saw a guilty expression flash across her face. "Vasti, who was the original director?"

She turned away. "Why do you ask?"

"It was you!" I guessed. "You were the director, weren't you?"

She hung her head, then nodded.

"You told us he quit because of a family emergency."

"It *was* a family emergency. Do you know what it's like trying to nurse a baby in the middle of rehearsal? I thought I had a director, but Sally Hendon got him for *her* show, so I figured I'd do it myself. I didn't think directing would be so hard, but nobody was learning their lines and the show was just awful. I had to do *something.*"

"Maybe so, but you didn't have to lie to me and Richard."

"I didn't lie. I just didn't tell you every little detail."

"Vasti—"

"You're not going to tell Richard, are you? I don't want him to make another scene."

"If he asks me, I'll tell him the truth, but I won't volunteer anything."

"Thank you, Laurie Anne. It's all for a good cause." Then she looked at her watch and said, "Look at the time! I've got to go pick up Bitsy at my in-laws' house. I only left one bottle of my milk, and it's nearly feeding time." She grabbed her purse and coat and stopped only long enough to say, "You'll keep an eye on things, won't you?"

"Sure," I said, but she was already out the door.

I looked around the room and sighed, mostly on my husband's behalf. Even though it was Richard's first crack at directing a play, I thought he deserved better than a stage in a worn-out recreation hall. The building was decades old, and over the years had hosted craft fairs, scout meetings, senior citizen's parties, and goodness knows what else. Half the chairs were broken, and I didn't completely trust the ones that weren't. The linoleum was worn near the doors and peeling up elsewhere. Somebody had decorated a dilapidated artificial Christmas tree with a dozen red satin balls, and hung a few straggly strands of garland around the walls, but that bit of holiday cheer only made the place look worse.

Of course, none of that would show once the house lights were out. What bothered Richard was the fact that the stage was only a few feet off the ground, which meant that sight lines for the audience were going to be horrible. My makeup mirror at home was more advanced than the lighting system, and there must have been whole generations of moths raised on the curtain. On the plus side, the acoustics were surprisingly good and the backstage space was decent, despite the layers of dust.

Junior Norton saw me and waved me over to an empty chair next to her. Junior's a little bit shorter than my five feet, two inches, but there's something about the way she carries her sturdy build that gets people's attention. Andy Norton had had his heart set on a little boy to pass on his name, but when the fifth girl arrived, he gave up and named her Junior. Of course, later on he got his boy, but since "Junior" was taken, the new baby was Trey, for Andy III. Junior had taken over from Andy as police chief, with Trey as her part-time deputy while he finished college.

"I take it that Richard is sticking around," Junior said.

"For now, anyway."

We watched the players at work for a few minutes in companionable silence.

Then Junior said, "You know, this is about as interesting as seeing grass grow."

"Or watching paint dry."

It was only my second day of rehearsal, but it seemed as if I'd been sitting in those hard plastic chairs for a month. I'd thought it would be fun to see Richard direct—nobody had told me how boring rehearsals are. Watching my husband run the cast through the same scenes over and over again was enough to drive me to drink.

I was just happy that I had a companion in boredom. Junior was spending some of her rare time off riding herd on the nieces and nephews who had parts in the show.

"Do you think Richard will throw another tantrum?" she said hopefully.

"It wasn't that bad," I said, defending him. "The cast is way behind where they should be. I don't blame Richard a bit for getting hot under the collar."

"I don't blame him either. I just wish it would happen again. If *something* doesn't happen, I'm going to fall sound asleep."

"I hear that," I said. "Maybe we should try to hunt down the practical joker."

"Hunt him down? I want to shake his hand. Those jokes and your husband's tantrums are the only things getting me through the day."

I was tempted to sneak off and go shopping or visiting or something, but I was afraid I might be needed to calm down the director again.

Back on stage, Richard stopped the action once more and ran his fingers through his already disheveled hair—a sign that agitation was building again. "David," he said, "can you try to look a little more cheerful? You're young Ebeneezer, Ebeneezer *before* he turns into a curmudgeon. It's Christmas, and you're having a wonderful time. You are not having root canal surgery!"

"Sorry," he said. "I'm trying my best." Other than his hair and bushy eyebrows still being reddish-brown, David Murdstone was the spitting image of his father, and his dual roles as Scrooge's nephew and Young Scrooge took advantage of the resemblance. David usually had his daddy's smile, too, but not right that minute.

"Just think happy thoughts," Richard said. "Florence, you make your entrance now."

Florence Easterly, in character as the young woman Ebeneezer was once in love with, floated onto the stage. Even as bored as I was, I could see David's face light up when he saw her. Though the two of them were fifty years old if they were a day, they'd only been married a few months, and it showed.

Richard must have seen the same thing I did, because he came up with a way to use it. "Here's an idea. Florence, I want you to be on stage when the Spirit of Christmas Past and Scrooge arrive."

"That's not in the book," David objected.

"If we were going to do exactly as the script says," Richard said patiently, "you people wouldn't need me. Just try it."

"Whatever you say, Richard," Florence said.

He said, "Let's start with Fezziwig shaking Young Ebeneezer's hand." They ran through the last part of the scene again, and this time it worked beautifully. Young Ebeneezer glowed with Christmas joy, and so did Richard.

Maybe he was going to pull it off after all. The players were still rough, but they'd improved so much already and they still had nearly a week before opening night. If Richard could just get Seth Murdstone to do a decent job with Scrooge, it might not be a total disaster.

Richard called out, "Spirit of Christmas Past and Scrooge, let's get you two into the picture."

Oliver Jarndyce, the round-faced man playing the first spirit to visit Scrooge, stepped out of the wings, but he was alone.

"Where's Scrooge?" Richard asked.

"He said he wanted a cigarette," Oliver said.

For a second it looked as if Junior might see her wish for another tantrum granted, but Richard swallowed whatever it was he wanted to say and instead said, "Mrs. Gamp, do you think you could find Seth and get him back on stage?"

"I sure will; Mrs. Harris probably knows just where he went," the cheerful, birdlike stage manager said, and she scooted away. Unlike most of the cast, she managed to be right where she needed to be whenever Richard called her.

Richard ran his fingers through his hair again. "While we're waiting for Scrooge, let's try something a little different."

My eyes glazed over at that, and I lost track of what was happening for the next few minutes. Then a scream rang out, and I jerked wide awake. Since when was there a scream in that scene?

The folks on stage looked as surprised as I was. I turned to ask Junior what had happened, but her reflexes had taken her nearly up onstage by then, and I took off after her as fast as five months of pregnancy would allow.

Richard saw me coming and helped hoist me up, and then we followed Junior as she chased a second scream. How she'd been able to judge the direction it was coming from in that cave of a building, I'll never know. To me it seemed to echo everywhere.

We went stage left and down the narrow, dimly lit corridor that led past the dressing rooms and ended at the back door. We found Mrs. Gamp about halfway down the hall, her fist pressed against her mouth as if to hold in any more screams.

Lying on one side on the floor in front of her was Seth Murdstone, blood seeping from a swollen lump on his head. I could tell he was dead even before Junior knelt to touch his wrist.

"As dead as a doornail," Richard whispered, quoting from *A Christmas Carol*.

All I could think of was that he'd promised a show that Byerly would never forget. It looked as if he'd succeeded even before the curtain went up.

Chapter Three

Junior barked, "All of y'all step back, and nobody touch anything!" We obeyed, and I looked away from Seth's body. Mrs. Gamp had started sobbing, and I pulled her away, then let her hold on to me while she continued to cry. More members of the cast and crew came down the hall toward us, but Richard waved them away. I don't know if they realized how serious it was or if they were afraid of another one of Richard's tantrums, but they moved back without questioning him.

Junior reached into her pocket, pulled out a cell phone, and dialed. "Hey, Mark. I've got something for you."

At first I was surprised Junior would hand over a murder to her deputy, but then I remembered that she was on vacation. Even though Junior was there on the scene, investigating Seth's death was going to be Mark Pope's job, not hers.

"You've got yourself a situation at the recreation center," Junior was saying. "The fatal kind. You know we're rehearsing a play down here? One of our actors got himself killed. . . . Seth Murdstone . . . Of course, the scene is secured. . . . I *am* going to let you handle it. . . . Yes, I touched something—how do you think I knew he was dead?" Junior's sigh was loud enough for Mark to hear it. "I'll be here when you get here." Junior broke the connection and put the phone back in her pocket.

The people down the hall started asking questions, and I realized that Junior, Mrs. Gamp, Richard, and I were blocking their view of Seth's body. "Richard, we can't let David and Jake see their father like this," I whispered. Both of Seth's sons were in the play.

"We're not going to let *anybody* see him like this," Junior said firmly. "Not yet, anyway." In a louder voice, she called out, "People, we've had an accident."

My Aunt Maggie yelled back, "What kind of accident? Who is it?"

Junior ignored the questions. "Help is on the way, so y'all can go on back to the auditorium." She added, "Richard, take Laurie Anne and Mrs. Gamp out, too, and make sure nobody leaves before Mark gets here."

"What do we tell them?" I asked.

"Exactly what I just said, and not one word more."

"They're going to figure out that Seth is missing," I pointed out.

"Probably, but it'll take them a while. Mark should be here by then, and he can worry about it."

Mrs. Gamp still had her head buried on my shoulder, and as I was wondering how I was going to extricate her, Junior said, "Mrs. Gamp, I sure would appreciate you looking after my sisters' children for me."

Once she had a job to do, Mrs. Gamp promptly dried her eyes, and said, "Don't you worry. Mrs. Harris and I will take care of them." She started marching down the hall, fluttering her hands to herd people in front of her. Richard followed, holding himself as wide as he could to block as much of the line of sight as possible.

I stayed long enough to look around. The wall of the hall was lined with shiny off-white tiles up to eye level, and then with beige-painted concrete blocks the rest of the way to the ceiling. The flat ceiling was painted a darker color and punctuated with ceiling fixtures. There were no new marks on the walls or elsewhere on the well-scuffed linoleum floor, and other than Seth's body, there was nothing in the hall but Junior and me.

"Junior, how did Seth hit his head?"

"You tell me."

"Maybe he slipped and ran into . . ." I looked around, but there was nothing he could have run into. "Maybe he hit the floor . . . or the wall."

"Look at the shape of that knot on his head. He didn't get that from a flat surface. I'm guessing it was something long and not too wide."

"But there's nothing like that in here."

"That's right. So unless whatever it was he hit himself on walked away afterward . . ."

"Then somebody killed him," I finished for her.

"That's what I'm thinking."

"But who?" I knew that nice people get murdered as often as nasty ones, but I couldn't imagine why anybody would have wanted Seth Murdstone dead. "Did the killer come in that way?" I asked, nodding at the door to the back parking lot. The smokers had been going out that way for cigarette breaks.

"Whoever it was had to have come through one of these doors," she said neutrally. "It's too soon to say which one."

I'd really wanted her to say that the killer must have come from outside, meaning that it wasn't somebody involved in the play.

"Laurie Anne, are you all right?" Junior asked.

"This isn't my first dead body," I reminded her.

"I know, but you've never been pregnant before. Mark will never let me hear the end of it if I let you get sick all over his crime scene."

"I'll have you know that I quit having morning sickness months ago."

"In that case, do me a favor and wait outside for Mark to get here, and send him in my direction."

"All right." Despite what I'd said to Junior, I was just as glad to get away from Seth's body.

Richard had everybody out of the hall by then, and I had to tap on the door at the end to get him out of the way so I could get through.

"Junior wants me to go meet Mark," I whispered to him.

"I'll hold the fort here." He leaned down to give me a quick peck on the cheek. "Are you all right?"

"I'm fine," I said firmly.

My great-aunt pounced on me then. Nobody is quite sure how old Aunt Maggie is. Her hair had been salt-and-pepper for as long as I could remember, though maybe there was a bit more salt than there used to be. I didn't know how Vasti had talked her into supplying props for the play, since she wasn't known for her willingness to volunteer or for her Christmas spirit. Her sweatshirt said, "BAH! HUMBUG!" in bright green letters, and she'd owned it long before she started working on the play.

She said, "Laurie Anne, what in the Sam Hill is going on? I heard Sarah Gamp scream like she'd seen a ghost, but all she'll say is that I shouldn't frighten the children."

I might have been tempted to tell Aunt Maggie the truth, just to ensure family peace, but there were too many people listening in. The entire cast and crew were clustered in the auditorium, and I could see Florence looking around as if trying to decide who was missing.

"There's been an accident," I said, going toward the door to the parking lot. "Just like Junior said."

"What kind of accident?" Aunt Maggie asked, walking along beside me.

"Help is on the way," I said, still moving.

"Laurie Anne . . ." Aunt Maggie said.

I dropped my voice to a whisper. "Junior asked me not to say anything until Mark Pope gets here."

"Why did she call her deputy for an accident?"

"Please, Aunt Maggie. Junior doesn't want people getting worked up."

"They're already getting worked up."

I just shrugged. She was right, but there wasn't anything I could do other than what Junior had asked me to do.

"All right," Aunt Maggie said, "but I expect you to tell me the whole story later."

"I will," I promised, and I finally made it out the door.

I stood on the sidewalk in front of the building to wait, again rubbing my tummy. "Well, baby," I said, "you've seen your first dead body. Okay, not seen, but been around. They do pop up now and again." That was true enough, but it sounded too flippant for the circumstances. "Not that Mama and Daddy go looking for murder victims, mind you, but we have gotten mixed up with this kind of thing before." That wasn't much of an improvement. "Sometimes Mama and Daddy solve mysteries." Great, the kid was going to think that her parents rode around in a van with a Great Dane named Scooby Doo.

Before I could confuse my unborn child further, a blue-and-white police cruiser tore into the parking lot, siren blaring. The driver didn't so much park as screech to a halt, blocking three parking places in the process. Then Mark Pope got out of the car.

Mark Pope is one of the most forgettable-looking men I've ever met. Medium height and build, with medium brown eyes and hair. If his job had ever called for following somebody on foot, he'd have been great, because nobody would remember him ten minutes after seeing him. He strode over to me, his hand perched on the handle of the nightstick at his belt.

"Where's the alleged body?"

I was tempted to tell him it was allegedly in the alleged recreation center, but I settled for, "Inside. Junior asked me to take you there."

"Good enough." Then he stopped, and looked me over. "You're one of the Burnettes."

"That's right." Actually, it was my mother who'd been a Burnette, but people around Byerly and Rocky Shoals tend to trace people back at least two generations in order to place them correctly. "I'm Laura Fleming."

"Right. Laurie Anne."

I winced, but I knew it wasn't worth the trouble to correct him any more than I could correct my family.

"You're the one who keeps butting into police business."

"You might say that." Richard and I had clashed with Mark after a flea market dealer was murdered. Mark had been on the wrong track entirely and hadn't been pleased when we beat him to the killer.[1]

"Is that what you're doing now?"

"No, I'm here because my husband is directing the play."

He didn't look convinced, but he said, "Let's get on with it," and started toward the door.

"There's something I should tell you. Mr. Murdstone's sons are inside, and they don't know he's been—that he's been hurt. I don't know how you want to handle it, but—"

"Well *I* know how I want to handle it."

"Whatever you say." I hadn't been trying to help him anyway—I'd only wanted to make things easier for David and Jake.

All conversation stopped when I led Mark into the auditorium. He swiveled his head around like a spotlight, as if relishing the attention. David and Jake were standing together, with Florence's hand in David's, and I was sure that they'd realized Seth was missing. Everybody watched while I showed Mark the way, but it seemed to me that the Murdstones were watching us more closely than the rest.

Richard was still guarding the door to the hall, but he stepped aside when he saw us coming.

"Junior is down—" I started to say, but Mark cut me off.

"I'll take it from here." He turned back to the people in the room and raised his voice much louder than was necessary. "I don't want any of you people leaving the premises until we sort out the situation, and nobody is to come down this way unless I tell them to. Is that understood?"

When nobody answered, he took that to mean that it was, and he went into the hall, shutting the door in our faces.

---

[1] *Tight as a Tick*

Chapter Four

" '**S**ecret, and self-contained, and solitary as an oyster,' " Richard said.

"That Shakespeare had something to say about everything, didn't he?" Aunt Maggie said, coming up to us.

"Actually, that wasn't the Bard. It was Charles Dickens in *A Christmas Carol*. Stave One, if I'm not mistaken."

Aunt Maggie raised one eyebrow. "Since when do you quote Dickens?"

"Since he decided to direct this play," I explained. As a Shakespeare professor at Boston College, Richard didn't know all the Bard's work by heart, but he came close, and was usually more than willing to share that knowledge. "You see, it's an old theater superstition that it's bad luck to quote *Mac*—"

"Don't say it!" Richard nearly shouted.

"Sorry. It's bad luck to quote that Scottish play, or even to say its name."

"The Scottish play?" Aunt Maggie asked.

Richard was still looking at me in alarm, and short of spelling it out, there wasn't any way I could think of to tell Aunt Maggie that we weren't supposed to say *Macbeth*. "I'll tell you which one I mean later. Anyway, just to make sure he doesn't accidentally quote from *that* play, he's sworn off quoting Shakespeare for the duration."

"Hence the use of Dickens, in honor of our production," Richard added.

Aunt Maggie shook her head. "Richard, did you ever think of just saying things like normal people?"

"Did you ever think of wearing shirts that don't tell people what's on your mind?"

"Fat chance," she said with a snort.

"My sentiments exactly."

She looked as if she wanted to say more, but she must have decided it wouldn't do any good, so she changed the subject. "Are you two going to tell me what's going on around here? It's Seth, isn't it?"

I hesitated, but decided it wasn't going to be a secret much longer anyway. Keeping my voice low so that nobody else could hear, I said, "Yes, ma'am. He's dead."

She nodded, her suspicions confirmed. "What happened? Florence says he had a bad heart. Was that it?"

"I don't think it was a heart attack," I said, but before I could say more, Mark stepped out of the door from the hall. "Is Mr. Murdstone's family here?" he said.

David stepped forward. "Deputy Pope, I believe you know my brother Jake and my wife Florence."

Mark nodded in acknowledgment. "I'm afraid I've got bad news for you," he said.

The two men stiffened and Florence gasped. I've known other women to gasp for effect, but with her it sounded genuine.

"Is Daddy . . . ?" Jake couldn't finish the question.

Mark nodded.

"Was it his heart?" David wanted to know. "Chief Norton said something about an accident, but my father does have a bad heart."

Mark hesitated, then said, "I'm not sure. Once the medical examiner gets here, I may be able to tell you more."

"Can I see him?" Jake asked.

"Not yet, but I'll tell you when you can. If y'all will excuse me, I need to notify the proper authorities." Closing the hall door quietly but firmly, he went back toward Seth's body.

Though we should have given them some privacy, I don't think anybody could resist watching the Murdstones. Florence grabbed hold of David, who was staring straight ahead, then reached out and pulled Jake into the embrace, too. Jake started to cry, deep sobs that must have hurt him.

That's when I turned away, rubbing my tummy again.

"I guess he broke it to them as best he could," Aunt Maggie allowed, "but he should have gotten them alone first."

"It wouldn't have made any difference," I said.

"Well, I think—" Aunt Maggie started to say; then she stopped. "I guess you know what you're talking about."

Junior's father, Chief Andy Norton, had been the one to tell me when my parents were killed in a car accident. I'd been visiting my grandfather Paw, and Chief Norton had asked Paw out onto the porch to tell him, giving Paw a chance to recover before they told me. But it hadn't really mattered. I'd known from the expression on Chief Norton's face that something was bad wrong.

"Sometimes being alone is worse," said a voice from behind us. It was Tim Topper, who was playing Bob Cratchit, and like me, he had reason to know. His mother had been murdered when he was just a little boy, so Chief Norton had come to visit him, too. Since Tim's father had been long gone, Tim was left to be raised by his aunt and uncle.

I looked down at my tummy, feeling the baby's kicks. Suddenly I was terrified that something would happen to me or Richard before our child could grow up—that some police officer would be wearing that same expression to give that awful news someday.

Richard somehow knew I was close to tears before I did myself, and he wrapped his arms around me. "It's okay, Laura," he murmured.

"It's just the damn hormones," I said angrily. "I didn't even hardly know Seth."

"I know," Richard said, rubbing my back. "Let's sit down." He led me to as quiet a corner as he could find, and made me put my feet up while Aunt Maggie got me one of the bottles of cold water I'd brought to rehearsal.

Part of me appreciated the attention, while part of me hated the feelings of weakness that pregnancy caused. The rest of me was watching the other people in the auditorium. They were probably starting to realize that Seth Murdstone hadn't died of a heart attack or from an accident—that he'd been murdered. I couldn't help thinking that there was a good chance that the murderer was in the room with us.

Chapter Five

Though Richard had known a fair amount about Dickens before he decided to direct *A Christmas Carol,* ever since then he'd been reading exhaustively, and as usual, he'd shared tidbits. That's how I knew that it's pretty easy to tell the villains in Dickens's books. They tend to be grotesque like Fagin, or repellent like Uriah Heep. Unfortunately, real-life murderers don't always look or act like murderers, but knowing that didn't stop me from looking over the cast and crew.

There was Aunt Maggie, of course, but as far as I knew, she'd liked Seth. Lord knows that she would have let us know if she hadn't, and even then, she would have been more likely to subject him to a tongue-lashing than to a bludgeoning.

She noticed me looking around and said, "Was it an accident, Laurie Anne?"

"It doesn't look like it."

She nodded, absorbing it more easily than most people would have. Maybe it was her age, but I've always thought that Aunt Maggie must have been born unflappable. "Do you think that somebody here did it?"

"I don't know enough to say. I don't even know these people that well." There hadn't been much time to meet everybody yet, and after Richard's tantrums, I thought some of them had been avoiding me. "Other than the triplets, of course."

Nearby were my cousins Idelle, Odelle, and Carlelle Holt. Though they don't always dress alike, they do it often enough that the rest of the family has gotten used to being confused. That day it was snug blue jeans and matching Christmas-colored sweaters: Idelle in red, Odelle in green, and Carlelle in green and red stripes. Vasti had brought them in to do costumes and makeup for the show, and since they have more clothes and wear more makeup than anybody else I've ever met, I thought they'd do a good job.

"What do you think, Richard?" I asked. "You know everybody."

"Only through their parts," he said.

Aunt Maggie said, "Y'all are talking like this is Boston. This is Byerly, Laurie Anne. You must know these folks."

"I don't know *everybody* in Byerly," I protested. "I haven't lived here in ten years." I'd gone up North to go to college and had ended up marrying Richard and staying there. "I only just met Seth." And I wasn't going to get a chance to get to know him any better, I thought sadly.

"You know Big Bill," Aunt Maggie said, nodding at an older man in a flannel shirt and blue jeans.

I nodded, though I could hardly believe that he was there. Big Bill Walters owned Walters Mill, which employed a good proportion of the people in Byerly. He also owned the bank, several apartment buildings, and I wasn't sure how much more of the town. Anything he didn't own, he ran by means of being head of the city council. I'd never seen him in anything less formal than a sport jacket, and I certainly would never have thought that he owned a pair of blue jeans, let alone would wear them in public.

I'd been hearing rumors about him and Aunt Maggie, but this was the first chance I'd had to ask her about them. "So are you two—?"

"We two aren't anything," she said emphatically. "He thinks he can make it up to me after trying to sell the mill to a bunch of no-good Yankees.[2] He just happened to be at the flea market when

---

[2] *Death of a Damn Yankee*

Vasti tricked me into doing props for the show, and when he said he'd be glad to help out, Vasti couldn't wait to give him a part."

Richard said, "He's playing Jacob Marley, Scrooge's dead partner."

"I hear he only took the part to be around you, Aunt Maggie," I teased. "It must be—"

"Don't say it!" she snapped.

"Yes, ma'am. I mean, no ma'am."

She gave me a look. "Anyway, he's been helping me out with the props." She glanced back in his direction. "He looks pretty darned good in those blue jeans, don't you think?"

I blinked. Though I knew that a person's sex life didn't come to a screeching halt at age sixty, I wasn't sure I was up to hearing my great-aunt critique Big Bill Walters's tail end.

Aunt Maggie said, "Did you meet the Murdstone brothers?"

"Briefly. Vasti introduced us yesterday, but David's been busy on-stage and Jake's been backstage."

Jake was playing the charity collector and building sets. He was in the furniture business with his father, which was why he'd been tapped to make sets. He didn't look much like his brother or his father. He was much thinner, which made him look taller, and his hair was jet black.

"Jake must take after their mother," I said.

"I don't remember what she looked like. She died when Jake was just a little thing," Aunt Maggie said. "You know Jake's boy Barnaby is the reason we're doing this play."

"I thought it was for charity." Most of Vasti's endeavors were for charity, though she was usually pretty vague about the actual cause involved. For some people, this would have meant that the work was its own reward. In Vasti's case, the reward was having a chance to order people around and make a big show.

"It *is* for charity. The money is going to the Shriners' Burn Hospital in memory of Barnaby. He died last month."

"There was another fire in Byerly?" I asked. The previous spring there'd been a rash of them.[3] What with the Burnette home place

---

[3] *Death of a Damn Yankee*

being firebombed and my coming uncomfortably close to burning to death myself, I was a little sensitive on the subject. "Don't tell me there's another arsonist at work."

"Nothing like that. Barnaby was hurt in an accident, one of those propane space heaters. I hear there were burns all over his body." She shook her head. "He wasn't but nine years old."

Richard solemnly said, " 'When Death strikes down the innocent and young, for every fragile form from which he lets the panting spirit free, a hundred virtues rise, in shapes of mercy, charity, and love, to work the world, and bless it.' *The Old Curiosity Shop*, Chapter Forty."

"So it's just the two of them now," I said. Though I didn't have any brothers or sisters, I had enough cousins, aunts, uncles, and other relatives that I couldn't imagine not being surrounded by family.

"And David's wife, Florence," Aunt Maggie said.

"Scrooge's girlfriend in the past, and Mrs. Cratchit in the present," Richard put in.

The petite blonde was sitting between Jake and David, but her eyes were only for her husband. Most women her age would look silly in pastels, but the fuzzy rose-colored sweater suited her fine. I knew she was tougher than she looked—she was the lawyer who'd helped my cousin Ilene when she was in trouble.[4] "I heard they got married. It must have been quite the shindig, with her family connections and all."

Aunt Maggie snorted. "Not hardly! She and David eloped, and the Junior League is still buzzing about it."

"Why? Because they didn't get another chance to dress up?"

"That and the fact that Florence married beneath herself." She must have seen the look on my face because she added, "I'm just repeating what they're saying. This 'marrying up' and 'marrying down' business is nothing but foolishness."

I nodded, though technically I'd "married up" myself. Richard was a full head taller than I was.

---

[4] *Trouble Looking for a Place to Happen*

"Florence is one of the few people Vasti didn't have to drag into this kicking and screaming," Aunt Maggie said.

"Since when does anybody need to drag in performers in Byerly?" I didn't know if all small towns had as many aspiring actors, musicians, singers, and dancers as Byerly did, or if we were just lucky. That didn't mean that people were good, but they were darned enthusiastic, and there'd never been a show without hotly contested roles.

"All the usual folks were already working for the competition," Aunt Maggie said.

"What competition?"

"The Byerly Holiday Follies. Since they got going early, they got the cream of the crop. No offense, Richard."

"None taken," he said with a grin.

"Even Dorcas Walters is going to be in the Follies," Aunt Maggie added.

"Really? Who's in charge of it?" I asked.

"Sally Hendon."

Ouch! Sally Hendon was a distant cousin of mine and Vasti's, and as far as Vasti was concerned, she wasn't distant enough. Once she became the county's leading saleswoman for Mary Kay cosmetics, Sally had set her sights on being the biggest social climber, too. She'd jumped onto any committee that would have her, helped with every charity event that came down the pike, and ingratiated herself with the society columnist in Byerly's twice-weekly newspaper. Since Vasti used the same techniques, they'd butted heads more than once.

For Sally to have gotten the jump on Vasti's theatrical aspirations must have been galling, and I realized now that it was probably Sally's show that had the high school auditorium booked up. Even worse, Vasti and Sally were both dying to get into the Junior League, and Dorcas Walters was the reigning president. Everybody in town knew Dorcas couldn't act, sing, or dance, but she still lusted after the spotlight. That Sally had managed to find something for her to do on stage was quite a coup, sure to improve her chances of getting into the coveted organization.

Aunt Maggie said, "Vasti's lucky she got Florence. She and David were on their honeymoon when Sally Hendon put out the word that she wanted performers, so her show was already full up when they got back. In fact, Vasti had been thinking of not even doing a show until she heard Florence was available."

"Is she that good an actress?" I asked.

"Excellent," Richard said. "One of the bright spots in the cast."

"You don't think Vasti picked her for that, do you?" Aunt Maggie asked. "All Vasti cares about is that Florence is the membership secretary of the Junior League."

Then Vasti wasn't completely off her game after all. "Did Vasti choose all the actors by what they can do for her?"

"Naturally. Not that some of those folks aren't good, but that's not why she picked them. You know how she got Florence, and when Florence said she thought her new husband would be interested, Vasti gave him a part, too."

I asked, "What about Seth as Scrooge? Was it because he's Florence's father-in-law?"

"That and the fact that the show's in honor of his grandson. Which is why Jake is in on it. You already know that a bunch of the Norton girls' kids are playing Tiny Tim and the other little Cratchits."

"So Vasti can get Junior and Trey to direct traffic?" I guessed.

"Got it in one."

"What about Bob Cratchit?" I asked.

"Tim Topper?" Richard said. "I thought it was quite brave of Vasti to cast a black man as Cratchit next to a white Scrooge, using American racism as an analogy for the British class system."

Aunt Maggie looked at him pityingly.

"It was the barbecue, wasn't it?" I said. Tim ran Pigwick's, one of Byerly's two barbecue houses. "Refreshments for the intermission? Catering for the cast party?"

Richard said, "You're serious, aren't you? Did Vasti even bother to hold auditions?"

"What for?" Aunt Maggie said.

"How could Vasti do this to a perfectly good play?" he moaned.

"What other favors is she after?" I asked Aunt Maggie.

"See if you can guess."

"Oliver Jarndyce is the Spirit of Christmas Past. He's in real estate, isn't he? Is Vasti still talking about buying a bigger house because of the baby?"

Aunt Maggie nodded.

Sid Honeywell, the plump and usually jolly man playing the Spirit of Christmas Present, had a gas station. "Door prizes from Sid?"

Aunt Maggie nodded again.

Pete Fredericks was one of Byerly's morticians and was all too appropriately cast as the Spirit of Christmas Yet to Come. "Do I want to know what she wants from Pete?"

"Don't worry. He's just bringing extra chairs for the show."

"That's a relief." I had to wonder if he was going to be taking care of Seth Murdstone. "What about Mrs. Gamp? She's not in the Junior League, is she?"

"Not hardly. They'd choke on their cucumber sandwiches before they'd let a trucker's widow in their precious club."

" 'Be wery careful o' vidders all your life,' " Richard quoted. "*Pickwick Papers*, Chapter Twenty."

Aunt Maggie ignored him. "Besides which, she probably wouldn't have time. She's too busy volunteering. At church, and at the schools, and up at the hospital in Hickory. She even volunteered to work on the play without Vasti having to chase her down. Mrs. Gamp does good work, even if she is a mite strange."

"What do you mean?" Richard said. "She and Mrs. Harris are the only things holding this play together."

"Richard," I said, "have you actually seen Mrs. Harris?"

"Not yet. Is there something wrong with her?"

"Not at all—other than the fact that she doesn't exist. There is no Mrs. Harris—Mrs. Gamp invented her."

"Are you serious?"

I nodded.

"Is she seeing a professional about that?" he asked.

Aunt Maggie looked at him as if he were the one with the imaginary friend. "What on earth for? Mrs. Gamp doesn't bother anybody. Neither does Mrs. Harris."

Before we could speculate further, we heard the sound of sirens. I think all of us jumped at the noise, but I wondered if one of us in the room was afraid to know that more police were coming.

Chapter
Six

Mark ushered a procession of medical and police personnel past us on their way to and from the hallway where Seth still lay. A county officer was stationed at the front door to make sure nobody unauthorized went in or out—and probably to keep an eye on us, too.

Eventually Junior came out from the hallway, looking as disgusted as I'd ever seen her.

"Junior?" I said, but she walked past me to where her nieces and nephews were still under Mrs. Gamp's wing.

"Thanks, Mrs. Gamp," she said. "I'll take over now."

Florence said, "Chief Norton, can you tell us anything more?"

"No, ma'am, I can't. This is a police investigation and I'm staying out of it."

"Don't be foolish!" Aunt Maggie said. "You *are* the police around here."

"Not this month," Mark said. He'd followed Junior out the door, and it seemed to me that I heard more than a little satisfaction in his voice as he said, "Chief Norton is off duty until the end of the year. Though I appreciate her help in securing the scene until the appropriate personnel could arrive, she's now welcome to go about her business as a private citizen." Actually, the way Mark said it made it sound as if Junior was *required* to do so.

Then he turned to the Murdstones and said, "If one of you could come with me, I need a formal identification of the deceased."

"I'll go," Jake said immediately.

"Let me do it, little brother," David said.

"We'll *all* go," Florence announced, and she took the two men by the hand to follow Mark.

There was dead silence for a few seconds, and then people started chattering, probably trying not to think about what the Murdstones were going through. I took advantage of the distraction to escape Aunt Maggie and Richard long enough to go to Junior. Her nieces and nephews seemed relatively unaffected and were playing with brightly colored Gameboys.

"Junior, what's going on?" I asked her.

"You heard Deputy Pope," Junior said, with extra-heavy emphasis on Mark's title. "He's in charge here—I'm just a private citizen."

"I heard it; I just didn't believe it. Since when do you let personal time get in the way of police business?" Usually it was the other way around. Junior had been using official excuses to get out of unwanted family and social obligations for years.

Junior frowned. "This vacation wasn't exactly my idea. I got a memo from the city council that I had some accrued vacation, and if I didn't take it I'd lose it at the end of the year. I wasn't going to worry about it, but Mark found out."

"Why did he care?"

"Didn't you know he's angling for my job?"

"You're kidding."

"Apparently he's been nursing a grudge ever since I took over for Daddy—he just did a good job of hiding it up until recently. He figures the more time he has in charge, the better his chances are of proving to the city council that they need a real man in the job."

"Is anybody dumb enough to buy that?"

"I hope not, but you know the council. Some of them think I'm going to up and quit as soon as I find myself a man to marry."

"Oh, please," I said, rolling my eyes.

"Anyway, Mark called my mama and told her I was working too hard. Mama has been complaining for years that I don't take enough time off at Christmas, and when she found out how much vacation I was going to lose, she tore into me about it. I tried to tell her about the mess that people get into over the holidays, like drunk driving and shoplifting and domestic problems, but she was a police chief's wife too long to be impressed. She said Mark can handle the drunks by himself, and he can get my brother to help with the domestics, and that nobody bothers to shoplift in Byerly when they can go to the mall in Hickory instead. So to make her happy, I told her I'd take the time off. Which means that, short of a major emergency, I'm not to even set foot in the station until after New Year's."

I know there are people who would think Junior was insane for letting her mother push her around like that, but those people don't have families. Or maybe their families aren't run by anybody as strong-willed as Mrs. Norton. I said, "We can always hope for an earthquake."

"Even that might not be enough to convince Mama. Though I might have been able to change her mind if we'd known you were coming down."

"What's that supposed to mean?"

"Laurie Anne, do you know how few homicides we get in Byerly, and what percentage of those homicides take place when you're in town?"

"Ha, ha," was the best response I could come up with. "Anyway, can't you get away with helping Mark on the sly? Without telling your mama?"

"I might could, but Mark won't accept so much as a suggestion from me while he's trying to impress the city council with how good he'd be as police chief."

"Isn't catching a killer more important than making points?"

"Of course it is, but Mark's bound and determined to prove what a big man he is."

"Playing politics shouldn't come between the police and solving murders."

"It happens all the time," Junior said. "I hear it's even worse in big departments, not to mention competition between the county mounties and state troopers, and federal versus local, and every other kind of authority. Fighting over turf is a fact of life. Besides which . . ." I waited for her to go on, but all she did was to shake her head and mutter, "It's probably nothing."

I knew I wouldn't get anything more out of her until she was ready, so I changed the subject. "Do you think Mark is up to handling the case?"

"We'll have to wait and see," was all she would say.

Vasti burst in then, completely ignoring the officer who was trying to stop her. "What in the Sam Hill is going on?" she said, looking at all of us accusingly. Then she saw me. "Laurie Anne, I told you to keep an eye on things. What did Richard do now? I saw an ambulance out there. Don't tell me he hit somebody!"

"Of course he didn't hit anybody!" I snapped.

Mark Pope appeared and said, "What's this about somebody hitting people?"

"Nobody hit anybody," I said; then I realized how ridiculous that was, considering what had happened to Seth. "I mean—"

"What she means is that her husband has been repeatedly losing his temper ever since he got here," Vasti said, "but I'd never have left him alone if I'd known he was going to get violent."

Mark actually pulled out a pad of paper and a pen. "Would you say Mr. Fleming had any particular animosity toward Seth Murdstone?"

"Lord, yes," Vasti said, rolling her eyes. "He's been picking on Seth ever since he got into town."

"Was the late Mr. Murdstone acquainted with Mr. Fleming before then?"

"I don't think so. Why—" She stopped. "What do you mean, 'the *late* Mr. Murdstone'?"

I said, "That's what I've been trying to tell you, Vasti. Somebody killed Seth."

"What?"

"Chief Norton said she'd told everyone it was an accident," Mark said, his attention suddenly on me.

"A child could have seen it wasn't an accident," I said in as scathing a tone as I could manage. "Besides which, Junior and I already discussed it."

"I wasn't aware Chief Norton was sharing information about the investigation," Mark said.

"Just one private citizen talking to another," Junior said.

Mark narrowed his eyes. "Then let's get back to Mr. Fleming. Mrs. Bumgarner, you were explaining how Mr. Fleming came to know Mr. Murdstone."

"I didn't even know they knew each other," Vasti said, flustered. "Laurie Anne never told me."

"They didn't know each other!" I said. The baby picked that moment to start kicking, and I was about ready to join in.

"Mark," Junior said, "if you ever get around to questioning witnesses, you'll find out that Richard was on stage when Seth was killed. I can vouch for him myself."

"Is that right?" Mark said, sounding disappointed as he shoved the note pad back into his pocket. "Then if you'll excuse me, I'll get back to the investigation." He stalked off.

"Thanks a lot, Vasti," I said. "You almost got Richard arrested for murder."

"Did I hear that correctly?" Richard said, joining us.

That led to two rounds of explanations: one to tell Vasti what had happened to Seth; and a second to tell Richard the ridiculous conclusion Mark Pope had come to.

"That idiot," I seethed. "How dare he think that about Richard!"

"It is his job to explore every possibility," Richard said mildly, "though I must admit I'd never considered myself the murderous type."

Then Vasti said, "But what are we going to do about the play?"

"Vasti!" I said. "A man's been killed."

"I know that, Laurie Anne, but we've made a commitment to the community, and to the Shriners' Hospital. Let's not forget about that."

"You mean, let's not forget about your getting into the Junior League!" I shot back. I was planning to keep going when Junior reached out and touched my arm.

"Y'all might want to hold off on that for now," she said. "They're bringing out Seth."

We quieted down and turned to watch as ambulance attendants rolled out a gurney with a black body bag on top. David, Jake, and Florence followed after, their eyes red from crying.

Feeling awful for arguing with my own cousin at a time like that, I reached out and rubbed Vasti's shoulders in silent apology. She nodded back and squeezed my hand as we watched the Murdstones accompany Seth outside. There were plenty of tears then, and I wasn't ashamed that I was one of the ones crying.

After that, I thought the question of the play would be moot, considering that we'd just lost our Scrooge and figuring that surely the other Murdstones wouldn't want to go on. But I'd underestimated Vasti.

At least she wasn't rude enough to bring it up again right then. Not that she had a chance. Once Seth's body was gone, a crew of county police officers started pulling people aside to question us about what had happened during rehearsal.

The humorless officer who interviewed me wouldn't tell me a thing, and at first I wondered if Mark had warned him about me. Then I realized that as far as he was concerned, I was a murder suspect. After all, I'd been outside alone for a while, and that could have been when Seth was killed. Maybe I should have been gratified that he would think a pregnant woman capable of murder, but I wasn't.

After having me go over my whereabouts about a dozen times, and then those of Richard, he wanted to know where everybody else in the crew had been at every moment of the rehearsal. I was more than a little embarrassed to have to tell him that I had no idea. I knew Richard had been on stage, and that Vasti and Junior had spoken to me at various points, but otherwise, it was just a blur. People had been wandering onstage, and backstage, and into the kitchen, and all over. When it came down to it, the only person I could really vouch for was myself, and I didn't have anybody to give me an alibi.

When he finally gave up on me, I was sent to sit down at a table with the other witnesses. Or maybe we were suspects, because an officer was standing over us, watching and listening. Mark was still questioning Jake, but everybody else was sitting around, looking bored, disgusted, or annoyed. Needless to say, Vasti was one of the annoyed ones.

"Can you believe that that officer had the nerve to ask if I went straight to my in-laws' house?" she said. "I told her that it was Bitsy's feeding time, but she seemed to think I could have snuck around back and killed Seth."

"It's theoretically possible," I said, "assuming you had a reason to want Seth dead."

She glared at me.

"I know you didn't do it, Vasti, but they don't." I'd been just as mad at the officer who interviewed me, but I did understand why he was acting that way. "They're just determining who could have killed Seth. Isn't that right, Junior?"

"That's what they're trying to do, anyway," she said, "but I don't think they'll have much luck. We all compared notes a minute ago, and nobody's in the clear except your husband."

"Really?"

There were nods all around.

Before I could ask anything else, Mark brought Jake back over. I was expecting Mark to say something about the case, but all he said was that the investigation was proceeding and that none of us should leave town. If I hadn't been worn slap out, I'd have tried to get more out of him, but it was awfully late and I was starving. So when he said we could go, I went.

My next thought was to talk things over with somebody in the family, but Aunt Maggie said she was going straight to an auction where she was supposed to sell, Vasti had to go get Bitsy, and the triplets had dates. So Richard and I made a quick stop at Hardee's for dinner, and though he and I halfheartedly rehashed the whole mess, neither of us really had anything to say that we hadn't heard already. I was relieved to fall into bed.

Chapter
Seven

Richard and I stay with Aunt Maggie when we're in Byerly, in the Burnette home place where I'd grown up. I don't know how many Burnettes have lived in that old white clapboard house, but going there makes me feel like I'm surrounded by family. When my parents were alive, we were always there visiting, and after they died, I'd gone to live there with Paw. Years later, when Paw died,[5] the house had passed on to Aunt Maggie, but she'd never hesitated to open the doors to me. She'd even left my bedroom the same as it had been when I left, so when I awoke late the next morning, it was in comfortably familiar surroundings.

I stumbled downstairs to the den in the basement, found Richard reading, and joined him on the flower-patterned couch. "Where's Aunt Maggie?" I said around a yawn.

"She was up at the crack of dawn as usual, pursuing her appointed rounds."

Though the flea market where she sold was only open on weekends, Aunt Maggie spent most of the rest of the week tracking down new merchandise at auctions, yard sales, thrift stores, and who knew where else.

[5] *Down Home Murder*

"I should have known." Then I caught a glimpse of the cover of the book in his hand. "What are you reading?"

He looked sheepish as he held it up. "It's one of Aunt Maggie's romances. I didn't bring anything to read other than Dickens and related material, and there doesn't seem to be any reason to finish them now."

"I'm sorry you won't get to direct the play," I said, hugging him, "but you'll get another chance."

"I suppose," he said. "It's not important now."

"Maybe you can hook up with one of the local theater groups when we get back home."

"I don't think there's going to be time before the baby arrives." He patted my tummy. "And I have a hunch this little one is going to be taking up a lot of my energy for the next few years."

"He or she sure is taking up a lot of mine now," I said, stifling another yawn. "What time is it?"

"Nearly eleven. You better hurry up. Junior will be here soon."

"Shoot, I'd forgotten about getting together with Junior," I said. Before everything had gone crazy the day before, Junior had asked me to go to lunch with her. "Do you think she still wants to go?"

"She called to confirm a little while ago."

"Don't you want to come with us?" I asked, not wanting to leave him there by himself.

"No, thanks."

"Then maybe I'll call her and cancel. I'm kind of tired after yesterday."

"No, you're not," he said with a knowing smile. "You just don't want me to brood about the play. But I'm not brooding—I just want to finish this book. Romances are really underrated. The plot of this one is incredibly complicated and I want to see how the author ties it all together."

I let him get away with it for two reasons. First, I was pretty sure that he'd say so if he needed me to stay. And second, he loved reading enough that he probably really did want to see how the book ended. So I headed upstairs to shower, dress, do my hair, and take my prenatal vitamin. When I heard Junior honking her car horn from the driveway, I asked again if he wanted to come, but by that point he was so immersed in the book that all he did was wave.

When I got into Junior's battered Jeep, the first thing I noticed was her outfit. I rarely saw her in anything but her police uniform and cowboy boots, but today she had on winter white slacks with a matching blazer, a pretty blue blouse, and flats. "You're looking spiffy today. I feel underdressed." Actually I'd felt underdressed most of the time I'd been pregnant. I had a couple of nice maternity outfits for work, but mostly I was relying on stretch pants and over-sized sweatshirts like what I was wearing. "Is that makeup?"

"I don't get many excuses to dress up. Besides, I was up early and didn't have anything better to do."

"This vacation is pretty hard on you, isn't it?" I said sympathetically.

"You don't know the half of it. Now that the play's been canceled, Mama wants me to help with the baking and wrapping and shopping and I don't know what all."

"Don't you enjoy getting into the Christmas spirit?" I teased.

"About as much as getting a tooth pulled. I like Christmas fine, but I've burnt every Christmas cookie I've ever tried to make, my presents have to be rewrapped before they're fit to be seen under a tree, and I'd rather face a riot than a mall at Christmastime. Riding herd on the kids at rehearsals was boring, but it beat the heck out of the alternatives."

"Any word about the investigation?"

"I'm just a private citizen, remember?" she said.

I quickly changed the subject. "Where are we going to eat?"

"Wherever you want."

"I'm dying for some barbecue," I said. "How about Fork-in-the-Road? It's closer than Pigwick's, and I'm about to starve."

She snickered. "Does being pregnant really make women that hungry?"

"Junior, I swear I dream of food. I wonder if Aunt Nora has started her Christmas baking yet; I could really go for some of her double-butter cookies."

"You can find out later. My mama asked me to drop by her house later and pick something up."

"Why don't we go now? I can wait that long for barbecue." Besides which, Aunt Nora's house was closer than Fork-in-the-Road and she always had food around.

"Let's not. I know you Burnettes—if y'all get to talking, we won't get out of there for an hour."

"Good point. Barbecue now, double-butter cookies later."

We made small talk about old friends from high school along the way, and in no time we were sitting at a table with a plastic red-and-white checked tablecloth, with iced tea, heaping plates of pulled-pork barbecue, and a basket of hush puppies in front of us.

I took a big bite of barbecue and sighed happily. "I really ought to take some of this home with me and let my Boston friends taste what they've been missing. They grill beef, put some ketchup or barbecue sauce on it, and think they've got something. They look at me like I'm crazy when I try to tell them they need a vinegar sauce, but if they had just one bite of this . . ."

"Laurie Anne, you know as well as I do that if you took any of this up North, you'd have it all eaten yourself before anybody knew you were back."

"Assuming that I didn't eat it on the airplane," I agreed.

After a few minutes of serious eating, Junior asked, "Are you and Richard going to be staying in town for the holidays? I mean, since he doesn't have a play to direct."

"We haven't talked about it, but I think we will. The family would be mighty disappointed if we didn't, and I hate to think what it would cost to change our plane tickets this time of year. How about you? Other than helping your mother, what are you going to do with the rest of your vacation?"

"That's up to you."

"It is?"

"I thought I might give you a hand."

"Give me a hand doing what?"

"Solving Seth Murdstone's murder."

I blinked. "What makes you think that I'm getting mixed up with that?"

"He's dead. You're here."

"I don't always spend my trips home chasing killers."

Junior didn't say anything, just raised one eyebrow.

I tried to come up with a time Richard and I had come to Byerly without a murder intervening, but I couldn't, so I took another approach. "I've had good reasons for getting involved before, but not this time. Nobody in my family is a suspect, and no one has asked me to step in, and I didn't even know Seth that long. Murder isn't a game to me, Junior."

"I know it's not, Laurie Anne. That's why I figured you'd want to investigate. You hate the idea of somebody getting away with murder as much as I do."

"You're right about that," I said. When my own grandfather was murdered, I'd started taking all murders more personally. I knew darned well that Paw's murderer would probably never have been caught without Richard and me.

Junior said, "I realize that Seth wasn't a friend of yours, and maybe nobody in your family is directly involved, but somebody is asking you to step in—me."

"Why?"

"Because Mark Pope is going to screw it up if you don't help."

"Mark's not that bad," I said halfheartedly. "I mean, he's not stupid or anything."

"No, he's not stupid, but I've got a hunch that he's going the wrong way on this one."

"Really?" Junior's hunches were legendary in Byerly—I'd never known her to have a wrong one—but still I wasn't convinced. "I don't know, Junior. I mean, look at me. I'm as big as a house, and my feet swell if I'm on them for more than ten minutes at a time. I spend half my time eating and the other half in the bathroom. Then there are my mood swings—if you think Richard's tantrums are bad, you really don't want to see one of my hormone attacks. This might not be the best time for me to go snooping."

"Your brain still works, doesn't it?"

"You tell me."

"And your mouth still works."

"Is that a comment on how many hush puppies I've eaten?"

Junior refused to rise to the bait. "So you can still go around and ask people questions and think about what they say. Most of the time that's all you do, isn't it? It's not like you go on stakeout or try to tail people or break into houses, so I don't see why your being pregnant makes any difference."

"Spoken like somebody who's never been pregnant."

"Look, Laurie Anne, I'm not going to try to talk you into anything you don't want to do. If you can sleep at night knowing that you've let Seth's murderer go free—"

"Like heck you're not trying to talk me into it!"

"Okay, I am trying to talk you into it. Is it working?"

"I'm not sure," I said. "I want to think about it."

"That's fine."

We ate for a few minutes without talking, and I figured that Junior had given up for the time being. I should have known better. I was just about to finish my barbecue when she said, "Would it help you any to know more about Seth?"

"Like what?" I said cautiously. "I know he was a widower with the two sons, and his grandson recently died in an accident. And that he was a nice man, of course."

"Do you know what line of work he was in?"

"He made furniture, didn't he?"

"Yep, but when he wasn't making furniture he was making moonshine."

"Moonshine!" I yelped. When I saw heads turn my way, I lowered my voice. "That sweet old man was a moonshiner?"

"That's right."

"How on earth could I have missed hearing about that?"

"Very few people know, and I'd just as soon it stayed that way, just in case I'm wrong."

"What do you mean?"

"My daddy has suspected Seth was running a still since before I was born. He just never managed to catch him at it."

"Really?" As good a police chief as Junior was, there were those in Byerly who insisted that Andy Norton had been better. I wasn't willing to go that far, but I knew that most of what Junior knew, she'd learned from her father. "I didn't think your daddy ever gave up."

"He didn't give up. That's why he passed the case on to me when he retired."

"Is he sure Seth was a moonshiner? I just can't picture it."

"Years back, Daddy started getting hints that somebody in Byerly was shipping shine up North. So he started hunting around, and more than once he came across spots where stills had been, but all that was left was bits of copper tubing and such. He even found an intact still once and kept watch to see who came back to it, but the moonshiner must have gotten wind of him being there, because he never showed. And he hadn't left a fingerprint or anything else to identify him. Eventually Seth Murdstone's name got attached to the rumors, and Daddy started keeping an eye on Seth.

"The problem was, Seth had too much sense to put the still on his own land. So even though Daddy managed to look over his property a few times, there was nothing to find. He tried watching Seth to see where he went, but every time he did, Seth spent all day in his workshop, making chairs. Or he'd manage to sneak out despite Daddy watching him, and the moonshine would go through just like before."

"I'd never have thought Seth was smart enough to stay away from your father," I said.

Junior shrugged. "He was either smart or lucky."

"You say he shipped the stuff up North?"

"That's right. There are plenty of bars that would rather buy illegal booze for cheap, charge regular prices, and pocket the difference. Daddy figured Seth was sending it up in the trucks with his furniture, but he could never catch him at it, no matter how many times he stopped the trucks."

"I can't believe word of this never got around town."

"Daddy was careful. He knew that if the rumor got out, it would hurt his chances of catching Seth. Not to mention the fact that without proof, Seth could have sued him for slander."

"Is he sure Seth was the one? Maybe somebody was trying to make it look like it was Seth."

"Daddy said he had a hunch."

There was no arguing with that. Like Junior's, Andy Norton's hunches were never wrong.

Junior said, "I've been sniffing around Seth ever since I became police chief, but I haven't had a bit more luck than Daddy did."

"Do Jake and David know about it?"

"They must. Those chairs of Seth's didn't put David through business school, and Jake was in business with his daddy."

"It's hard for me to get my mind around this," I said. "I wouldn't have suspected Seth of doing anything worse than speeding."

"He probably did that, too, when it was time to get his product to market."

"Do you think Jake is going to keep the business going? The moonshining part, I mean."

"Probably, though I can't ask him."

I shook my head, amazed that none of this had ever made it into the Byerly rumor mill. There were other bootleggers around, but people knew who they were, and who had the best product and prices. Even I knew some of them, though the one time I'd tasted moonshine had been more than enough for me. "How on earth did he ever keep it a secret all these years?"

"Seth may not have been a good actor onstage, but he could play parts offstage like nobody's business."

"Do you think the moonshining had something to do with his death?"

"Could be. There's money in moonshine, and when you mix money and criminals, you tend to get killings."

"Rival moonshiners? Seth not delivering the booze on time?"

"Something like that. Maybe he was shipping watered booze, or not greasing the right palms along the way, or even running into bigger sharks in the water."

Now Junior was starting to scare me. I could understand personal killings. Revenge or jealousy or fear—those things I'd run into before. Killing for business was something different. "If that's what it was, I don't want to get anywhere near this one," I said flatly. "Dealing with organized crime is not my idea of a good time."

"Hey, that's just one possibility, and if that's what it was, you're right to stay away. Solving that kind of killing is best left to the professionals."

"Is Mark investigating from that angle?"

"That's what I suggested to him. Of course, he knows about Seth, because he was in on the original investigation with Daddy, and he's been involved in mine. But he didn't seem to think much of the idea."

"Why not?"

"I don't know. Mark isn't telling me any more than he has to. Besides, he could be right. People get killed all the time without having anything to do with moonshining. I just wanted to let you know what you're getting yourself into."

"I appreciate that, but I still haven't made up my mind."

"Right. I imagine you'll want to talk to Richard. I know y'all work together, but I don't have a problem with being a third wheel." The waitress dropped our check on the table and Junior reached for it. "Let me pick this up."

"Are you trying to bribe me?"

"Will it work?"

I took the last hush puppy. "With food as good as this, it just might."

Chapter Eight

I was considering Junior's request as we drove to Aunt Nora's, so we didn't talk much. The idea that Seth's murderer might go free did bother me. I'd been worried about it ever since I found out Junior was letting Mark handle the case. I still didn't quite understand why she didn't just tell her mother the situation had changed and go back to work, but since I'd foregone my own Christmas plans for my family, I couldn't very well criticize Junior.

Still, I wasn't sure if I should even be thinking about murder while carrying a baby. The doctor had told me to stick as closely as possible to my normal routine, but I didn't think she expected murder to be part of that routine. Though I'd never really been hurt during my investigations, I'd come close, and Richard had been shot. Did it make sense for me to risk my baby's life? And the baby was Richard's too. I had to speak to him before I decided anything.

"Junior," I said, "do you mind dropping me off at Aunt Maggie's before you go to Aunt Nora's? I really need to talk to Richard." As Junior had said before lunch, we were likely to be over there a while, especially since I hadn't seen Aunt Nora since I'd been in town.

"I would, Laurie Anne, but Mama told your aunt I'd be there by two. It's nearly that now, and Nora knows you're with me."

"Rats!" If we didn't go straight there, Aunt Nora would think we'd been in a car crash or there was a problem with the baby or who knows what.

"Besides, I thought you wanted some of her cookies."

"That's right," I said, brightening. Talking to Richard could wait. I spent the rest of the drive happily imagining those cookies and hoping that Aunt Nora would pack me a box of them to take with me. Maybe I'd even save a couple for Richard.

With cookies on the brain, I was moving pretty fast when we got to Aunt Nora's house, and I didn't notice that Junior was letting me go ahead of her. The door was unlocked as usual and I went on in, meaning to call for Aunt Nora on my way to the kitchen.

Except Aunt Nora was in the hall waiting for me. So was Aunt Daphine, Aunt Edna, Aunt Ruby Lee, Aunt Nellie, and Aunt Maggie. As soon as I stepped in, they yelled, "Surprise!"

Beyond the aunts, I saw a cluster of female cousins and other lady relatives and friends. Pink and baby blue streamers were every-where, with matching balloons stuck in every conceivable niche. There was a table stacked high with presents wrapped in pastel-colored paper, and every available surface had some sort of party favor: miniature baby carriages, giant baby bottles and pacifiers, plush storks, and cardboard rocking horses. If it wasn't a baby shower, it was an awfully good imitation.

"Junior, were you in on this?" I said.

She just smiled. Now I knew why she was dressed so nicely.

I happily hugged everybody who came within reach: motherly Aunt Nora; tall Aunt Nellie, dressed dramatically as always; buxom, blue-eyed Aunt Ruby Lee; Aunt Edna, who'd only recently trans-formed from drab to vivacious; and the always smiling Aunt Daph-ine. Then I assured everybody that I was completely taken by surprise, and started the time-consuming process of catching up on family gossip.

We were expecting a lot of weddings over the next few years, and the family was trying to decide who'd go first: Aunt Nora's boy Thaddeous, Aunt Ruby Lee's son Clifford, or maybe Aunt Ruby Lee's daughter Ilene. Aunt Edna had a head start on all of them because she was already engaged to her beau, Caleb, and had a beautiful diamond to prove it.

Unsurprisingly, Uncle Ruben and Aunt Nellie had a new business. Their previous businesses, of which there'd been more than I could remember, had lasted an average of three months. This time they'd joined the Internet revolution. Though folks were vague on the details, it sounded to me as if they were sending spam all over the world.

Everybody told me how wonderful I looked, and asked whether I'd picked out names, and said the other things people say to pregnant women. And of course, they had to pat my tummy and compare my size to how big Vasti had been at that point of her pregnancy.

"Where is Vasti?" I asked, finally realizing we were a cousin short.

"She's running behind," Aunt Daphine said. "Bitsy slept late, and Vasti had to feed her before she could get dressed."

Talk about feeding babies reminded Aunt Nora that I hadn't eaten yet, and even though I protested that I'd just come from lunch, she pushed me into a big armchair so she could fill up a plate for me. Obviously she believed in eating for two. She brought tiny pimento-cheese sandwiches, little country ham biscuits, carrot sticks with creamy onion dip, fruit salad, potato salad, hunks of cheese on crackers, some of the double-butter cookies I'd been hoping for, and a big glass of milk to wash it all down. Then she actually said, "Don't forget to save room for dessert."

Not wanting to hurt her feelings, I ate every smidgeon of it, and had just finished when Aunt Daphine said, "Who's ready for party games?" We spent the next hour or so playing a ludicrous assortment of games including a baby-diapering race using dolls borrowed from Sue's youngest girl; coming up with baby names using the letters from the parents' names; and the baby-bottle-sucking relay race. I'd never seen so many grown women making such fools of themselves, and I've rarely laughed so much.

When I thought nobody could hear me, I patted my tummy and said, "See all the fuss people are making over you?" Then I looked up and saw Junior grinning at me. So much for not being heard.

"I bet y'all have been playing Mozart to your belly to make the baby a genius," she said.

"We have not," I said, seeing no reason to admit that Richard had been reading Shakespeare out loud ever since I'd found out I was pregnant.

"I've seen expecting parents do sillier things," she said.

"Since when are you an expert on babies?" Junior had started helping out her daddy at the police station almost as soon as she could walk, so she hadn't worked as a babysitter like most of the girls in Byerly.

"Are you serious? I've delivered a baby, which is more than you can say."

"That's right. I haven't even gone to childbirth classes yet."

"Besides which, I've got four big sisters, and they all have kids. I've been to every one of their baby showers, and since I've got friends with babies, I've been to most of their showers, too. Do you have any idea of how many showers that makes?"

"Quite a few," I said, wondering if I'd be able to survive eating that many pieces of pastel pink-and-blue cake.

"So I've heard every old wives' tale, newfangled improvement, and cockamamie theory about babies that you can imagine."

"I had no idea. Now I understand how you did so well in the bottle-drinking contest." I only wished I had a picture of Junior sucking down apple juice through a rubber nipple.

"It's all in the way you hold the bottle," she said loftily.

"You were pretty fast with those diapers, too."

"I've had plenty of practice. But only with the girls. It's too nerve-racking with a boy. You never know when he's going to cut loose."

"I hadn't thought of that," I said, wincing. "Aunt Maggie says mine is a girl, so I'm safe."

"This time, anyway."

"This time?" I said, thinking about the five months I'd already gone through and the four still to come. "I don't even want to think about going through this again."

"You'll feel differently when you hold that baby in your arms,"

Aunt Nora said, bringing me another glass of milk. "You'll forget all about the stretch marks and swollen feet once you look in that little face and hold those little hands."

"Are you sure?" I asked doubtfully.

She just laughed and patted my tummy before heading back toward the kitchen.

"Junior, with all your vast experience, can you tell me why is it that everybody wants to pat my tummy?"

"To make sure you're not faking?"

I had to laugh.

We were about to start in on the stack of presents when Vasti burst in the front door, looking more than a little harried. There was a run in her stockings, she'd forgotten to put on lipstick, and her shoes didn't match her skirt. Instead of an extravagantly wrapped gift, she was carrying a wrinkled Belk's shopping bag. Motherhood was really taking its toll on my cousin.

"I'm sorry I'm late," she said, though she made it sound as if it was our fault for starting without her. "I was on the phone all morning, and Bitsy was so cranky that it took me forever to get her fed, and Grandmama was late getting to my house." She stopped just long enough to take a breath. "Then Bitsy threw up all over my dress, and I had to change into the first thing I could find."

"You look fine," Aunt Daphine said. "Come sit down and I'll get you a cup of punch."

Vasti let herself be led to the couch, and in an aggrieved tone said, "I suppose Laurie Anne has told you all about Seth Murdstone."

No wonder she was aggravated. She wasn't worried about being beaten to the punch bowl; she was worried about being beaten to the punch with the news.

"Actually, I hadn't mentioned it," I said, trying not to smile when her face lit up. "I wasn't sure it was appropriate to talk about it at a baby shower."

Her face fell again. "Maybe I shouldn't talk about it either—"

"We've already heard the news," Aunt Nora said, "but we don't know all the details." She and Vasti looked at me hopefully.

"It's not going to bother me to talk about it," I said—especially since Junior and I had already discussed it over lunch. Besides, I was afraid that Vasti would burst if she didn't get a chance to tell the tale.

Everybody listened in as Vasti told us about Seth's death, and I was impressed that she gave such an accurate recitation of the facts. She hadn't even been there when Seth was found, and besides, she usually embroidered the facts to make a better story. Of course, knowing that several of the rest of us had been there may have kept her on the straight and narrow.

"That's awful," Aunt Ruby Lee said. "Seth was such a nice man. To have that happen in broad daylight . . ."

"Do they have any idea of who might have done it?" Aunt Nora asked.

"I talked to Mark Pope a little while ago," Vasti said. "He hasn't made any arrests yet, but he thinks it's mighty interesting that Seth was found right next to a door to the outside."

I knew Vasti was waiting for a cue, but I had to ask, "Meaning what?"

"Isn't it obvious?" Vasti asked. "Somebody came in that door, thinking there was nobody around. Must have meant to make off with whatever he could find. When he saw Seth standing there, he panicked and hit him. Or maybe Seth caught him in the act."

I looked over at Junior to see her reaction to this piece of speculation, but she avoided my eyes. "Is that the best Mark can do?" I asked. "Somebody just happened to come by—in broad daylight, like Aunt Ruby Lee said—and walked in the door at the exact moment when Seth was standing there. And he just happened to be carrying something heavy enough to hit Seth with, which he did so quickly and quietly that nobody noticed it."

"Maybe nobody heard anything because Richard was having one of his tantrums," Vasti shot back.

"Maybe," I said through gritted teeth, "but I think it's darned unlikely that a thief would be stupid enough to break into a building with all our cars parked outside."

"Then why do you think the killer came in that door?"

"Maybe he didn't come in the door."

"You don't think it was somebody in the play, do you?" Aunt Nora asked anxiously.

"I don't know," I said, "but if it was somebody from outside, Seth must have arranged to meet him there."

"What do you think, Junior?" Aunt Daphine asked.

Junior said, "Haven't you heard? I'm on vacation, so I'm not entitled to an opinion."

I think everybody was so surprised that Junior was really going to stay away from a murder investigation that nobody had anything else to say. After a minute or two of uncomfortable silence, Aunt Nora said, "I'm just sorry that it ruined your play, Vasti."

"Oh, don't be sorry," Vasti said. "The play is back on!"

"Are you serious?" I said. "There's no way the Murdstones are going to want to be in that play now."

"Yes, they are," Vasti said triumphantly. "That's part of the reason I was on the phone so long this morning."

"Vasti!" Aunt Daphine said. "You shouldn't have bothered them about a silly play at a time like this."

"I didn't bother them," she said, trying to look innocent. "I only called Florence to make a condolence call, and to see when the services were going to be. Then we got to talking about what a shame it was that the play couldn't go on now, what with it being in honor of poor Barnaby. Florence said she wished there was something she could do, but I said that of course nobody would expect her and Jake and David to take part after what had happened. Then I told her I had to go because I had to call the Shriners' Hospital. I'd promised free tickets for the show to some of the children there, and I needed to tell them they couldn't come. Well, Florence said not to say anything to them right away, and that she'd call me back in a little while."

She stopped and took a swallow of punch. "A few minutes later, Florence called back. She'd spoken to David and Jake and said that when they thought about Barnaby, they just couldn't stand to let him down. They knew that Seth would have hated to have been the cause of canceling a play in his own grandson's honor, so they decided to do their best to keep going." Seeing the expressions of everybody else in the room, Vasti added, "Naturally, we'll take time off for the funeral."

Aunt Daphine just shook her head, but she couldn't have been all that surprised. It was vintage Vasti.

"I've called everybody else in the show and they're all willing. It took a while to convince Junior's sisters that the kids would be safe, but I told them that Junior would be there and that she wouldn't let anybody else get killed. Right, Junior?"

"I'll do my best," Junior said dryly.

Vasti said, "The only folks I haven't called are y'all here at the shower, but now we're all set!"

"Haven't you forgotten something?" I asked.

"What? I called Mark Pope to make sure he was done at the recreation center so we could get back in for rehearsal this evening." She checked her watch. "You better hurry up and open your presents, Laurie Anne; I've got lots to do before then."

"What about . . . ?"

"Oh, don't worry about Richard. He's ready and raring to go. Though he's got to do something about that temper of his."

"Vasti," I said, "we don't have anybody to play Scrooge."

She waved the objection away. "Oh, we'll find somebody."

"Who? I thought that Sally had everybody else in town committed."

"Then we'll shuffle around the people we've got. You're being a Scrooge yourself, Laurie Anne. Don't you want your husband's play to be a success?"

"Of course I do, but—" I stopped because there wasn't any real reason to argue. If anybody could produce a Scrooge out of thin air, it was Vasti.

After that, Aunt Nora steered us to opening presents, and talk turned to sleepers, booties, and rattles. It's amazing how a pair of sneakers suddenly becomes adorable when sized for a newborn. I'd never said, "Oh, how cute!" so many times in my life. The present I liked best was the bassinet I'd slept in myself. It had been freshly sanded, painted, and cushioned, and it matched perfectly the baby furniture Richard and I had picked out.

Once the presents were opened, I caught Aunt Ruby Lee cuddling the stuffed bear dressed like Sherlock Holmes that Junior had given me. She said, "You ought to put this up for yourself, as a memento. I know you're going to miss solving mysteries once the baby gets here."

"What do you mean?" Though I knew I had to take it easy while pregnant, I hadn't been worried about changes to my life after that. But Aunt Ruby Lee looked shocked, as did the other mothers nearby.

"You won't have the energy, for one," Vasti said. "You have no idea how rough nighttime feedings are."

"And forget about spare time, especially if you keep working," my cousin Sue put in. "By the time you put the baby to bed, and maybe clean up a little, you're not going to want to do anything but sleep."

"You and Linwood must do something other than sleep," Ilene said with a giggle, "or you wouldn't have but the one kid!"

Everybody laughed at that, but even though I joined in, I felt unhappy. Was it really going to be that bad?

Aunt Nora must have realized what I was thinking. She put an arm around me and said, "Don't you worry. You know Vasti and Sue always make things out to sound worse than they are. Your life isn't going to change that much."

"Did things stay pretty much the same for you and Uncle Buddy when y'all started having babies?" I asked.

"Lord, Laurie Anne, that was so long ago I can hardly remember," she said with a laugh. "Sure, the boys kept me busy, but I knew then they wouldn't be little forever, and once they got big enough, I'd be able to do whatever I wanted to."

"How big is big enough?" I asked. Richard and I liked going to movies, and to plays, and to all kinds of places. Were we going to have to put all of that on hold until the baby hit high school? What if we had another baby? How many years would that add to our sentence?

"Now don't get yourself worked up," Aunt Nora said. "Look at Vasti. She's still doing what she likes to do."

"True." Of course, she didn't work full-time, and goodness knows the play wasn't up to her usual standards.

"What are you two looking so serious about?" Aunt Daphine asked.

"Laurie Anne's worried that she won't have any time to herself once the baby shows up," Aunt Nora said.

"Y'all are the ones who said I wouldn't be able to do the things I've been doing," I objected.

"You don't mean messing with killers, do you?" Aunt Daphine said. "Why would you want to do that once you've got a baby?"

Now they were making it sound as if my helping people in trouble had been a twisted replacement for motherhood. "All I'm saying is that I don't see why having a baby will change everything. I'm going to be the same person, aren't I?"

"Of course you are," Aunt Daphine said. "It's just that you're going to be a lot busier than you are now. Your priorities are going to be different."

"So other than me having no time to sleep or do what I like to do, and suddenly having a completely different set of goals, everything will be the same. Is that right?"

My two aunts looked at each other uneasily. Aunt Nora said, "You knew things were going to change once you had a baby, didn't you? You and Richard did plan this baby."

"Of course we did, and we knew things were going to be different." I looked down at my tummy, thinking how Richard had said that the play might be his last chance to direct for a long time. "I guess I'm just starting to realize how different. I'm not sure I'm up to it." Despite myself, my eyes started to tear.

The two of them converged on me in a double hug.

"Don't even think that!" Aunt Daphine said. "You're going to be a wonderful mama."

"You bet you are," Aunt Nora said, nodding vigorously. "You're just tired out from all the excitement. Carrying a baby is hard on a body, you know. Vasti says she read that when you're pregnant, just sitting down is as much work as climbing a mountain when you're not."

Aunt Daphine said, "My moods were up and down the whole

time I was pregnant with Vasti—that's all that's happening with you."

"Pregnant women worry about everything, especially the first time," Aunt Nora said. "You just need something to take your mind off yourself."

Aunt Daphine snapped her fingers. "I know just the thing! What about Seth's murder? You've got one last chance to go after a killer!" She said it the way you'd suggest a trip to the park to a bored child during summer vacation, but before I could complain, Aunt Nora broke in.

"I don't know if that's a good idea, what with Laurie Anne being as far along as she is."

"She's made it through the first trimester, which is the worst time," Aunt Daphine pointed out, "and she'll have Richard with her to make sure she stays out of trouble."

"But Daphine, Richard is going to be busy with the play!"

"That's right. What about Thaddeous? Laurie Anne said he was a big help when he was in Boston."[6]

Aunt Nora shook her head. "Don't you remember? He's gone to Boston with Michelle to visit her family and won't be back until Christmas morning."

The two of them turned toward me as if I were a particularly sticky problem they had to solve, but they still didn't bother to ask what I thought. I was trying to come up with a polite way to tell them to mind their own business when Junior walked up.

"How are y'all doing?" she asked, far too innocently. I'd lay odds that she'd heard our entire conversation.

"Junior?" Aunt Nora said, looking at Aunt Daphine.

"Junior!" Aunt Daphine replied, nodding.

"Yes?" Junior said, looking from one to the other.

Aunt Nora said, "Junior, you're just the person we want to talk to. Seth Murdstone's killing might be Laurie Anne's last chance to solve a murder for a while, but Richard's going to be busy with the

---

[6] *Country Comes to Town*

play, and in her condition, she doesn't need to be running around on her own. We were thinking that you and she could work together on this one, seeing as you're on vacation."

Junior pretended to consider it. "I'm supposed to be keeping an eye on my nieces and nephews. . . ."

"That's no problem; the triplets can help. Those children are as good as gold anyway."

"It might work," Junior said, rubbing her chin. "If it's all right with Laurie Anne, I'd be glad to help out."

"Of course it's all right," Aunt Nora said, beaming. "Doesn't that make you feel better, Laurie Anne?"

"Much better," I said. I don't know if the smile on my face looked at all real, because I was steaming on the inside.

The two aunts went to tell Idelle, Odelle, and Carlelle what they'd just committed them to, and once they were out of earshot, I said, "Junior, did you put them up to this?"

"Not me," she said, still trying to look innocent.

"Can you believe this? First they say I won't be able to do this anymore. Then they decide I can, but only this one last time and only if I have a chaperon. Since when does being pregnant mean that I don't get to make my own decisions?"

"They're just worried about you."

"I know that, but it's still aggravating."

"Families are like that. So don't feel like you have to tackle this if you don't feel up to it."

"Of course I feel up to it," I snapped. "I'm pregnant, not an invalid." I knew I was contradicting what I'd said to Junior over lunch, but I was too mad to care.

"That's fine," Junior said. "Of course, you don't have to work with me. I'll come up with an excuse for your aunts, and you can go ahead on your own."

"Come on, Junior, maybe you didn't orchestrate this with my aunts, but you sure as heck laid the groundwork. If I don't let you in on this, I'll never hear the end of it—from them or you."

"That's true." She grinned, abandoning all pretense of innocence.

I glared at her. Of course it was a good idea. Even if I hadn't been

pregnant, it wouldn't have been smart to go asking possibly dangerous questions without backup, and with Richard back at work on
the play, Junior was the best candidate around. It could even be fun
to work with her; goodness knows we'd worked *against* each other
before. "Let's give it a shot."

"That would be great," she said. "The fact is, I've always wanted
to see how it is you go about solving a case."

"Really? I always figured you thought I was going about everything ass-backwards."

"I never argue with results, and you've gotten them time and
time again—even when I've been completely in the dark."

"Thank you," I said, but now I was getting suspicious. Though
Christmastime is usually green in North Carolina, I was smelling
snow. A snow *job,* that is. "Junior, you're not just wanting to do this
because you're bored with vacation, are you?"

"That's part of it."

"And part of it's because you want to get back at Mark Pope for
trying to get your job?"

"You bet," she said, not at all repentant.

Something was still niggling at me, but I didn't know what.
"There's more to it, isn't there?"

Now she stopped smiling. "If I told you that there was, but that I
couldn't tell you what, would you back out?"

I thought about it for a minute. I'd known Junior a long time, and
we'd been through a lot together. There'd been times when I'd
asked her to trust me and she'd done it. Surely I owed her the same.
"No, Junior, I wouldn't back out."

"Then let's leave it at that."

"Okay," I said, and I stuck out my hand. "Partners?"

Junior gave my hand a firm shake. "Partners."

Chapter
Nine

I would have liked to corner Aunt Nora then. Since she'd pushed me so hard, the least she could do was provide gossip on Seth and his family. But the shower was winding down, so everybody pitched in to load the presents into Aunt Maggie's battered Dodge Caravan. Of course, Aunt Nora couldn't resist sending along enough leftovers to feed a small army. Or one pregnant Burnette, I thought to myself as I snagged another deviled egg. Maybe my child was going to be born up North, but I was going to do my best to make sure she ate like a Southerner.

Richard met Aunt Maggie and me at the door, smiling widely.

"You knew about the shower, didn't you?" I said accusingly.

"Of course," he said as we started unloading the car. "But that's not why I'm so happy. Have you heard the good news?"

"That the play's back on?" I asked. "Vasti couldn't wait to tell us. But what are you going to do about Scrooge?"

"I'm not sure," he admitted. "Vasti seems to think it will work out."

"Vasti assumes things will work out because she can't imagine the world spinning in any direction other than hers."

"Generally speaking, she's right."

I had to admit that he had a point.

Once everything was inside, naturally I had to show it all off to him. He admired everything, but then he said, "Laura, do we need all this stuff for one little baby?"

"Are you kidding? There's more stuff being shipped up North, and Vasti said this isn't nearly as much as she got at her baby shower."

"How kind of her to point it out," Richard said. "Are we going to fit it into the new place?"

"We'll manage. By the way, I've got some other news for you." I explained how Junior and I had decided to tackle Seth's murder.

"I must admit that I assumed you'd be going after Seth's killer sooner or later," he said when I was finished.

"Why does everybody think I'm dying to go after every killer that comes around?"

"Why won't you admit that you like it?" Richard countered. "You don't even admit it to me."

"I don't like . . ." In all honesty, I had to stop. "Okay, maybe I do like it. At least, I get some sort of satisfaction out of it. That's weird, isn't it?"

"No more so than for cops and private eyes to get satisfaction out of their work."

"They get paid for it."

"Lots of people enjoy things they don't get paid for. My directing this play is a case in point."

"I guess." For a minute I wondered why I liked chasing killers so much, and then I wondered why liking it bothered me.

Richard said, "Anyway, I'm glad you're not going at it alone."

"Why's that?" I said, tensing. If Richard said one word about my not being able to handle it while I was pregnant, I was going to have a mood swing that would turn his hair white.

"Because with the play back on, I'm not going to be able to do research or run around and question people with you."

"Don't you think I could work alone?"

"You probably could, but I wouldn't be able to concentrate on the play if you were." Before I could take offense, he added, "No more than you could concentrate if I were working without backup."

"True enough."

"And if the killer is in the cast or crew, I want a competent set of eyes keeping watch. Having two competent sets of eyes is even better."

As usual, he'd given exactly the right answers. If having an undiscovered killer in Byerly worried me, having one locked in a recreation center with my husband and various members of my family made me downright nervous. "That's me, the defender of the innocent," I said more lightly than I felt.

"I don't know that I'm exactly innocent," he said, putting his hand on my tummy, "but Laura, you can defend me anytime."

We cuddled for a few minutes after that. It's more awkward to cuddle when you're five months pregnant, but just as much fun.

Richard said, "You and Junior working together . . . Oh, to be a fly on the wall."

"Why do you say that?" I said. "I think we'll be a good team."

"If you don't kill each other."

"We're not the ones who've been throwing tantrums."

"Touché. But you two are strong-willed women."

"Since when are strong-willed women a problem?"

"When both of them are trying to be in charge. I can't picture Junior blithely following your lead, and I'm sure you won't follow anybody's but your own."

"I'm not sure how it's going to work either," I said. "I just wanted to make sure you weren't going to make any jokes about cat fights or hormones."

"What kind of sexist pig do you think I am?"

"No kind at all," I said, "or I'd never have let you knock me up."

"That's better," he said, mollified.

We cuddled a while longer, but when I caught Richard peeking at the wall clock, I realized that it was nearly time to head to rehearsal. We both had work to do.

Chapter Ten

It was a subdued crowd that night at the recreation center, and I saw more than one person sneaking glances at the door to the hallway where Seth had been killed. Still, it looked as if Vasti really had convinced everybody to come back. Admittedly, everybody jumped every time there was a loud noise, but they were there.

I'd expected Junior's nieces and nephews to be nervous, but they seemed fine. I didn't know if it was because death didn't mean as much to them at their age, or if having a deputy, a police chief, and several former police chiefs in the family had given them a different viewpoint. Instead, it was Sarah Gamp who showed the most strain, but then again, she'd been the one to find Seth's body. I thought it was awfully brave of her to come back at all.

Unless . . . Hadn't I read that the person to find a body is frequently involved? I tried to remember how long Mrs. Gamp had been gone when she went looking for Seth. Surely she'd had enough time to bludgeon him to death, and it wouldn't have taken her but a minute to hide the weapon. Then all she would have had to do is scream for help and pretend to be upset. Heck, she would probably have been upset if she'd just killed a man.

I didn't know why she would have wanted to kill Seth, but then again, I didn't know why anybody would have wanted to. Somebody had, so why not Mrs. Gamp? That's when I noticed Junior standing by my chair.

"Checking out the field?" she said as she sat down next to me.

"Just speculating," I said, a little embarrassed for suspecting a little old lady.

Richard hopped up onto the stage, and once everybody quieted down, he said, "The show must go on. We've all heard that. The show must go on." He paused, making eye contact with various people. "The fact is, the show doesn't have to go on. As much as I love the theater, there are countless good reasons to cancel a performance. The loss we've had is as strong a reason as I've ever known." He nodded at the Murdstones. "Yet every one of you has decided to get past that loss, to come back in here to do the job you promised to do. For that I applaud you." He actually clapped, and when he said, "Now applaud yourselves," darned if we didn't join in, even the Murdstones. As the sound started to dwindle, he said, "I hope you all get used to that sound, because that's what you're going to be hearing on opening night."

"This is almost as much fun as one of his tantrums," Junior whispered, but I shushed her. I'd sat in on enough of Richard's lectures to know he was a good teacher, and I'd seen him on stage so I knew he was a decent actor, but this was the first time I realized that he would have made a dandy preacher.

Then David Murdstone stood up. "Richard, may I say something?"

"Of course."

David turned to face the room. "I know some of you are surprised that Jake, Florence, and I are here tonight. Quite frankly, it was very difficult to come back. But this is what Dad would have wanted. He loved his grandson Barnaby, as did we all, and honoring him this way was extremely important to him. So for Dad's sake, and for Barnaby's, we decided to go on. In their names, thank you for being here with us."

There was no applause as David sat down, but there were some wet eyes.

"Thank you, David," Richard said. "Now I won't lie to you people. We have a monumental task in front of us. Not only have we suffered the personal loss of Seth, we've also lost our leading man. If we're going to continue, we have to find another actor willing to take on the role of Scrooge."

There were murmurs and people looking around the room. As for me, I glared at Vasti. She'd implied that finding another Scrooge would be easy; now it was time for her to pull a rabbit out of her hat. Unfortunately, from the expression on her face, she was fresh out of rabbits.

"Why don't you do it, Richard?" Carlelle said. "I bet you've got all the lines memorized already."

I could tell he was flattered, but Vasti burst in. "Oh, no, you don't! We need Richard right where he is."

"Vasti's right," Richard said. "Directing you people is more than enough work for me."

"What about Sid? Or Oliver?" Tim asked.

Sid shook his head vigorously. "I couldn't do that. I've got all I can do to remember my own lines." I'm sure Richard was relieved. The roly-poly man was perfectly cast as the Spirit of Christmas Present, but he was a worse fit for Scrooge than Seth had been.

Oliver Jarndyce, who mangled his lines terribly, stood up eagerly, and I was sure I saw Richard flinch. "I'd be happy to jump in," he said. I had to wonder if he'd be as eager once he realized he wasn't going to be able to wear his reddish-brown toupee for the role.

"That's generous of you, Oliver," Richard said, "but that would still leave us with a hole in the cast. We need a Spirit of Christmas Past."

Oliver started to say something else, but Aunt Maggie piped up, using that tone of voice that carries over and through other voices. "What about Big Bill? He's been training for the part of Scrooge for years."

There were laughs, but to give Big Bill credit, he joined in.

"But he's already got a part, too," Oliver said indignantly. "He's Marley's ghost."

"True," Richard said. "Of course, Marley is a small role; somebody else could double up."

Oliver brightened up again. "In that case, perhaps I could—"

"Why not let Pete Fredericks play Marley?" Idelle said. "He doesn't have any lines as the Spirit of Christmas Yet to Come, and you can't see his face in the robe I made him, so nobody will know he's doubling up."

There was agreement from everybody but Oliver. All he seemed able to manage was, "But . . . but . . . ."

Richard took pity on him. "Oliver, if you're really willing to take on another part . . ."

"Anything!" Oliver said.

"Vasti only cast one charity collector, but generally two are used. There aren't any additional lines, but—"

"I'll do it!" Oliver said, and he sat down, looking quite pleased with himself.

"Then we have our cast." Big Bill, I realize you'll have to work from a script tonight, but—"

"Actually," Big Bill said, "before I agree to the part, I have one condition."

"Oh?" Richard said. He looked concerned, and Vasti looked downright panic-striken.

"As some of you may know, I've been trying to regain the affections of this lady here." Big Bill put his hand on Aunt Maggie's shoulder, and she promptly pushed it off again. "If she agrees to go out to dinner with me, I'll play Scrooge."

"Oh for pity's sake," Aunt Maggie said, "are you that desperate for a date?"

He didn't answer, just smiled.

Aunt Maggie could see that everybody was looking at her, and in Vasti's and Richard's case, they were staring beseechingly. "I suppose one dinner couldn't hurt anything," she finally said.

"One dinner for each curtain call," Big Bill persisted.

She rolled her eyes, but said, "All right, one dinner for each curtain call, whatever that is. But don't expect me to dress up!"

"Maggie, you look fetching no matter what you wear."

Aunt Maggie snorted particularly loudly.

Big Bill turned back to Richard and said, "Mr. Director, I accept the role with pleasure." For the second time that night there was applause.

Richard brought Big Bill onto the stage so they could discuss the part, and the other people either mingled or started work on whatever it was they were doing for the play. That meant that it was as good a time as any for Junior and me to get going. Only when we turned around, Mark Pope was standing right behind us. I hadn't even realized he was in the building; he must have come in during Richard's pep talk.

"Hey there, Mark," Junior said.

"Junior," he said. "I'm kind of surprised to see all of y'all here. When Mrs. Bumgarner called about my releasing the crime scene, I thought she just wanted a chance for everybody to get their belongings, but now I hear that y'all are going through with this thing after all."

"Apparently so."

"Do you think that's a good idea? A man was murdered here."

"It's not my decision," she said. "Besides, I heard that you decided it was a burglar who killed Seth, and no sneak thief would come back here now." She lifted one eyebrow. "Or have you changed your mind?"

"I haven't closed the investigation yet," Mark said stiffly.

"Then I guess it's a good thing you're here to protect us."

"What about you?"

"You said you wanted to handle this case on your own—you go ahead and handle it."

"And Mrs. Fleming?" Mark asked.

"What about her?"

"Is she planning to interfere in my investigation?"

"What Mrs. Fleming does is her own business," Junior said firmly.

"Not if she hinders a police investigation."

"She's never hindered an investigation in Byerly before. I don't expect her to start now."

Mark looked at me suspiciously, but all I did was smile. Though I didn't like being talked about as if I weren't there, I thought I'd do better to stay out of the conversation.

Mark must have realized that he wasn't going to get anything else out of us, because he nodded and said, "I think I'll take another look outside."

"Keep an eye out for sneak thieves," Junior said. "Or maybe you can catch that practical joker that's been bothering us."

He stiffened but didn't answer as he left.

Once I was sure he was out of earshot, I said, "Junior, what in the Sam Hill is going on?"

"What do you mean?"

"Since when does Mark talk to you like that, and since when do you put up with it?"

"Remember what you said at your aunt's house today? About your not backing out even if there was something I couldn't tell you?"

I didn't like it, but I said, "I remember. But let me get this straight: we're not telling Mark we're investigating?"

"Right."

"Even though he's going to figure it out soon enough?"

"That's right."

I looked at her, hoping she'd tell me something more. She didn't. So I said, "Well, if we're going to interfere in a police investigation, let's get going."

Chapter
Eleven

"What do we do first?" Junior asked.

"What would you do if you were officially on the case?" I countered. Despite what Junior had said about wanting to see me in action, I was feeling a little self-conscious about working with an actual police officer.

"I'd examine the crime scene. Which Mark has released, if you want to take a look."

I didn't, but it was the logical place to start. "Let's go." As Junior and I made our way to the hallway, I saw Mark watching us with a frown on his face. Junior saw him too, but she didn't say anything as she pulled the last scrap of yellow crime-scene tape off the door.

The hall was empty. I suspected the rest of the cast was avoiding that part of the building. I would have too, given a choice. Other than Seth's body being gone, it looked pretty much the same as it had the day before. Thankfully, somebody had cleaned up the stains on the floor.

"Can I safely assume that you looked around while waiting for Mark to show up?" I asked.

Junior just grinned.

"So what exactly do you look for in a crime scene?"

"Anything I can find," she said, "though most of what I find doesn't mean a thing. In this case, I didn't have much time. I didn't want to move Seth's body around before the coroner got here, but I did make sure there was nothing under him that wasn't supposed to be there. Then I looked around for a murder weapon, but couldn't find one or even a good place to hide one. I was starting to think about how the killer got into and out of the hall when Mark showed up."

"Did you come to any conclusions?"

"Not a one."

There were six doors leading from the hallway: one to the auditorium, four to other rooms, and one to the outside. I looked longingly at the door leading outside. Despite what I'd said to Vasti at my baby shower, I really hoped the killer had come through that door. Though I knew it would make investigating a lot harder, I preferred that to having to suspect somebody I knew. "Was the back door unlocked?"

"Yes, though that doesn't tell us much. The smokers in the cast had been coming in and out all day, so it was left unlocked. I locked up after we found Seth, to make sure nobody could sneak in behind me."

"Was there any sign of anybody coming in that way?"

"Mark didn't tell me."

I just looked at her.

"Okay, I took a peek, but I didn't see anything that would help. There were a lot of cigarette butts on the ground, but none of them were still burning. It's all paved out there, so there couldn't be any footprints, and there was no blood trail or sign of a murder weapon. We could go look again, but the forensic people have been all over it, so there's not going to be anything left."

"Let's not bother." Next I tried to remember exactly where Seth's body had been.

Junior said, "The door wasn't what hit him, if that's what you're thinking."

"Just a thought." I had another one. "If Seth was there," I said, pointing, "doesn't that mean that he was between the door and the killer?"

"That's how it looks," Junior said, "but the killer could have walked past him and turned around. Why?"

"I was just wondering about these other rooms. Did you look in them?"

"Just to make sure there was nobody hiding in there, so it wouldn't hurt to look again."

The first two doors had hand-printed signs identifying them as "Men's Dressing Room" and "Women's Dressing Room"; the third was being used to store props and scenery flats; and the fourth was tiny—barely big enough for the sink and cleaning equipment it held.

"All of the windows are intact," Junior said.

"The locks have been painted shut," I added, looking them over. "Nobody came in or out that way. What about the kitchen?" The door that led from the auditorium to the kitchen was just a few feet away from the door to the hallway.

But Junior shook her head. "I looked in there the first day of rehearsal to make sure there wasn't anything in there my nieces and nephews could get into. There's an emergency exit, but it's got an alarm on it. All the windows are the louvered kind; they're not big enough for anybody to get through."

I looked up at the solid ceiling. "No way to get through the roof."

"Not without a wrecking ball," Junior agreed.

"That means that whoever it was either came from outside or through the auditorium." I was still hoping to blame somebody from the outside if I could come up with something halfway reasonable. "Are we both agreed that Mark's idea of a sneak thief is completely bogus?"

"Do you even have to ask?" Junior said dryly. "I'll admit there are some pretty dumb criminals out there, but I don't think that we have any that dumb running around in Byerly."

"Seth could have set up a meeting with somebody, and told him to come to the door."

"I suppose, but I don't see how Seth could have known he was going to be free at that particular moment. He would have still been on stage if Richard hadn't thrown that tantrum."

"Could he have provoked Richard just to make sure he was free?"

Junior just looked at me.

"Never mind. Still, it's possible he set something up."

"Or another cast member could have gone outside and come back in again."

"Good point," though I wasn't thrilled about more evidence pointing to the cast. "I suppose it's theoretically possible that somebody snuck in the front door. . . ."

"Without anybody noticing?" Junior said skeptically.

"You're right; I don't believe it, either." I wasn't happy about it, but I was going to have to face facts. "So it does look like the killer was somebody involved with the play."

"That's what I think, unless we find something to point us in another direction," Junior said.

With that decided, I moved on. "Was there anything about Seth's body I should know?"

"Just what you already know: he was hit over the head with something. I'm no medical examiner, but it looks to me like it was long, like a bar or a stick, rather than round like a ball or square like a brick. Whatever it was, the killer probably brought it with him, because there wasn't anything that would fit the bill in the hallway beforehand or afterward."

"Then Mark hasn't found the murder weapon?"

"I don't think so, but I don't know for sure. Not only is he not telling me anything; he's doing all the work himself so even Trey doesn't know anything."

"Rats!" I'd been hoping we could use Junior's little brother as a source of information.

"Laurie Anne, you're going to have to stop using such strong language after the baby comes."

"Don't start, Junior," I said. "So we've examined the scene, and we've learned absolutely nothing. What would you do next?"

"Normally I'd have witness statements, and possibly the autopsy report. Had any physical evidence been found, I'd usually have more information on that."

"It must be nice to have so much to work with."

"How do you manage without it?"

I carefully kept my face straight. "Oh, I usually break into your office at night and take a peek at the files. Or hack into your computer and get the information."

She blinked. "Are you serious?"

"Of course I'm not serious," I said, laughing. "If I can't get it from you, I do without."

She relaxed. "Lord, you scared me there for a minute."

"Though if you want me to hack into Mark's computer—"

"I'd just as soon you didn't."

"Suit yourself."

"As I was saying, I'd have a lot of information to go through, but I'm not sure that any of it would help in this case. Maybe I don't have the autopsy report, but I was there when the doctor gave his preliminary opinion that Seth died from a blow to the head—possibly in combination with a bad heart—and I know about when he died. Whoever hit him did it from the front and was right-handed. It was a hard blow, but not so hard that any adult couldn't have done it."

"That lets your nieces and nephews out."

"I was kind of leaving them off the list, anyway," she said. "I don't think there was any useful trace evidence. No muddy footprints or blood drops or anything like that. Any fingerprints on the walls and door knob and such would be meaningless, because so many people have gone up and down that hall."

"If there were anything obvious, Mark would have made an arrest by now."

"I would hope so. Now, I haven't talked to everybody who was here when Seth was killed, but I've talked to enough of them to know that everybody was moving around so much that we can't rule out anybody as the killer."

"Except Richard."

"Right. He was on the stage pretty much the whole day, except when he stomped outside, and Vasti was watching y'all then because she was afraid he was going to leave. But the rest of us were milling around like ants on an anthill. There's not a single alibi that would hold up."

"Wonderful."

"It's not that bad. It would be better if we could eliminate some of the possibilities, but I do hate playing the alibi game. Who left where when, and whose watch is set fast, and all that mess. What we've got is this: nobody knows exactly when Seth came down this hall, and that means that pretty much anybody in the building could have come after him."

"Great."

"Though I'm assuming that you're in the clear, too."

"Thanks," I said. "I'll return the favor. While we're at it, I'd just as soon we leave the rest of my family off the list."

"I can go along with that. That leaves us with everybody else in the cast and crew."

"I guess we should be grateful that the cast isn't any bigger than it is. So, having exhausted all your reports, what would you do next?"

"I'd go talk to the folks who knew the victim: his family, friends, neighbors, and so on. So I'd start with the Murdstones."

"What if they won't talk to you?"

"Laurie Anne, I'm chief of police. People talk to me, or I'll know the reason why."

"That definitely gives you an advantage," I said. "People can blow me off anytime they want to, and they don't have to give me a reason. So I start by talking to people who will talk to me, and hope that they know something about the victim."

"What if they don't?"

"I talk to somebody else. Eventually I find somebody who both knows something and will talk to me."

Junior looked doubtful and I didn't blame her. "What can I say? It's haphazard, but it's worked before."

"That it has. Since I'm just a citizen this time around, we'll try it your way. I take it this means we won't be talking to the Murdstones right off."

"Lord, no. They've just had a murder in the family. I wouldn't want to intrude at a time like this."

"What if one of them is the killer?"

"Then I don't want to talk to them before I know more." We left the hall and went back into the auditorium, where I surveyed the prospects. Aunt Nora and Aunt Daphine were usually my best sources of gossip, but neither of them was there. Vasti knew lots of gossip too, but she got as much wrong as she got right. "Let's go talk to the triplets," I finally decided. "They've been around the rehearsals long enough to have gotten a feel for everybody."

"I'll just listen in if that's all right."

"Richard usually takes notes for me."

She didn't say anything, but the look she gave me was answer enough.

"Okay, we'll skip the notes," I said.

Idelle, Odelle, and Carlelle had taken over a corner of the auditorium for their costumes and sewing equipment, with a long rack to hang clothes on. When Junior and I got there, Idelle was consulting a stack of papers on a clipboard while Odelle pulled a coat off the rack and Carlelle put together a stack of shoes, socks, and other garments.

Odelle held a tattered morning coat up for her sisters to see. "We're going to have to completely remake this."

Carlelle threw her hands up. "When am I supposed to do with that?"

"Problems?" I asked.

"Hey, Laurie Anne, Junior," Idelle said, looking up from her clipboard. "We just realized how much work it's going to be to make Scrooge's costume fit Big Bill."

"I hadn't thought about that," I admitted. Seth had been a big man, in height and in girth. Big Bill, despite his nickname, was shorter and much trimmer, which was why he looked so good in blue jeans.

"And we're going to have to come up with a whole new costume for Oliver to be a collector," Odelle said.

"That's right," Idelle said, flipping furiously through her papers. "It's all well and good for Richard to hand out parts like they were candy; he doesn't have to dress everybody!"

"Vasti told me y'all were renting costumes," I said.

Idelle rolled her eyes. "Don't get us started! We ordered from

Morris's Costumes in Charlotte, and don't you know it took some sweet-talking! Do you know how many productions of *A Christmas Carol* there are at this time of year? But they promised us they'd get them to us—even claimed it was the last available set in the state. Only the costumes never showed up."

"Personally, I think they took something under the table to rent them to somebody else," Odelle put in.

"I wouldn't be surprised," Idelle said. "In the meantime, they're claiming the costumes were delivered, and even faxed us a copy of the signature of the person who signed for them. It's completely illegible, so it wasn't one of us."

I nodded sympathetically. Everybody knew that the triplets had beautiful handwriting. I'd gotten them to address the invitations to my wedding.

"So with us going round and round with them, we decided to bite the bullet and make the costumes ourselves," Odelle said. "Which wasn't as bad as it could have been because we'd already planned to make some of them."

"Easy for you to say," Carlelle grumbled as she started picking at the seams in Scrooge's coat. "You're not the one doing the sewing."

"Who was it who spent half a day with a glue gun putting chains on Jacob Marley's costume?" Odelle retorted.

Then the three of them stared at one another in horror. "Marley! We've got to redo his costume, too!"

Idelle frantically consulted her list. "Maybe not. Pete Fredericks is only a little smaller around than Big Bill. We can pin him in if we have to."

"Maybe we won't even have to do that!" Carlelle said excitedly. "He's dead, isn't he? His clothes should be hanging on him."

"You're right!" Idelle said.

"What about the length on the pants?" Odelle wanted to know. "He's a couple of inches taller than Big Bill."

Carlelle's face fell again.

"Can you fray the hems?" I suggested. "If you've got enough threads hanging loose, people won't be able to tell it's too short."

"That might do it," Idelle said speculatively. "Odelle, go get Pete to try on the pants and see if it will work." While one sister rushed off, the other two went back to their respective lists and sewing.

"I had no idea that doing the costumes was so much work," I said.

"It wouldn't be so bad if we were doing something modern," Idelle said. "Sally Hendon's show is all contemporary costumes. They're buying most of them off the rack. We had to do research on Victorian clothes, and figure out what colors we could use, track down patterns, and all kinds of trouble. Plus making everything from scratch."

"Which would be a whole lot easier if I could use my sewing machine when I need to," Carlelle said, glaring up at the stage. "But every time I get going good, Richard makes me stop because I'm disturbing his concentration."

I really didn't want to have to apologize for my husband again, so I sidestepped the issue. "Why don't y'all use one of the back rooms so the noise won't bother anybody?"

"We tried that," Idelle said. "But after *somebody* wadded up a stack of costumes that I'd just finished ironing, and *somebody* hid every cotton picking spool of thread so we couldn't find them for an hour, we decided to keep our things out here where we can keep an eye on them."

"That prankster is getting pretty bad," I said. "Any idea of who it could be?"

Idelle shook her head. "If we did, we'd have a word or two with him. I like fun as much as the next person, but we don't have time for this!"

"You sure don't," I said sympathetically. "Is there anything I can do to help?" Admittedly, I was doing well to sew on a button, but surely there was something suitable for unskilled labor.

"Aren't you sweet to ask?" Idelle said. "But don't you worry about us. You know doing something like this isn't any fun unless we fuss about it. Aunt Daphine, Aunt Edna, and Aunt Nora have volunteered to come over to our place tonight and finish up the sewing."

"Besides," Carlelle said, "don't y'all have another project?" She looked at us significantly.

"We were hoping y'all would be too distracted with the play to notice," I said.

"Laurie Anne, you've been living up North too long if you believe that."

"I said we were hoping, not that we believed it." I wasn't really surprised. It's not like a five months pregnant woman and a police chief aren't noticeable. Besides, the triplets had been at the baby shower, and I was sure that everybody there knew what we were up to.

"Assuming that y'all didn't come over here just to chat, what do you want to know?" Carlelle said.

"Are you sure you're not too busy?" I asked.

"Lord, Laurie Anne, I can sew in my sleep; sewing and talking at the same time is nothing."

"Good enough." I pulled a chair over next to Carlelle's, and Junior did the same. "I want to know about the Murdstones. You must have seen a lot of them since the show started. Starting with Seth."

Carlelle said, "I spent right much time with him when I was working on his costume. I liked him, too. He was an awfully nice man—friendly and easy to talk to."

"What did y'all talk about?"

"This and that. He was a bit of a flirt, to tell you the truth, though I think he'd have passed out from shock if I'd taken him up on it."

"What about his business?"

"You know he makes porch chairs and little tables to go with them? I was thinking about getting a set for Mama and Daddy's anniversary, and he said he'd do them for me for nothing. Isn't that sweet? Only I'd have to let him know right away, because he was thinking of retiring soon."

"How come? He wasn't that old, was he?"

"He turned sixty-four in June," Junior said.

"I guess that's nearly retirement age," I said, "but so many people work later these days. He must have done well to have put away enough money to retire early."

"He talked like he did," Idelle said, "but I imagine the real reason was because of what happened to his grandson. I think Seth blamed himself."

"I thought it was an accident," I said.

"It was, but Seth said he'd told Jake that old space heater wasn't safe to use around an active boy like Barnaby. He said he should have tossed it out himself before anything could happen. Besides, Seth was the only adult there when it happened. He and Jake shared a house, with Seth upstairs and Jake and Barnaby downstairs.

"Anyway, Seth heard Barnaby scream, and ran down and found him. Then he panicked. He realized afterward that he should have called an ambulance, but all he could think of was getting the boy to the hospital. So he wrapped him up in a blanket, put him in the truck, and took off for Hickory."

"Would it have made any difference if he'd called the ambulance?" I asked.

"Not a bit," Idelle said, "and Seth knew that, but he said he kept going over and over it all in his head, thinking that he could have done something to save the boy."

I could understand that; I'd spent plenty of late nights replaying mistakes in my head. At least none of mine had ever led to a child's death. Then I put my hand on my tummy, wondering what mistakes I would make with the baby.

"What about Jake?" I asked. "He's the one who left his nine-year-old son alone with a dangerous space heater."

"He didn't know the heater wasn't safe," Carlelle objected, "and he wouldn't have left Barnaby if Seth hadn't been there. Seth said he tried to get Barnaby to come upstairs with him, but Barnaby was playing computer games and didn't want to. Nobody could have known that would happen."

"I suppose not," I said.

"Poor Jake was so torn up about it," Idelle said. "The little fellow didn't die right away, you know. He was in the hospital for nearly a week, suffering. Mrs. Gamp volunteers up there, and she said he was just the bravest thing she ever saw. They thought he was going to make it, but he got an infection and that's really what killed him. It was just terrible."

I nodded, resolving never to leave my child alone or own a space heater. Then, eager to change the subject, I said, "Jake and Seth must have gotten along well to have worked together and lived in the same house."

"They seemed to," Carlelle said.

But Idelle added, "Most of the time, anyway. I saw them going at it one time last week."

"What were they arguing about?" I asked.

"I wasn't close enough to hear much of it," she said, sounding regretful, "but I think it was something to do with business. Seth said something about local competition, and Jake said they couldn't afford to just give everything up. It didn't last long, and they seemed all right the next day, so it must not have been all that serious."

"What would Jake have done if Seth had retired?" I said. "For that matter, what will he do now that Seth is gone?"

Carlelle said, "I would think he'd keep the business going, since that's the only job he's got, but I don't really know."

Though killing one's father to gain ownership of a chair company didn't seem like a compelling motive to me, it might look different from Jake's perspective. Or had they been arguing about moonshine and not chairs? "Seth didn't seem bothered by anything from what I saw of him. Did he say anything to y'all about being worried, or being in danger?"

The two sisters looked at one another, then shook their heads.

"What about David and Seth?" I asked. "Did they get along?"

"I guess," Carlelle said hesitantly.

"But?" I prompted.

"It's not like I saw them fighting, but they were awfully different. David being in business and being married to Florence Easterly and all. He's so serious, and Seth was so funny. Listening to the two of them together was like listening to two acquaintances talking, not a father and son. They didn't seem to have much in common."

"Same planet, different worlds," I said. Sometimes I felt that way myself. Goodness knows I'd led a very different life from the rest of my family. Not only was I the first Burnette to go to college; I was the first to move up North and the first to marry a Yankee. There'd been a time when I wasn't close to any of my relatives, and it had taken work on all of our parts to get over that. It was a shame that Seth and David weren't going to have that chance.

I looked at Junior to see if she had any other questions, but she shook her head. So I thanked Idelle and Carlelle for their help and left them to their costumes.

Chapter
Twelve

"I don't get it, Junior," I said. "Killing Seth was like killing Santa Claus."

"Seth wasn't a saint, Laurie Anne, and Santa Claus doesn't run a still."

"I know, but it still seems nuts to me."

I was trying to decide who to talk to next when the door opened and a woman came in. Her hair was platinum blond and permed, and though the coat slung over one arm was navy blue, everything else she had on was the same shade of pink: skirt, blouse, purse, even her boots. It had been a while since I'd seen Sally Hendon, but a color scheme like that was impossible to forget.

"It's true!" she exclaimed in a voice loud enough to draw the attention of everybody in the room. "I didn't believe it, but it's true."

Vasti dropped whatever project she'd been supervising and rushed over to stand in front of Sally, her hands on her hips. "What do *you* want?" she demanded.

"Vasti, aren't you looking well? How's that baby of yours? How can you *stand* to leave her alone? I'd have thought you'd want to spend as much of her first Christmas season with her as you could."

Vasti refused to rise to the bait. "What are you doing here, Sally? I thought you had a show to put on."

Sally waved a hand in the air. "We've got everything under control over at the high school. I swear, my people are so organized, we could go on tonight." She looked pointedly at the chaos that reigned around us. "I heard that you hadn't given up on your little play after all, and thought I'd come over to see if I could help."

"We don't need any help from you!" Vasti said. "We're doing just fine."

"Oh, Vasti, we're family. You don't have to put on a brave face in front of me. I know things must be falling completely apart."

I could see the steam starting to shoot from Vasti's ears, and I wondered how long it would be before she threw a tantrum that would completely erase the memory of Richard's outbursts. I didn't think she'd get physical, but just in case, I moved closer to the two of them. Junior came, too, but I suspect she just didn't want to miss anything.

Vasti must have realized that others were watching—particularly Florence. So instead of the verbal attack I was expecting, she adopted a syrupy tone to match Sally's. "That's so sweet, but I just can't imagine what help you could be here. You better head right back to your own rehearsal before things get out of hand. You know what they say: while the cat's away, the mice will play."

Other than a slight emphasis on the word *cat*, I thought Vasti had done a fine job of insulting Sally sweetly—just the kind of performance that the Junior League expected of its members. But Sally wasn't giving up.

"Vasti, everybody knows that you can't put on a show without a leading man. The loss of poor Mr. Murdstone is tragic in so many ways." She pulled a sad face for a few seconds, then snapped her fingers as if something had just occurred to her. "I know! Why don't we combine shows? We'll add a skit to my show, something short so your people won't have any trouble learning their lines. And you'll be able to go back home and tend to that darling daughter of yours."

Junior League or not, Vasti was about to lose it, so I thought I'd better step in. "That's kind of you to offer," I said, "but we've found a replacement for Seth."

"Who?" Sally snapped. Then she forced a smile. "I mean, I understood that all the town's capable actors were already busy."

"Hadn't you heard?" Vasti said, knowing that even Byerly's rumor mill couldn't have spread the word yet. "Big Bill Walters is going to play Scrooge."

Sally's mouth opened, but nothing came out for a good thirty seconds. Finally she visibly pulled herself together and said, "Is that right? How wonderful." There wasn't anything else Sally could say without implying criticism of the leading family in town, and as a dedicated social climber, she knew better than to do that. "Are you sure there isn't something I can do to help? You must be worn out. I can tell your little girl isn't sleeping through the night."

Ouch. Vasti was so good with makeup, I hadn't really noticed the bags under her eyes until then. After all her years selling Mary Kay, Sally must have learned how to spot the signs.

"I'm just fine," Vasti said through gritted teeth.

"But surely—"

Before Sally could repeat herself, I heard Aunt Maggie bellow, "Sally, if you really want something to do, come help me unload these boxes of props. And bring a rag with you—the dust on some of this stuff must be an inch thick."

Sally froze, then reached into her purse. "Oh, darn, there goes my pager."

"I didn't hear anything," Vasti said suspiciously.

Sally made a show of looking at the display of her beeper, though I noticed she held it so that nobody else could see it. "I've got to run. Vasti, you be sure and call when you need my help."

She hurried out the door, but not before Vasti muttered under her breath, "When pigs fly." I knew Sally must have heard it, because the color that rushed to her face didn't come from Mary Kay.

People got back to work after that, but even though I'd had a good dinner, I was hungry again. So I excused myself from Junior and went to find the package of snacks I'd left in the kitchen. I ate the fruit and drank water for the baby, then had a cookie for myself. I was coming back into the auditorium, wiping crumbs from my shirt, when Sid Honeywell came in the front door and called out, "Did anybody ask for something to get delivered here?"

"Like what?" Vasti asked.

Sid said, "There are some big old boxes out here that I don't think were here before."

Looking mystified, Vasti followed him outside. Junior and I went along, too.

Sure enough, three large cardboard boxes were stuck in an alcove outside, not too far from the nook the play's cigarette smokers had taken over since Seth's murder.

"I could have missed them," Sid said, "but I swear I think I'd have noticed something this big."

"What in the Sam Hill is this?" Vasti said, and reached out to grab one.

"Hold it," Junior said. "Why don't you let me take a look first?"

Vasti jumped back. "You don't think it's a bomb, do you?"

Junior said, "Bombs aren't usually this big," but I noticed that she didn't touch anything right away. Instead she pulled a tiny pocket flashlight and let the light shine onto the ground around the boxes. "The ground's too hard to hold prints, but it looks like somebody dragged them over from the parking lot."

Once she pointed it out, I could see the bent grass and scuff marks on the hard red clay that covered most of the area.

Junior moved closer, still not touching anything, and looked at the side opposite us. "According to this label, these boxes were supposed to be delivered to the Byerly Auditorium."

There was no Byerly Auditorium; the high school auditorium and the recreation center itself were the closest we had to such a thing. "Does it say who sent them?" I asked.

"Morris Costumes in Charlotte."

"Morris Costumes!" said a voice behind us. I hadn't realized it, but a crowd had gathered behind us. Idelle burst out and, if Junior hadn't stopped her, would have opened the boxes right then and there. "These are the costumes we ordered!"

"Where did they come from?" Odelle wanted to know. "They were supposed to have been delivered a week and a half ago."

"There's no way they've been here all this time," Carlelle declared. "We'd have seen them."

"Besides which," Junior added, "it rained late last week, and these boxes are bone dry."

"It's safe to open them, isn't it, Junior?" Idelle asked.

"Give me a minute first." She walked around all three boxes, looking closely at them. "They should be all right. It doesn't look like the tape's been messed with since they left Charlotte."

The triplets gleefully ripped open the boxes and, after making sure they'd finally gotten what they'd ordered, drafted a couple of helpers and gleefully carted off their prize.

Vasti just stood there with her arms folded tightly across her chest, tapping her foot. "It was that Sally Hendon. I bet they got delivered to her show by mistake, and she didn't bother to tell anybody. She must have dumped them off when she was here."

"Why do you say that?" said a voice.

I jumped as Mark Pope stepped out. The way the man appeared from nowhere was getting on my nerves.

"Isn't it obvious?" Vasti said. "She shows up without being invited, and as soon as she's gone, we find these boxes. Do you know how much time's been wasted making new costumes?" She sounded as indignant as if it had been her own time that had been wasted. "Not having costumes could have ruined the show, which is what Sally wants. She thought the play was canceled, so she must have figured it wouldn't hurt to give them back now." She wagged a finger at Mark. "You ought to arrest her."

Aunt Maggie, who'd come out with the others, said, "Maybe it wasn't Sally. It could have been our practical joker." She turned to Mark, too. "It seems to me that you ought to be able to do something about this troublemaker before somebody gets hurt."

"In case y'all have forgotten, I've got a murder investigation to tend to. I don't have time for playing games with . . ." He paused. "On second thought, tell me more about these jokes."

Between them, Vasti and Aunt Maggie gave him a rundown on all the pranks I'd heard about, plus a few others, and Mark actually took notes. I looked at Junior, but she looked as confused as I was that Mark would take it so seriously.

"It seems to me that we've got a pattern here," Mark finally said.

"What kind of pattern?" Junior asked.

"The way these pranks have been escalating. You've been worried that somebody might get hurt. Maybe somebody already did. Maybe what happened to Seth Murdstone wasn't a murder after all."

"You think he died because of a practical joke?" Junior said, not bothering to hide her skepticism. "The man wasn't hit over the head with a whoopee cushion."

Mark shot her a look. "Even an innocent bucket of water propped on a door can cause harm if it falls the wrong way."

"I didn't see any bucket near Seth's body."

"I didn't say it was a bucket, only that it could have been. There are all kinds of ways it could have been rigged. Obviously the prankster found Seth first, and removed the evidence."

"Maybe it's obvious to you—" Junior started to say. Then she stopped herself. "Never mind me. You go ahead and handle this however you want."

Mark looked as if he wasn't sure he could take her at her word, but he turned back to Vasti. "Is there anything else you can tell me?"

"I've already told you who it is," Vasti said. "Sally Hendon must be behind all the pranks. I want you to arrest her!"

"I can't do that," Mark said slowly.

"Why not?" Vasti said.

"Because Mrs. Hendon didn't leave these boxes here."

"How do you know?"

"It just so happens that I was examining the grounds when she arrived, and I was still here when she left. At no time did she unload any boxes."

"Are you sure?" Vasti said, clearly deflated. "Maybe she left them earlier. It was nearly dark when we got here; maybe we missed them."

"Possibly," Mark allowed, "but there are other possibilities. If you don't mind, I think I'll go inside and see what I can find out about these so-called practical jokes."

Most of the others followed him inside, with Vasti speculating loudly that everything from a broken nail to low air in her tires could have been sabotage.

I waited with Junior until they were gone, then said, "What do you think? Could Seth have died by accident?"

"It's possible," Junior said, "but it doesn't seem to fit. All of the other practical jokes were pretty easily fixed. It was a pain untying those ropes, but it's not like any of them were cut. In fact, none of the other practical jokes have been dangerous. Missing thread and toilet paper isn't the kind of thing to get anybody hurt. Offhand, I can't think of any practical joke that would have killed Seth without leaving some sign of it."

"What about what Mark said? The prankster could have found Seth first and then removed the evidence."

"That's mighty cold-blooded for a practical joker."

"True," I said, "and come to think of it, this new prank kind of blows the idea, anyway."

"How's that?"

"Suppose I was a practical joker, and even though one of my stunts had gone so badly wrong as to kill somebody, I'd managed to get away with it. The last thing I'd want to do is to play another joke. I'd swear off them for life!"

"Then again, you might develop a taste for killing, the way serial killers do."

"In that case, I'd set up something else that could kill somebody. I wouldn't bother messing with costumes."

"That makes sense to me. So what do you say we leave the practical jokes to Mark? He probably won't catch the killer, but maybe the joker will get nervous and find somebody else to bother."

Chapter Thirteen

Junior and I had intended to corner somebody else when we got back inside, but Richard had all of the cast onstage to give them comments on their performances, and most of the crew was helping the triplets unpack the newly delivered costumes. Besides which, Mark was poking around, and the way he kept looking our way made me nervous.

"Do you suppose he's going to be hanging around like that to-morrow?" I asked Junior.

"There's no telling."

"Maybe we could go someplace where we won't have him around."

"What did you have in mind?"

"We could go visit Aunt Nora. She might have gossip about Seth. Or we could go to Aunt Daphine's beauty parlor. A lot of good stuff gets told there."

"That might be interesting," Junior said, but she didn't sound enthusiastic.

"You think it would be a waste of time, don't you?"

"I wouldn't say that exactly."

"What *would* you say?"

"I'd say that I'm tired, and kind of discouraged."

"I'm doing my best, Junior."

"It's not you, Laurie Anne. It's me. I'm used to doing things a certain way; that's all."

"And I'm used to doing things my way," I said, feeling a bit discouraged myself. "Maybe I'm the wrong person for this murder, what with Seth being a moonshiner. I don't know the first thing about moonshine."

"Officially, moonshine is any corn whiskey that hasn't been aged, but generally speaking, it's the illegal kind that gets people's attention," Junior said with a grin.

"Ha, ha. I know what it is, but I don't know anything about the business."

"I'm glad to hear that, Laurie Anne." She was still grinning.

"All right, laugh it up. But since you obviously know all about it, wouldn't you like to enlighten poor ignorant me?"

"As a matter of fact, I don't know a whole lot about the nuts and bolts of bootlegging myself, but there is somebody who might help us."

"Your daddy?"

"No, I'm talking about somebody in the business. When does rehearsal start tomorrow?"

"Richard wants everybody who can to come in first thing in the morning."

"Do you suppose anybody will mind if we're not here?"

"Probably not. I'll just tell folks I've got morning sickness. Nobody will question that."

"I thought you weren't having morning sickness anymore."

"You know that and I know that, but not everybody else needs to know."

Junior and I decided to meet at the recreation center after she'd dropped off her nieces and nephews, and she recruited Mrs. Gamp to watch the kids while we were gone. By the time that was settled, Vasti was impatiently waiting to lock up, and we all headed home.

I'd hoped to be able to talk things over with Richard on the way back to Aunt Maggie's and then in bed, but though he tried his best to pay attention, clearly his mind was still on stage. Finally I took pity on him, kissed him good night, and let him go to sleep.

I tried to wrestle the facts into a pattern myself, but I just couldn't come up with anything without my usual sounding board. Like Junior, I was used to doing things a certain way. I eventually gave up and went to sleep myself.

Junior was waiting for me when we got to the recreation center the next morning, and after a quick good-bye kiss for Richard before he started rehearsal, I climbed into her Jeep and we headed out.

Despite what I'd told Junior the night before, I did know a little about moonshine. I don't suppose there are many Southerners who don't. Most good-sized gatherings I'd attended in Byerly, whether wedding or funeral or family reunion, included a questionable bottle of corn whiskey being passed about. I'd even tasted the contents of one of those bottles. I could still remember how it burned its way through my body, and the way my cousin Linwood had laughed when tears ran down my face. After that, I'd been happy to stick to beer and mixed drinks, so I'd never bothered to learn exactly how people went about obtaining the stuff.

Still, there was something vaguely romantic about bootleggers, as if they were the Southern versions of Robin Hood or Zorro. I'd listened to the tales of their pulling the wool over the eyes of government agents—invariably Yankees who were rude to Southern women—and then dashing through back routes and dirt roads to get their product into the willing hands of other independent men. The sport of stock-car racing had evolved from those midnight chases; Junior Johnson, one of the all-time greats, had spent time in jail for making moonshine runs.

With all that cultural history, I was looking forward to seeing just what kind of man Junior was taking me to see. Admittedly, Seth Murdstone hadn't fit my notions of what a moonshiner should be, but I felt sure that Junior's connection would be the rogue of my imagination.

I was glad Junior was driving, because even with her directing, I don't know that I would ever have found the place. She took us down roads I'd never been on before, and had to turn around twice before getting us on the right one.

"Are we still in Byerly?" I asked her once she seemed satisfied that we were on the right path.

"This patch isn't part of any town," she said. "That's the way the Todger family likes it: nobody local has any interest in shutting them down, and nobody federal can find them."

"Is that why you haven't shut them down yourself? Because they're not in Byerly?"

"Nope. It's because they're retired. They used to go through an awful lot of corn, but these days all they make is wine: elderberry wine, blackberry wine, and so on."

"Is that legal?"

"It would be, with the proper paperwork, which they don't have. But the wine isn't for sale anyway. It's all given away to family and friends. Of course, family and friends like to return the favor with a load of groceries or a tank of heating oil or whatever they happen to have on hand."

"Making it technically legal."

"Just barely."

Junior stopped the car, but all I could see was a wide spot in the road. "Are we there? I don't see anything."

"It's not polite to show up without announcing ourselves." She pulled her cell phone out of her pocket and dialed a number. "This is Junior Norton. I was wondering if I could come pay my respects. . . . No, I'm not alone. A friend of mine is with me. Laurie Anne Fleming. Her mama was Alice McCrary, one of the Burnette girls. . . . That's right, she's expecting."

"Can they see us?" I said, looking around nervously.

Junior pointed up above the car. Darned if there wasn't a security camera aimed in our direction. She waved at it and nudged me until I did the same.

"Yes, I'm sure she'd like some molasses cookies. Is it all right if we come up to the house? . . . No, we don't mind if you finish up what you're doing first. Just give me a call when you're free. You've got my cell phone number, don't you? . . . Then we'll wait to hear from you." She broke the connection.

"Do they want us to come back another time?"

"No, they just want us to sit here until whoever is in there leaves. Which means that we've got to close our eyes."

"You're kidding."

"They're watching us through that camera, and if we don't cover up our eyes until a car goes by, not only will we not get inside their place today, but I'll never get in there again."

"Junior, you're scaring me."

"Don't worry. They're just private, and a bit ornery. They know I don't have any jurisdiction here, so they don't have to let me on their land if they don't want to. That means that I play by their rules if I want to talk to them."

It wasn't the strangest situation I'd ever been in, but it was darned close. Still, if Junior trusted them, I would too. "What do I do?"

"Close your eyes and then put your hands up over them." She demonstrated.

I obeyed but had to say, "What's to keep me from peeking?"

"Two things: One, they've got a zoom lens on that camera, and chances are that you'd get caught. And two, I gave my word years ago that I'd never peek and that nobody I ever brought with me would peek."

I got the message; I wasn't even tempted to peek after that. Well, I was tempted, but not enough to actually do it.

We stayed like that for what seemed like an awful long time, though it was probably no more than five or ten minutes. "Is it all right to talk?" I asked Junior.

"Sure, though I can't guarantee that they don't have a mike set up. What do you want to know?"

"Do you come up here often?"

"No, but every now and again I can get information from the Todgers that I can't get anywhere else. That camera up in the trees isn't the only one they've got, and they keep a close eye on this part of the woods."

"Are you sure they're not a militia group? Or a cult?"

She chuckled. "Just a mite more eccentric than most. Which I've got to admit is saying something around Byerly."

"I can't believe I've never heard of these folks."

"You're too young," Junior said. "Years ago, Todgers' liquor was all over these parts. When they got out of the business, they got more intent on privacy."

"You mean paranoid."

"Call it whatever you want."

Just then we heard a car approach ours, then pass on by.

"Can we open our eyes now?" I asked.

"Not yet." Maybe a minute later, Junior's phone bleeped, and she answered it with her eyes closed as far as I knew. "This is Junior. . . . Thank you kindly. We'll be right there." I guessed that she hung up, because she said, "All right, Laurie Anne, you can look now."

I did so, blinking a bit at the morning glare. "Junior, you do know the most interesting people."

"Somebody recently said that same thing to me. Only we were talking about you."

I tried to decide if I'd been insulted, complimented, or just accurately described, as we drove on through the woods, emerging in front of a fence that must have been ten feet tall. "How many bottles of wine did it take to pay for this?" I asked as the gate opened.

Even after we'd driven through, I couldn't see any buildings. The land inside the fence was as thickly wooded as the land outside. It wasn't until we'd driven another full minute that the house came into sight. After all the build-up, I'd been expecting something along the lines of Robin Hood's tree house, or even a castle. In fact, it was an ordinary split-level brick house with yellow shutters, and it would have fit in perfectly in any suburb in the country. There was a lawn surrounding it, with bushes and a collection of cheerful lawn gnomes. I could see a normal assortment of tools, hoses, and clutter inside the open garage door. Even the wreath on the door and the electric candles in the window screamed *"normal."*

I still didn't give up on my dreams of a dashing bootlegger until the front door opened and a fiftyish woman in jeans, a burnt-orange-striped blouse, and Keds waved at us.

"Don't tell me that's the moonshiner," I said to Junior.

"That's Clara Todger," Junior said. "What were you expecting?"

I was so glad I hadn't said anything about Zorro or Robin Hood. "From what you said, I thought she'd be older."

"She's the granddaughter and daughter of the real moonshiners," Junior said. "They made some good shine in their day and delivered it themselves a lot of the time. Daddy says the Todger women are the best drivers he's ever seen."

As I climbed out of Junior's car, I rubbed my tummy and silently promised the baby that I'd try to stop making assumptions about people I hadn't met.

Clara Todger met us at the door. "Hey there, Junior."

"Hey there. Clara, this is my friend Laura Fleming."

Clara's response struck me as oddly formal. "Any friend of Junior's is welcome here."

"Thank you," I said.

Junior and I followed her through the house to the kitchen. I only caught glimpses of the other rooms, but everything seemed ordinary to me, from the furniture to the messy stacks of Christmas cards. The kitchen wasn't at all ordinary. It was huge, for one thing, and had the biggest stove I'd ever seen outside a restaurant. There were big copper pots and pans hung on one wall, and I could tell they were there for easy access, not decoration. The counters were covered with bowls of berries and various gadgets for removing seeds, stems, and such. Obviously this was where the Todgers made their wine.

Clara waved us toward chairs around the solid oak table, where glasses and a plate full of cookies were already waiting.

"It's just grape juice," Clara said when I hesitated. "I know you shouldn't drink anything stronger in your condition, and Junior is driving."

I took a swallow. It was delicious, and I didn't have any idea that it came from a grocery store.

"When are you due?" Clara asked.

"Around the middle of April," I said.

"Boy or girl?"

"We haven't found out."

She nodded in approval. I'd noticed that most people thought it was a good idea to wait, but most people found out early when it was their own baby. I had no idea why.

We all took cookies, which were just as good as the grape juice, and talked babies for a little while. Clara said she had three daughters of her own, but I was happy to find out that she wasn't one of those who thought it was necessary to share every detail of labor. I'd already heard enough gruesome tales to make me wonder why anybody ever had a second child.

Eventually Clara said, "This is lovely, but I'm guessing y'all didn't come all this way to eat cookies and discuss potty training."

"Not that these cookies wouldn't be worth the trip," Junior said politely, "but actually, we want to talk to you about the family business. The former family business, that is."

"Then either Laurie Anne here is thinking about getting into that business, which I doubt, or this is about Seth Murdstone."

"It's about Seth," Junior said. "I imagine you heard about him getting killed."

Clara nodded.

"I was wondering if you'd heard anything else about that through the grapevine. I know you wouldn't tell us anything if Seth were still operating, but since he's gone . . ." She let her sentence trail off, giving Clara a chance to think about it.

"There's been some talk," she said slowly. "You know that Seth was in the habit of sending the fruits of his labor up North?"

"I could never prove it, but that's what I figured."

"There are others in the state who do the same thing, and some of them have mentioned problems up there. Someone is trying to take over all the available venues, and they're hoping to cut out everybody else."

"Who?"

"I've heard that they were Italian, but somebody else said Puerto Rican," Clara said. "Whoever they are, they're a lot more organized than the run-of-the-mill smalltime operators."

"Like Seth?"

"Exactly. Seth stayed as far down the food chain as he could and still make a decent living. So I don't think he would have wanted to go head-to-head with the big boys. It would have been too much of a gamble for him."

"Did they threaten him?" I asked. "Physically, I mean."

"I don't know about Seth specifically, but there have been threats made. Everything from destruction of property to breaking legs. Makes me glad to be out of the business."

Junior looked pointedly at the open pantry door, where we could see rows and rows of neatly labeled bottles, but she didn't say anything about them. Instead she asked, "Have any of the organized types come down here?"

"That I don't know. People are spooked right now, so they're seeing Al Capone with a tommy gun behind every tree. Every time there's an accident at a still, somebody claims it's mob sabotage, when probably it's nothing more than sloppy maintenance." To me she added, "Moonshiners in general aren't known for their common sense."

Junior asked, "Do you know what Seth was planning to do? Was he going to retire?"

"Rumor has it that he had been advised to switch to distributing locally, but that he hadn't decided one way or the other."

"Wouldn't that hurt business for the people already distributing around here?" I wanted to know. "Did any of them threaten Seth?"

Clara said, "Not that I know of. Which isn't to say that they might not have done something later, but right now they're more concerned with the people from up North."

"Did any of them have any feuds with Seth?"

"No. As I said, Seth stayed out of trouble. He had a handful of distribution deals and was happy with them. He stayed friends with everybody and made sure not to cut into anybody else's business, so nobody had any quarrels with him that I knew about."

I shook my head ruefully. "Who would kill a man that everybody likes?"

"I didn't say I liked him," Clara said.

"Didn't you?"

"As a matter of fact, I didn't."

"Why not?"

"It was something that happened a long time ago. Lord, it must be twenty years now." She stopped, but I waited her out. Eventually she went on. "It was one of those icy winter nights when sensible people stay home, and one of our men was out on a delivery. To keep from being seen, he was driving one of the back roads with no lights on. Unfortunately, Seth Murdstone was doing the same thing on the same road. He rear-ended our man's car, and sent it into a tree. Our driver was killed."

"What about Seth?" I asked.

"Only bruised, so he could have stayed to help."

"He didn't stop?"

"He didn't even admit it until he had to. When my sisters and I went to check on the delivery, we found the car, but it wasn't until we asked around that we found out that Seth had been out that same night. When we tracked him down, he said he'd stopped, but when he saw the driver was dead, he thought he better leave before the police came. He even said he thought he heard sirens. Which would have been reasonable—if he'd really heard sirens."

"You don't think he did?"

"I can't say, but I do know the police didn't find the wrecked car. Of course, it was certainly an accident, and it looked as if our man died instantly, so there was no real harm done. But I never quite trusted Seth after that." She gave me a tight smile. "I didn't decide to avenge our driver all these years later, if that's what you're thinking. If I'd wanted Seth Murdstone dead, he'd have been buried a long time ago."

Junior didn't comment, and there was something about Clara's tone that made me believe her. "What about the driver's family?" I asked.

"His wife never knew Seth had anything to do with it. There didn't seem to be any reason to stir up trouble."

I nodded. As much effort as the Todgers went to in ensuring their privacy, I could see why they wouldn't have done anything else.

Junior finished up her grape juice. "One other thing, Clara. Do you know where Seth's still is? I don't want it laying around to be found."

"I'm afraid I can't tell you."

I noticed that she hadn't said that she didn't know—only that she couldn't tell—and I was surprised that Junior didn't call her on it. Obviously the two of them had rules when dealing with each other.

Clara looked at the two of us. "Can I get either of you anything else before you go?"

It was a polite dismissal, made even more so when she offered us both bundles of molasses cookies to take with us. Junior refused just as politely, probably so it wouldn't look as if she was taking a bribe. As for me, I took both bundles.

The three of us chatted just a bit more about babies on the way out, and then I asked something I'd been wanting to know ever since Junior told me about the Todgers. "This doesn't have anything to do with Seth, and I know it's none of my business, but why did y'all quit bootlegging?"

Clara got still, and for a moment I expected her to order us off her property, or at least take back her cookies. Instead she said, "I decided it wasn't worth the risks. We didn't have the problems with Northerners then, but there was always the ATF to worry about. And the police, of course."

"Glad to hear that we hindered you a little," Junior said.

Clara went on, "But the real reason is that dead man I told you about. I was the one who had to break the news to his wife. She was pregnant at the time, and she lost the baby afterward."

I felt a cold breeze, and wasn't sure whether it was real or not.

"I decided then that it was time for a change. It took a while to talk the rest of the family into it, but eventually they agreed it was for the best."

"But if y'all aren't in the business anymore, why the cameras and fences?"

"After generations of being moonshiners, we Todgers prefer our privacy." Her smile told me that was all the answer I was going to get.

Chapter
Fourteen

Once Junior had driven us out the gate, and I was reasonably sure that there weren't any cameras aimed so that anybody could read my lips, I said, "Was Clara telling the truth about the family just wanting privacy?"

"Heck if I know, Laurie Anne," Junior said. "I do know that the Todgers were originally mountain folk, and a lot of mountain folk keep to themselves, so that may be all there is to it. Then again, some people say they've got a cult in there, snake handlers or people speaking in tongues. Others claim there's a battered women's and children's shelter, or a retreat for ex-hippies to hide from the FBI. All I know is that an awful lot of food and supplies go in there."

"Weird," was all I could say. "I was surprised she was still protecting Seth's still, especially since she didn't like him."

"She wasn't," Junior said. "She was protecting Jake. Maybe David, too, but probably just Jake."

"What did I miss?"

"Clara won't give up anybody in the business. You remember how she talked about the delivery man but never mentioned his name, and he's been gone for twenty years. If I hadn't already known Seth was a moonshiner, and if he weren't dead to boot, Clara would never have admitted it."

"Really?"

"By the same token, she won't reveal the location of a working still, and you can bet she knows the location of every working still around here."

"So by her *not* telling you where Seth's still is, this tells you that it's currently in use, and since Jake worked with Seth, he's the one who'll be using it."

"Right. I wasn't really expecting to find out where the still is. I just wanted to know if Jake was going to stay in the business. Now I know."

I replayed the conversation in my head, trying to decide if I'd missed anything else. "Clara kind of talked in circles when you asked what Seth had been planning on doing. What do you think that means?"

"I'm not sure," she admitted, "but I was wondering about what your cousins said about that fight between Jake and Seth."

"Do you think Jake might have wanted Seth to start selling their stuff around here instead of shipping it up North?"

"Could be."

"That really puts Jake in the running as Seth's killer, doesn't it?" I said. "Because they'd been fighting, and because now Jake can run the business any way he wants."

"Right."

Then I thought of Jake's reaction when told Seth was dead. "I don't know, Junior, he really seemed to be upset about his daddy's death."

"What if he'd killed Seth accidentally?" Junior pointed out. "Say Seth said he was going to close down the still, which would leave Jake without a way to make a living. Jake could have tried to talk him out of it, and when that didn't work, he got carried away and hit him. He'd been working on sets, so he could have been holding a piece of wood when he went to talk to Seth."

I said, "Do you suppose he would have realized Seth was dead? Maybe he thought he was just knocked out, and hoped Seth wouldn't remember who'd hit him." I'd read that head trauma tends to play games with memory, especially the memories of how a person came to be knocked out.

"I think I'd have known right off," Junior said, "but I've had more experience with dead bodies than Jake has."

"Unless bootlegging is a whole lot more dangerous than I thought." I went back over some of what Clara had told us. "You know, Clara is the first person I've run into that didn't like Seth."

"I know, and that bothers me."

"Why?"

"Because I liked him myself. Daddy liked him, even though Seth kept running circles around him. I don't know if you realize it, but cops sometimes do like the people we're going after. Sometimes it's a matter of respect for another professional."

"Like you and Clara?"

"Exactly. Daddy knew Seth was moonshining, and Seth knew Daddy knew, but that didn't stop them from being friendly when they ran into one another. When Seth's wife passed away, Daddy even sent flowers."

"Maybe Clara misjudged him. She said herself it was just because of that accident, and I can't blame her for that. It must have been awful."

"It might have made a decent motive, too, if it hadn't been so long ago."

"I suppose so." Then I thought of something. "You know, if Seth did cause that accident, then he's indirectly responsible for the Todgers getting out of moonshining. Could that be a motive? Maybe not for Clara, but somebody else in the family."

"Laurie Anne, do you remember how Clara said that if she'd wanted Seth dead, he'd have been gone long ago? That goes for her whole family."

"That's scary."

"You bet it is," Junior agreed. "I'm just glad they've never wanted anybody dead—that I know of, anyway."

I shivered. I'd run into people who'd killed for one reason or another, but each of them had killed for emotional reasons. Clara was the first person I'd ever met who I thought would kill calmly. And the funny thing was, I liked her.

"Well, we didn't get a whole lot out of the visit," I said, "though that stuff about organized crime could be promising. A sneak thief probably couldn't have snuck in on Seth, but a professional hit man could have."

"We still have the problem of how a hit man knew where Seth was going to be."

"What about my idea of them setting up a meeting?"

"They could have done that," Junior said, "but considering how careful Seth had been all his life, why would he have arranged something like that in the middle of a rehearsal? Where anybody from the town's biggest gossip to the chief of police could have walked in on him?"

"True. Umm . . . when you talk about the town's biggest gossip, you do mean Vasti, don't you?"

"Laurie Anne, I've never thought you were a gossip. Nosy, yes, but not a gossip."

"That makes me feel so much better."

She ignored me. "Besides, why would Seth have been a big enough threat to any Mafia types for them to kill him? According to Clara, he was either going to shut down or start distributing locally, which is exactly what they would have wanted him to do."

"You're right. It just sounded like a nice, neat answer. In fact, I'm surprised Mark hasn't jumped on it. He could still claim it was an outsider and not be expected to actually find the killer. Nobody would hold it against him if he couldn't track down a Mafia hit man. Of course, that assumes that he's heard about these guys being around. Does he know Clara?"

Junior shook her head. "I've never told anybody about the Todgers other than you, and Daddy never told anybody but me. But if the other moonshiners are as nervous as Clara says they are, Mark could have picked up on the rumor easily enough."

"I wonder why he hasn't. Or do you think he's keeping it quiet?"

"I keep telling you, I don't know what Mark's thinking," she said sharply.

"Sorry," I said.

After a few minutes of strained silence, she said, "I'm sorry, too,

Laurie Anne. This situation's got me on edge. I don't like not being in charge."

"That's all right." I patted my tummy. "With the little one here, I feel out of control myself. According to my aunts, once the baby arrives, I'm not going to be in control of much of anything for a long time to come."

Chapter Fifteen

We got back to the rehearsal just in time to stave off another tantrum—not from Richard, for a change, but from Kyle, one of Junior's nephews. Kyle was playing Tiny Tim and was refusing to use his crutch because he claimed it hurt him. He'd just thrown it down from the stage when we walked in, and Junior immediately took charge of him.

On stage, Richard was running his fingers through his hair as he watched the other young Cratchits indulge in a shoving match while their onstage parents tried not to laugh. "Could somebody please retrieve Tiny Tim's crutch?" he said in a tight voice.

"I'll get it," I said, and picked it up. I was surprised Kyle was putting up such a fuss. Up until then, he'd been delighted to have the plum child's role, and had practiced walking with a limp so much that I'd almost forgotten he wasn't crippled. The crutch's arm piece was padded with foam rubber, which was admittedly not authentic for the Victorian era but should have been fairly comfortable. Since I'm not exactly tall, Kyle wasn't much shorter than I was, so I tucked it under my arm for an experimental step. And yelped.

"Now what?" Richard snapped.

Instead of answering him immediately, I poked at the armrest. There was something sharp in there! "Richard, somebody stuck a pin or something into the crutch." I reached under my shirt to feel my arm pit, and brought my finger back with a drop of blood on it. "I'm bleeding."

"What!" Richard hopped down from the stage and took the crutch from me. "Idelle, will you bring me a pair of scissors?"

All three triplets came over and watched as Richard cut away the chamois cloth covering the armrest. My husband's not much of a cusser, but he cursed loudly when he saw what was under the material. Somebody had stuck a thin nail, like a carpet nail, right where it would prick whoever used the crutch. Without taking it out, he looked at it carefully. "I don't see any rust, but . . ."

"I had a tetanus booster last year, remember?" Then I called out, "Junior, has Kyle had a tetanus shot?"

"Does this have something to do with this gash under his arm?" she called back, and brought him in our direction. Kyle's eyes were red from crying, and he was holding his arm gingerly. Having felt that nail myself, I didn't blame him.

"It looks as if our prankster has struck again," Richard said, showing Junior the crutch.

"Is Kyle all right?" I asked.

"I think so," Junior said. "I was just going to put a Band-Aid on him, but I better check on his shots first." She pulled out her cell phone and stepped far enough away so that she could call her sister.

"Kyle," Richard said solemnly, "please accept my apologies. I had no idea that crutch was booby-trapped."

"That's all right," the boy said, red-faced at being the center of so much concern. "You didn't know."

"No, but I should have listened to you when you said it hurt you. What good is a director who doesn't trust his performers—especially one of the stars?"

Kyle's eyes glowed. "Me? A star?"

"Absolutely," Richard said. "Who do people think of when they hear the title *A Christmas Carol?* Scrooge and Tiny Tim. Your role is key. I only hope you can forgive me and carry on."

"Yes, sir, I sure can." He wiggled his arm. "This ain't nothing but a scratch."

"Kyle had a shot the year before last," Junior announced. "He's in the clear, or will be as soon as I get him a Band-Aid."

"I don't need any Band-Aid," Kyle said loftily, his tears gone.

"No, let your aunt take care of it," Richard said. "An actor has to be in peak physical condition to give his best performance."

Junior looked at me, one eyebrow raised, but went off to get the supplies. Kyle stood by with a determinedly stiff upper lip when Junior doctored him; then he followed Richard back to the stage as if nothing had happened.

"I don't know what Richard said to him," Junior said to me, "but it sure did the trick."

"Just practicing to be a daddy," I said proudly. "Is your sister upset?"

"Some," Junior admitted. "I didn't tell her I wasn't here when it happened, but I think she guessed. So, if you don't mind, we better do our investigating here for the rest of the day."

"No problem." I looked at the crutch I was still holding. "I'd like to find out how this happened."

"Oh, we're going to find that out, I guarantee you. Whoever rigged this thing knew damned well that Kyle was the one who was going to be using this crutch. Running off with toilet paper is one thing, hurting my nephew is something else." From the look in Junior's eye, I wasn't about to get in her way.

Unfortunately, after talking to just about everybody, all we found out was that just about anybody could have put the nail in Kyle's crutch. Since the triplets were in charge of costumes, we went to them first to find out where the crutch was kept overnight. Only Odelle told me it wasn't part of Kyle's costume. It was a prop. So we tracked down Aunt Maggie, but she told us it wasn't the crutch that she'd dug up for Kyle to use, because hers had been modern and Vasti had said it didn't look right. We found Vasti, and she said that Jake had made the authentic-looking one out of scraps from building sets.

Jake was sitting backstage all alone, not even pretending to use the hammer in his hand, and I hated to interrupt what I was sure was mourning, but Junior asked him about the crutch anyway. It turned out that Jake hadn't kept up with the crutch after he made it—just handed it to Kyle during an earlier rehearsal. This led us back to Kyle, who admitted that he'd been in the habit of leaving it lying around when he left at night.

That meant that anybody could have sneaked away with it for long enough to stick in a nail.

We finally gave it up as a lost cause and retreated to chairs, where I could put my feet up and Junior could keep an eye on the kids. I had my usual ice water and tried not to envy Junior her can of Coke. "That was a waste of time," I said.

"Most police work is, when you come right down to it."

"Same with my nosing about." I rubbed my tummy idly. "What is it with these pranks? What's the point?"

"Why does anybody play practical jokes?" Junior said. "For the attention. To cause trouble. To embarrass people."

"Usually, I'd agree with you." An ex-boyfriend of mine had loved playing practical jokes, and in the long run, it had gotten him killed.[7] "It just seems like these tricks are for a reason."

"Don't tell me you think Vasti's right, and that Sally Hendon is trying to close down the play."

"I'm sure Sally would love to see Vasti fall flat on her face, but since Mark cleared her of leaving those costumes, she must be innocent. Though somebody else might want to shut things down."

"Why?"

"Let's look at the idea of practical joker as murderer again." I could tell Junior wanted to argue the point, but I waggled my finger at her. "Just listen for a minute. What if the earlier jokes were camouflage, just stirring things up until the killer got a chance to actually kill Seth? Maybe he'd planned to let it look as if Seth died as a result of a practical joke gone wrong if he got caught."

"As a fallback position?" Junior said.

"Exactly. But he got lucky and nobody caught him."

"So why didn't the jokes stop after Seth died?"

[7] *Country Comes to Town*

"He could be muddying the waters some more."

"Kind of risky, since every stunt he pulls increases his chances of being caught."

"True." I took a different approach. "Maybe he really is trying to shut down the play."

"Why?"

"Because of you and me. As long as rehearsals continue, we've got lots of access to the witness and suspects. If the show were canceled, we'd have a harder time tracking people down. And I don't have to tell you how unreliable memories are. The minute people get out of here, they're going to start forgetting details, and it might be those details that will help us solve this thing."

"Except that nobody remembers any useful details."

"Not yet, but they might. Or maybe we've already heard something and it just didn't register." I looked at her, trying to read her expression. "What do you think?"

"It's interesting."

"Is that a punch line?" I said suspiciously.

"Pardon?"

"Don't you remember that old joke? Two women who haven't seen each other in a while get together to catch up. The first one says her husband's a doctor and makes more money than God, and the second one says, 'That's interesting.' Next the first says her husband bought her a new Cadillac and a fur coat, and the second says, 'That's interesting.' Then the first says their house is huge and they've got umpteen servants, and the second says, 'That's interesting.' Finally the first one asks what the second one's been doing, and the second one says she went to charm school, and the first one wants to know what she learned. The second one says she learned to say 'That's interesting,' instead of 'Up yours, bitch!' "

Junior laughed so hard she blew Coke out of her nose. When she'd calmed down, and wiped her nose, she said, "No, Laurie Anne, that's not what I was thinking. But I still don't buy it. Seth's death didn't look premeditated to me. You see, head injuries are tough to predict. Just a light blow to the back of the head can cut off blood flow and kill a person, and other people survive massive wounds without any permanent damage. Now Seth was only hit once. Obviously it did kill him, but there was no way to know for sure that it would. If I'd gone to all the trouble to set things up so I could kill somebody, I'd have picked a method that would guarantee that he died."

"You're right," I admitted. "I just keep trying to link the murder to those silly tricks—" Remembering that Junior's nephew had gotten hurt through one of those tricks, I changed it to, "I mean, those nasty tricks. Maybe they really aren't connected."

"And maybe they are. We just don't know yet." She patted me on the arm. "But I do like the way your mind works. What next?"

I spotted Vasti greeting Aunt Nora at the door. "In my unprofessional opinion, we should eat, because I smell fried chicken."

Aunt Nora had brought some of her fried chicken, which is so delectable that if Colonel Sanders were still alive, he'd have been beating the door down to find out how she did it. Not only had she cooked enough to feed everybody, she'd brought along all the fixings, too: mashed potatoes and gravy, green beans, biscuits, and double-butter Christmas cookies for dessert. With all that, she had the nerve to apologize for not having been able to find decent corn on the cob in December.

Needless to say, Richard put an immediate halt to the rehearsal. If he hadn't, he would have had a mutiny on his hands. Once our plates were filled, I dragged him into a corner so we could talk. Or rather, I talked, telling him what Junior and I had found out so far. Richard nodded, ate, and made encouraging noises in the appropriate places. When I finished, he said, "It sounds as if you two are making progress."

"You think so?" I said doubtfully. "We've been shooting down theories faster than we can come up with them."

"I have complete confidence in you, and having Junior around can only help."

Just then I looked up and saw Mark watching us. "Has he been here all day?"

"In and out," Richard said. "I suppose he's investigating, but I haven't seen any progress from him."

"What's going on with him, anyway? He can't possibly be as stupid as he's been acting."

"Maybe he's trying to lull suspects into a false sense of security."

"If he's that good an actor, you should cast *him* as Scrooge."

"Don't even think of messing with my cast again," he warned me. "I've finally got the right Scrooge, but pulling this off is still going to be tough."

"Don't worry. You concentrate on the play and let Junior and me play detective."

"Have you two mapped out your next step?"

We hadn't, but he'd given me an idea. "I'm planning to question somebody who spent a lot of time with Seth recently, and who just happened to be nearby when he was killed."

"Great! He should be able to tell you a lot."

"I hope so." I looked at him expectantly.

A second or two later, he got it. "Oh, no, you don't! The deal was that you and Junior do your thing—I've got a play to direct."

"I'm not asking you to *do* anything. I just want to ask you some questions."

"Really?"

"Really."

"What if I don't cooperate?"

"I'll have to get tough."

"Whips? Chains?"

"Richard Fleming! This is a whole new side of your personality."

"We temperamental director types always live large."

"I can borrow Junior's handcuffs if you insist, but for now, how about bribery?"

"What did you have in mind?"

I tried for a husky whisper. "What about some cookies?"

"Aunt Nora brought cookies?"

After I brought him a plate-full, Richard was willing to tell me anything he knew. The problem was, he insisted that he didn't know anything that could help.

"Seth and I didn't discuss anything other than the play," Richard said in between mouthfuls. "I was working so hard to get him to stop being himself and start being Scrooge, I didn't want him to say anything personal. Even if he had been worried that somebody wanted to kill him, I wouldn't have given him a chance to talk about it."

"Rats," I said. "What about the rest of the cast?"

"The same goes for them. Half the time I don't even remember their real names. I just call them by their characters' names."

That made me think of something. "According to what Aunt Maggie said, Vasti pretty much let people pick their parts. Right?"

He nodded.

"Don't you think that the part a person picks says something about him?"

"Is this one of those pop psychology tests where you analyze people by finding out which Beatle they like best?"

"Probably, but play along anyway. After all, you did accept my bribe."

"So I did," he said, licking colored sugar off of his fingers. "Who first?"

"How about Tim Topper?"

"Bob Cratchit. Honest, and loyal to a fault. Loves his family. As far as I know, this also applies to Tim. None of which precludes his being a murderer, of course." He paused. "There is one thing. I don't think he liked Seth."

"Why do you say that?"

"As I said, Cratchit is loyal to Scrooge beyond reasonable expectations."

"I always figured he really needed the job."

"Partly, but Dickens created lots of characters who put up with cruelty because they're good. Most of them eventually get rewarded, at least in his early work, though in later—" He stopped himself. "Sorry, I get carried away."

"I understand." I'd known he was an English professor when I married him, so I could hardly blame him for acting like one.

"Anyway, Cratchit asks Scrooge for better treatment, but doesn't seem to resent it when Scrooge refuses."

"Right."

"Tim's performance didn't reflect that. His Bob seemed angry at Scrooge. Admittedly that's a more reasonable reaction, but it's not what the part calls for."

"Maybe Tim doesn't realize how it's supposed to be played."

"That's what I thought, and I was planning to address the problem when I got a chance, but after Big Bill took on the role, it wasn't necessary. Tim started playing it the way it was written."

"So either he really disliked Seth, or he really likes Big Bill," I speculated.

"Or maybe he reread his part," Richard said. "Who else?"

"Florence Murdstone. Now that I think about it, I'm surprised she didn't keep her maiden name."

"Most women do still take the husband's name, even in these enlightened times. You did."

"I know, but there are other customs from less enlightened times. Around here, when women marry down, they generally either keep their maiden name or go by both names, like Florence Easterly Murdstone."

"Marry down? I shouldn't quote Dickens so much. The Victorian era is going to your head. Tell me, was our marriage considered marrying up or marrying down?"

"Up because of that Harvard ring of yours, but down because you're a Yankee. So it evens out."

"I'll accept that," he said. "What does Florence's choice tell us? Or rather, both of her choices, since she's playing Scrooge's old girl-friend Belle and Mrs. Cratchit."

I thought for a minute. "Start with Belle. She's trying to make Scrooge realize what's really important in life. From Aunt Maggie's gossip, Florence blew off her society friends to marry the man she loved. Right?"

"What about Mrs. Cratchit?"

"My take is that she had more common sense than her husband. She knew Scrooge was using Bob, but she couldn't do anything about it. If this represents Florence's relationship with Seth, it doesn't sound as if she liked him."

"Maybe all it means is that there are only two decent roles for women in the play."

I punched him gently. "Play nice. I'm carrying your baby, and look how swollen my ankles are."

"Put your feet up and I'll rub them."

"And?"

"And I'll play nice."

"Good." I allowed him to massage my feet for a few minutes before going on. "Next, David Murdstone as Scrooge's nephew Fred, who keeps trying to redeem Scrooge. Since there's no mention of Fred's father, can we assume that Scrooge is a father figure to Fred?"

"Nothing in the text says that," Richard said, "but nothing disputes it, either."

"Then isn't it indicative that Fred tries to change Scrooge? I heard that David didn't get along with his father."

"They did seem very different," Richard admitted. "Jake and Seth were much closer. Does that make David a more likely candidate for Seth's killer than Jake?"

"Not necessarily. Sometimes it's the people who are alike who fight the most."

"True, but there's a problem. David didn't pick the role of Fred. He only took it because Florence talked him into it. She wanted him to be in the play with her, and she thought he'd be good as Fred."

"Oh." I stopped. "Does this psychobabble make any sense, Richard?"

He didn't answer—just kept rubbing my feet.

"I get the hint. I'll hush up and enjoy the foot rub." I did hush, and I definitely enjoyed the foot rub, but I kept going over the suspects in my head. It was aggravating. I just couldn't come up with a reason compelling enough to commit murder over. Then I thought of newspaper articles about people being killed for nothing more than cutting off another driver in traffic. Maybe our murderer didn't have anything like what I would consider a good reason.

"Richard," I said, "what would it take to get you to commit murder?"

"Other than losing another cast member?"

"Seriously."

"Somebody threatening you or our child. Or me, of course."

"That would be self-defense, or wife and child defense, not murder. What else?"

"I don't think I'd kill for money, but if I were desperate enough, maybe I would. The same for revenge: I don't consider myself a vengeful person, but who can tell? I don't know, Laura. Quite honestly, I hope I never find out."

"Fair enough. I can't say that I've got a better answer." Like Richard, I wasn't sure I wanted to find out either. I looked around and noticed that people were finishing their lunches. "Looks like it's about time to get things rolling again."

"So it does. If you'll excuse me, I think I'll hit the men's room." He gave me a quick kiss and headed off.

Aunt Nora was starting to pack up her things, so I went to give her a hand.

"The chicken was wonderful," I said.

"I'm so glad you enjoyed it." She patted my tummy. "Did the baby get enough, too?"

"Lord, yes. I ate enough for me, the baby, and six or seven other people." Then I virtuously added, "I had lots of vegetables, too."

She beamed. There's nothing quite so satisfying to Aunt Nora as a bulging waistband. "So," she asked with studied nonchalance, "how's your project coming along?"

"Junior and I are still working on it. While you're here, let me pick your brain. Do you know of any reason why anybody would have killed Seth?"

Before she could answer, I heard Richard call out, "Would whoever it was who ran off with the soap dispenser from the men's room please return it?" There were a few snickers, but most people just looked irritated.

"Are y'all still having problems with practical jokes?" Aunt Nora asked.

I nodded. "At least this one is harmless." I told her about the nail on Tiny Tim's crutch.

"That's terrible," she said. "I like a good joke as much as the next person, but there's no excuse for hurting a child."

"You'll get no argument from me. But we're having even less luck catching the prankster than with catching Seth's killer."

"I don't know that I can help you with either, but I will tell you what I know about the Murdstones."

"Great." I sat down and got comfortable. Aunt Nora isn't known for fast talking.

"I didn't know Seth well, but I did know his wife. We were on a couple of church committees together. Of course, that was before she got sick and stopped leaving the house."

"She had cancer, didn't she?"

Aunt Nora nodded. "Liver cancer. She was already pretty far gone before they found it, so there wasn't a whole lot they could do to help her. Some of us up at the church would take meals and things by for her and the boys, and it about broke our hearts. Her just wasting away, and poor David moping around, looking nearly as bad as she did, because he knew what was happening. Jake was younger, so it didn't hit him the same way."

"What about Seth? How did he take it?"

"He was worse off than David in a way. He didn't seem to believe that his wife was dying. Everybody in Byerly knew it was only a matter of time; she was so bad off she couldn't even go to the bathroom by herself. But he'd talk like she was going to get better and hop up off that bed."

"Maybe he was just trying to make her feel better."

"No, he was in denial."

I blinked. Even though they watch *Oprah* in Byerly just like everywhere else, it always surprises me when one of my aunts uses words like that. "What did he do when she died?"

"I've never seen a man take on so. What with him and the boys, it was the saddest funeral I'd ever been too. Seth fell apart, and David closed himself up, and Jake was mostly confused about what was going on. The other women at the church and I had to help them with just about everything: going through his wife's things, and cleaning the house, and making sure the boys got fed. Seth didn't pull himself out of it for months."

"He never remarried?"

"Everybody encouraged him to, since he had the boys to raise, but his heart was in the grave."

"I beg your pardon?"

"Don't you know that expression? It means he was still so much in love with his first wife that he couldn't bring himself to fall in love again. Which was a shame, because there were a couple of women who thought a whole lot of him." She nodded at somebody. "There's one of them right there."

I looked in that direction. "Mrs. Gamp?"

"Her husband died not long before Seth's wife, and since she didn't have any children of her own, she'd have been a good mother to his boys. Everybody thought sure he was going to marry her, but then he broke up with her and started going around with somebody else." She lowered her voice. "It was about then that she started talking about Mrs. Harris."

"Really?" I said. "He must have really hurt her." Of course, most scorned women act right away, not years later. "Did anybody else have a grudge against him? Maybe somebody else in the play?"

"Did you have anybody particular in mind?"

"What about the Christmas Spirits? Oliver, Sid, and Pete."

"Oliver?" She thought for a minute. "I don't know of any feud between Oliver and Seth, but it seems like there was something with Sid. You remember Tom Honeywell, don't you?"

"How could I forget?" Tom, a born troublemaker, had dated my cousin Ilene, and she was later accused of his murder.[8] Though Sid was a wonderful man, everybody in town pretty much thought Tom had gotten what he deserved.

"Tom worked for Seth for a while, but there was some kind of problem and Seth fired him. I think he said Tom stole from him, but I don't remember the details. I can't imagine he would have

[8] *Trouble Looking for a Place to Happen*

taken any of the chairs. It must have been tools or something like that."

Or maybe it had been moonshine. I was only surprised Tom hadn't blabbed what Seth was up to all over town, but then again, he couldn't have without admitting his own involvement.

"Sid was pretty hot at the time," Aunt Nora said. "He didn't want to believe his son would steal. Then Tom stole from him, too, and he realized Seth had been right after all. But that would have been more a reason for Seth to be angry at Sid than the other way around."

"If either of them held a grudge, I didn't see it," I said, "and since they had scenes together, I think I would have. What about Pete Fredericks?"

Aunt Nora giggled despite herself. "This is terrible, Laurie Anne, but all I can think of is that he might have done it to drum up business."

"I know, I've thought the same thing. Poor old Pete. I bet he's sorry he left the mill to become a mortician. He must have to put up with a lot."

"You know he does, but there aren't many places in Byerly where he could make as much money as he does at the funeral home. It's a shame, too, because he's got a degree in chemistry from NC State."

"I didn't know that." Could there be a connection there? Wouldn't a chemist have been helpful to a bootlegger, helping set up the distillations and testing the product for proof? Junior hadn't mentioned anything about Pete being involved, but there was a lot about Seth's operation she hadn't known. Then I pictured Pete delivering whiskey in his hearse, and started snickering again.

"What?" Aunt Nora wanted to know.

"Nothing," I said. "It was a silly thought."

She must have decided it was a pregnancy thing, because she let it slide. "Anybody else?"

"Only if you know about any other scores people might have wanted to settle." I looked around the room to see whom I hadn't asked about. "What about Big Bill?"

"Big Bill Walters with Seth Murdstone? Lord, Laurie Anne, I don't know that the two of them ever spoke until this play came up.

They didn't exactly travel in the same circles, you know." She stopped herself. "No, wait. It seems like I heard recently that Big Bill wanted to buy Seth's house. Or at least the land. He's got a couple of acres."

"Was Seth going to sell?"

"That I don't know. But why would Big Bill kill somebody over a piece of property? He already owns most of the town."

"That's never stopped Big Bill. Besides, when you always get what you want, it must be all the more frustrating when you find something you can't have."

"I suppose. Do you think that's why he keeps chasing after Aunt Maggie?"

"You think he wants to buy the Burnette home place?"

"I'm not talking about real estate."

"Aunt Nora," I said in mock indignation, "you have a dirty mind!"

"I didn't say a word," she said, trying to look innocent.

"You've said enough that you ought to be ashamed of yourself."

She just laughed. As for me, I refused to speculate further. "If you can get your mind out of the gutter," I said, "is there anybody else who had a reason to kill Seth?"

She thought it over but finally shook her head. "I'm sorry, but I can't think of a thing."

"I appreciate you trying to help, anyway. Speaking of helping, can I help you carry the leftovers out to your car?"

"No, thanks. I'm leaving everything here in case any of y'all need a snack later on. I'll come back tomorrow to pick up what's left."

"Aunt Nora, I can personally guarantee that there won't be anything left tomorrow but fond memories."

Despite Aunt Nora's objecting that I didn't need to be toting boxes, I did help her carry leftovers into the kitchen before she left.

Chapter Sixteen

One of the few advantages of using the recreation center was having a kitchen available. Mrs. Gamp kept the coffeepot full and made sure there were cookies and other treats for every rehearsal. I'd been keeping bottles of water in the refrigerator, plus a bag of fruit. I was eyeing the leftover cookies, trying to decide if I had room for one more, when Florence came in. So I grabbed a cookie and leaned nonchalantly against the counter, figuring that calories consumed in the line of duty didn't count.

"Hey there, Laurie Anne," Florence said. "Won't you join me for a cup of tea?" She started pulling out the fixings.

"No, thanks. The doctor's got me staying away from caffeine for the duration."

"What with everything else going on, I haven't had a chance to congratulate you on the baby," she said. "You and Richard must be so excited."

"Absolutely. At least, when we're not in stark terror."

Florence smiled. "Don't you worry. Y'all are going to make wonderful parents."

"Thank you. And while we're congratulating, belated congratulations on your marriage." I winced. "I mean, best wishes."

"Don't apologize. I know you're not supposed to congratulate a new bride, but as long as it took me to get David to marry me, I think I deserve congratulations. Do you know I chased that man for ten years?"

"Really? Y'all are so clearly in love now."

"Oh, we were in love the whole time. He just didn't believe that I loved him as much as he loved me." She shook her head. "Men can be so silly. He had it in his head that there was no way that one of the Easterlys could be interested in plain old David Murdstone. As if I cared one bit that his father wasn't a banker or a lawyer. There isn't a thing wrong with making furniture."

I nodded, but I had to wonder if she would have been that understanding if she'd known what else her father-in-law made.

"Besides, it was David I married, not Seth, and he's as much a gentleman as any man I've ever known."

Darned if her eyes didn't glow when she said that, and I smiled, remembering the way I'd felt when Richard and I first got married. Come to think of it, I still felt that way.

She said, "Oh, I dated other men, and I've had my share of proposals, but I knew David was the man I wanted. And it's like my daddy says, once I've made up my mind, don't get in my way, or you'll have a Florence-sized hole in your middle."

"Then your family accepts David?"

"Absolutely. They know quality when they see it."

"How about David's family?"

"It did take some time to win Jake over," she admitted. "I think he figured I was too high and mighty to really be interested in David, and that I was toying with his brother's affections. But he came around. Even though Jake's rough around the edges, he's got a good heart."

"And Seth? He must have been delighted when David finally got married, at his age and all." Then I realized what I'd implied about Florence's age. "Not that David's old—"

Florence just laughed and patted my arm. "That's all right, Laurie Anne, I know I'm not the usual blushing bride. Goodness knows my family has reminded me of that fact more than once. Seth did seem happy that David was settling down. In fact, he joked that if David hadn't married me, he'd have proposed himself. I'm glad that we married in time for him to see it. Their family—my family now—has seen so much sadness. David's mother, and then Jake's little boy, and now Seth."

The Murdstones had lost a lot, and I suddenly felt ashamed of grilling Florence. "David must be so glad he has you to help him through this."

"No more so than I am to be here for him. He's everything to me, Laurie Anne. I'm sure you know what I mean." She finished her tea. "If you'll excuse me, I think I'm going to visit the little girls' room."

"That sounds like a good idea to me, too." I stopped long enough to cover up the cookies so they wouldn't go stale, but I couldn't have been more than half a minute behind her. That put me right at the bathroom door when I heard Florence shriek, and then a loud thump.

I yanked open the door, saw Florence on her back, and started inside, but she said, "Don't come in! You'll fall!"

Looking down, I saw that the floor was coated with pale pink liquid, and I realized that I'd found the soap that had been stolen from the men's room.

Chapter Seventeen

David came running when he heard that Florence had fallen, and it was he who made his way cautiously across the slippery tiles to check his wife for broken bones before lifting her into his arms. Only when he was sure that she was all right, other than a few bruises, did he let his fury show.

"I demand to know who is responsible for this!" he roared.

Nobody spoke, which wasn't surprising. Had I spilled that soap, I would have been afraid to admit it in the face of so much anger.

"You heard the man!" Richard added. "Who the hell is playing these damned games?"

I blinked, surprised by my husband's reaction. Then he took my hand, and I understood. If I'd gone in first instead of Florence, I would have been the one to fall instead of her, and in my condition, I might have suffered more than a few bruises. I could have lost the baby. Suddenly, all I wanted to do was wrap my arms around my tummy and hide.

"Are you all right?" he asked.

"I'm fine," I said in as strong a voice as I could manage.

"Let me take a look in there," Junior said, and strode past us. She stayed in only a minute or two, then came back with an empty soap dispenser in her hand. "Nothing fancy. Whoever it was just spilled the soap on the floor. No way to tell who."

"What's wrong now?" somebody said. Mark Pope was pushing his way in.

"Another prank," Junior said.

"One hell of a prank," David snapped. "Florence could have been seriously hurt. Something has to be done."

"Damned right!" Richard said. He told Mark what had happened to Florence, and finished with, "This is on top of what happened to Kyle this morning."

"Did anybody see anything?" Mark asked. "Who was the last one to go in there?"

It took a bit of sorting, but we finally figured out that the triplets had taken Junior's two nieces in there at ten-thirty for a costume fitting, and that they'd been in there at least half an hour. Jake had gone to the men's room during that time, and the soap dispenser was still intact then. Richard had discovered the missing soap right before one o'clock, so the trap had been set some time during those two hours.

Once again, pretty much anybody could have done it, because everybody had been busy during that time.

"It had to have been a woman," Oliver insisted. "Somebody would have noticed a man going into the ladies' room."

"No more so than a woman going into the men's room to get the soap," Aunt Maggie shot back.

"Maybe nobody went in," Junior drawled.

"What do you mean by that?" Mark asked sharply.

"The bathroom window is open, there's no screen, and there's a splash pattern around the spot where I found the dispenser. I'm guessing that whoever it was went outside and threw the dispenser in. Otherwise they would have left tracks in the soap." She pointed to the path David had left when carrying out Florence, and lifted one foot to show the soap smeared on the bottom of her boots.

Mark said, "Then there's absolutely no way of knowing who it was. People, I'm sorry, but I don't have time to babysit you in the middle of a murder investigation."

"You could have fooled me," Aunt Maggie said. "I can't see that you've done a thing all day."

Mark ignored her. "I've half a mind to close down this show just to make sure nothing else happens."

"You can't!" Vasti said. "There's—I've got—you can't!"

"I understand how you feel, Mrs. Bumgarner, but in the interest of public safety . . ."

"In the interest of public safety, you had better find out who is doing this!" a voice boomed. Big Bill was standing in front of Mark. I'd gotten so used to him being one of the gang that I'd almost forgotten that he was Big Bill Walters. Apparently, so had Mark.

"But Mr. Walters, surely you don't want to risk—"

"Deputy Pope, it's your job to investigate *all* crimes in Byerly, not just the ones that make the newspaper. If you can't handle the job, then perhaps Junior would be willing—"

"No, sir, I can handle it." He took a deep breath. "Don't worry, sir, I'll take care of it."

"Good. Then I suggest you get to work. I assume that's why you're here."

"Actually, I came to let the Murdstones know that the coroner has released Mr. Murdstone's remains so they can make the necessary arrangements."

"Thank you, Deputy Pope," Florence said. Then she said, "Mr. Fredericks? How long would it take to prepare the services we discussed?"

"I can have everything in place by as soon as tomorrow evening," Pete said.

"That'll do fine."

"I'll have your father-in-law picked up immediately." I was glad Pete wasn't wearing his Spirit of Christmas Yet to Come costume. It would have been too creepy for words.

"Thank you." Florence raised her voice. "While everybody is here, I want to let you know that the visitation for my father-in-law will be at Giles Funeral Home at seven-thirty tomorrow evening, with the funeral there at ten the next morning." To Richard she added, "I'm sure you realize that David, Jake, and I will miss rehearsal."

"I'm canceling rehearsals for both those times," Richard assured her.

"Thank you. Then let's take advantage of the time we've got."

"I think I should take you home, darling," David said.

"I don't think that's necessary," Florence said. "My big scene is coming up."

"But—"

"You are the sweetest man to be concerned, but if you'll let me stand up, I'll show you that no harm was done."

Sure enough, she wasn't even limping once she got on her feet again.

"Are you sure?" he asked.

"Absolutely. Though I'll feel so much better if you stay by my side."

"Of course," he said happily.

I heard Mrs. Gamp say, "Aren't they the sweetest couple?" at about the same time Aunt Maggie snorted.

Then Richard said, "Laura, don't you want to go back to Aunt Maggie's house? To take a nap or something?"

"Aren't you the sweetest thing?" I cooed.

"All right, I get the message. I just don't want you or the baby getting hurt."

"And I don't want *you* getting hurt. The next prank could just as easily be set for you."

"You're right. I'll be careful if you are."

"It's a deal." I kissed him and then pushed him toward the stage. "Now get to work." Not that I wasn't nervous, but I was even more angry. Whether the trickster had anything to do with Seth's murder or not, now I was bound and determined to find him.

I said as much to Junior a few minutes later.

"Then we're on the same page. I thought I'd wander around and make sure nothing else goes wrong."

"Do you think he would try anything else today? He's got to know that you and David will string him up if we catch him. If Richard doesn't get to him first, that is."

"Whatever else he may be, he's been pretty gutsy up until now. So I'll see if I can fade into the background a while."

"I'll come with you."

She didn't say anything. She just looked down at my tummy.

"I guess I'm not in any condition to fade, am I?"

"Maybe you should keep on talking to people instead," she suggested tactfully.

I didn't like it, but she was right. So while Junior lurked, I looked around to see who I might talk to. Tim Topper was sitting by himself, drinking coffee, and I remembered what Richard had said about him not liking Seth. Since I had nothing better to do, I figured I might as well find out why.

"Hey, Tim," I said, taking the chair next to him.

Tim was a big man, around my age, with caramel-colored skin, hazel eyes, and untamed eyebrows. "Hey, Laurie Anne," he said. "How's the little mama?" He reached out toward my tummy, then stopped himself with an embarrassed grin.

"Go ahead," I said. "Everybody else in town has already patted us. I don't want you to feel left out."

He laughed, but he patted. "Have you decided on names yet?"

"Richard and I are still negotiating. He's thinking Portia for a girl or Mercutio for a boy, but I'm partial to Scarlett or Rhett."

He nodded but didn't say anything.

"Tim! I'm kidding!"

"Whew!" he said with a loud sigh of relief. "I didn't know how long I was going to be able to keep a straight face."

"You know us better than that. Scarlett?" I shuddered, especially knowing that Vasti had put that one on her short list for Bitsy.

"People do get creative with their children's names. I'm mighty grateful my mama went with something simple like Tim. And Laurie Anne is a real pretty name."

Actually, my mother always called me Laura, but the rest of the South was stuck on Laurie Anne, and I'd given up on changing their minds. So I just said, "Thank you." Then, wanting to edge the conversation toward something more useful, I said, "Are you enjoying your acting debut?"

"I'm having a great time. You know I've got a weak spot for Dickens."

I looked up on the stage, where Big Bill was practicing the jig

Scrooge dances upon realizing that he hasn't missed Christmas. "Big Bill seems to be having fun, too. Maybe I shouldn't say so, but I think he's a lot better in the part than Seth Murdstone was."

"A whole lot better," Tim said emphatically.

"It is terrible what happened to Seth. Did you know him well?"

"Never met him until we started on the play, and even if he hadn't been killed, I don't expect I'd ever have spoken to him again afterward."

"Really? Did you not—"

Tim downed the rest of his coffee. "Excuse me, Laurie Anne, but I better head on up to the stage. Richard's going to be calling for me any minute."

He was gone before I could point out that Richard had just backed up a couple of scenes, meaning that Tim wasn't going to be needed for a while yet. I frowned, not happy with the implications. Not only had Tim not liked Seth, but he wasn't even willing to talk about the man. I hated to be suspicious of him, but it looked as if I had to be.

Chapter Eighteen

I must have been looking as nonplussed by Tim's reaction as I felt, because Mrs. Gamp appeared at my elbow and asked, "Are you all right, dear?"

"I'm fine."

"Are you sure? Mrs. Harris says you shouldn't be too careful when you're in the family way."

"She's probably right." Then, recognizing an opportunity, I said, "How are you doing? I mean, after the upset of finding Seth and all."

She shook her head back and forth. "That poor man. It's a terrible thing to be murdered to death that way. Mrs. Harris hasn't been able to sleep a wink since it happened."

"Bless her heart," I said sympathetically, though I wondered if Mrs. Gamp had stayed awake with Mrs. Harris. She was looking a bit worn around the edges. "It must have been a shock for you. Somebody told me that y'all used to date."

"Is that what they call it now?" Mrs. Gamp giggled. "We used to call it sex."

I blinked, not sure if I'd heard that right.

"We were both lonely, don't you know," Mrs. Gamp said. "His wife had passed over, and Mr. Gamp was gone. So Seth and I had sex for a while, just to pass the time."

"Oh." It was an inadequate response, but I couldn't imagine what would have been a better one.

"We eventually broke it off. Seth wanted people to think it was his idea, but I'm the one who wanted to stop. He wasn't very nice."

"Really?" I said, thinking I'd found somebody else who didn't approve of Seth. "Most everybody I've spoken to liked him."

"Oh, I don't mean he wasn't a nice man. I mean he wasn't nice in bed. Not much of a lover."

I gave up on words and just nodded a few times.

"Too much in a hurry, if you take my meaning. Not like my Mr. Gamp. He knew how to satisfy a woman."

I nodded some more.

"How's your husband?"

"I beg your pardon?" I squeaked.

"Sorry, dear, was I mumbling? Mrs. Harris says I'm always mincing up my words." In a louder voice, she said, "How's your husband? Is he enjoying working on the play?"

"Oh, yes, very much," I said, happy to change the subject. "He's always wanted to direct."

"That's nice. I do enjoy seeing you two together. So much in love. Just like Mr. Gamp and I were." She sighed. "He's been gone such a long time."

"I'm sorry," I said. "Was he ill?"

"No, dear, and that's a blessing. Mrs. Harris says being sick takes such a toll on a person's health. Mr. Gamp was making a delivery on wet roads and lost control of the car."

"I'm sorry," I said again. "My parents died in a car crash, too."

"It's hard to lose somebody suddenly, don't you think? Though at least it's quick. Not like some of the poor souls I see at the hospital. Lingering for weeks or even days before passing on."

"At least they get a chance to say good-bye to their families."

"Yes, and that's something I wish I could have had from my dear husband, but not if it meant he had to suffer. Like poor Barnaby Murdstone."

"I heard he lived quite a while after the accident."

"Over a week. Burns are so painful, but Barnaby truly believed that he'd get better, and that can make all the difference. The doctor had told him there was a chance he'd be home for Christmas, and Barnaby was hoping for that. He wouldn't admit it, but I think he was afraid that Santa Claus wouldn't find him if he was in the hospital." She smiled. "You don't often find a boy his age who still believes. I even helped him write a letter to Santa."

"That's sweet," I said, but I couldn't help but feel badly for the boy that Santa would never find.

"Now, now, dear," Mrs. Gamp said, "don't mourn for Barnaby. He's in a better place, just as Mr. Gamp and your parents are. I truly believe that."

"I do, too," I said, "but I still miss them."

"Just try to remember the good times. Every time I'm feeling lonely, I think about Mr. Gamp's last gift to me."

"What was that?"

"The dear man had signed up for a life insurance policy just before the accident, almost as if he'd known something was going to happen. I've been living off of the proceeds ever since."

"Really? That must have been some policy."

"With the baby coming, I'm sure you understand what a blessing security is. In fact, when Mr. Gamp passed away . . ." She stopped. "Anyway, it was such a relief when Miss Todger told me about it."

"Miss Todger?" I said. "Clara Todger?"

"Do you know her? My husband worked for the Todger family, and the policy was arranged through work. Every month the insurance company sends them a check, and then they send me one."

I nodded, but I couldn't believe that Mrs. Gamp was that naive. Didn't she know what the Todger family did, or where that money really came from? Though I didn't know much about bootlegging, I was fairly sure they didn't have group insurance plans. Besides, the payoff for life insurance was typically a lump sum, not monthly payments. While the settlement from my parents' death had paid most of my way through college, it had run out years before.

"You should be looking into insurance, too, for your little one.

You never know what could happen, so you have to plan for it." She patted my arm and said, "I have to get back to work now. Mrs. Harris says idle hands are the devil's work."

It was just as well that she left—I needed a few minutes to catch my breath. First, she'd given me far too much information about her relationship with Seth, but at least I was reasonably sure that she hadn't been a woman scorned after all. Then she turned around and gave me a much better motive for her to want Seth dead. Her husband must have been the Todger deliveryman who'd died. Not only had Mrs. Gamp been left a widow, but she'd lost her baby, too.

The question was, did Mrs. Gamp realize that Seth had been the cause of it all?

Chapter Nineteen

After all that, I needed a drink, even if it couldn't be anything stronger than water. I found Junior at the kitchen sink, elbow deep in soap suds.

"What are you doing?" I asked her.

"What does it look like I'm doing?"

It looked like she was washing dishes, which was completely out of character, but I didn't know if she'd appreciate my mentioning it. I reached into the refrigerator to get a bottle of water.

"Is that bottle sealed?" she asked before I could open it.

"I think so." I checked the plastic screw-top to be sure. "Why? What happened?"

"Nothing, but something almost did. I came in to get a cup of coffee, and was about to take a swallow when I noticed that it smelled funny."

"Poison?"

"I don't know about that, but there was something in there that wasn't supposed to be. It smelled like dishwasher soap."

"Is that dangerous?"

"Heck if I know, and even if it is, I don't imagine people would have drunk more than a swallow, but I'm taking no chances." She reached into the soapy water for the coffeemaker's glass pot and carefully rinsed it. "I'm going to warn people to be careful of what they leave open; I'm not eating or drinking anything that's been left unattended unless it's sealed."

I checked the screw top again, just to be sure, then opened it to take a drink. "This is crazy," I said.

"It's not the only thing I found while I was lurking. Jake's got a workshop backstage to put sets together, and I got to thinking that tools can be dangerous at the best of times. So I took a look and noticed that the guard on his circular saw was so loose it was just barely staying on."

"You lost me, Junior." In fact, she'd probably have lost me if she'd mentioned any tool other than hammer, pliers, or screwdriver.

"You know what a circular saw looks like?"

"Sort of."

"The guard is the round metal piece that covers up the blade until you start cutting. It's supposed to help you guide the saw and protect you from pieces flying up. If the guard fell off while you were using the saw, you'd probably ruin whatever it was you were working on, not to mention what it could do to your hand."

"Jesus, that's scary."

"Not as scary as knowing that there might be other traps that I haven't found yet." She finished washing up and dried off her hands. "I sure hope you've found something that will tell us who killed Seth."

"No such luck. All I've got is more maybes."

"Can't you come up with a yes or no once in a while?"

"How many definite answers have you come up with?"

"Only that I definitely hate practical jokes. What have you got?"

I told her about Tim first, ending with, "I know it's not much, but other than Clara Todger, he's the only one we've found who didn't like Seth."

"The only one who admits it, anyway," Junior pointed out. "Chances are that the killer wouldn't come out and say he hated the man."

"Granted. But I wish I knew what Tim had against Seth."

"We'll see what we can do about that," Junior said. "Who else?"

"Would you believe Mrs. Gamp?"

"At this point, I'd believe Mrs. Harris."

I told her what Aunt Nora had told me about Mrs. Gamp and Seth dating, then repeated what Mrs. Gamp had said about it.

"You are kidding me!" Junior said.

"I wouldn't have believed it myself if I hadn't heard it, but that's what she said."

Junior scratched her head. "Just when I think I've heard everything . . . Anyway, if she's the one who dumped Seth, doesn't that let her out of the running? Unless you think she was lying about it."

"I don't think she was. It was what she told me next that I'm thinking about." I explained how I'd figured out that Mrs. Gamp's late husband must have been Clara Todger's delivery man. "So she had a whopping big motive to kill Seth."

"Maybe," Junior said doubtfully.

"You don't think a hit-and-run makes a good motive? Not to mention the miscarriage."

"Sure, either of them could lead to payback when the emotions are running hot. But not this many years down the road."

"Revenge is a dish best served cold."

Junior raised an eyebrow.

"All right, it's hard to imagine Mrs. Gamp carrying a grudge all this time and not doing something about it."

"Not to mention the fact that she'd hardly have slept with the man if she'd known he killed her husband. So we've got no reason to believe Mrs. Gamp knew it was Seth who caused the accident. She didn't even know her husband was carting moonshine."

"It doesn't sound reasonable to me either, but you've got to admit that a grown woman with an imaginary friend might do unreasonable things now and then."

"There's crazy and then there's *crazy*."

"Is that something Mrs. Harris says?"

Junior didn't answer. "What else have you got?"

I ran through the other gossip I'd gotten from Aunt Nora, but without much enthusiasm.

Junior wasn't enthusiastic either. "Either Sid hit him for being absolutely right about his son a long time ago, or Big Bill got tired of trying to buy his property. Yeah, either one of those would drive me to kill a man."

"I'm doing the best I can," I said, irritated. "How did you think I work?"

"I didn't know, but I didn't expect you to come up with silly ideas like these."

"Why don't you go see what *you* can find out?" I snapped. I shouldn't have, but my feet were swelling and I was hungry again.

"Don't be that way, Laurie Anne," Junior said. "If this is the way you work, then that's the way we'll do it."

I didn't say anything.

"You want me to get you something to drink?"

"That might be nice," I allowed.

She fetched a bottle of cold water for me, a Coke for herself, and some cookies for us to share. "Do you feel better?" she asked once I'd eaten more than half of the cookies.

"Yes, thank you," I said sheepishly. "I'm sorry for snapping. Blame it on the hormones."

"That's all right. I'm sorry for calling your ideas silly."

"They were silly," I said. "At least, this batch was. Most of my theories are pretty outlandish. But when I dig into something, eventually something starts to make sense."

"And that'll be the answer?"

"Of course not. The sensible one is never the answer. It's always something even more ridiculous, which makes me feel like a complete idiot for not seeing it in the first place."

"This is something you do for fun?" Junior asked. "Why do you keep doing this, Laurie Anne?"

"Why do you?" I countered.

"It's my job."

"You could get another job."

"I suppose I could, but I like being a cop. The thing is, I like the whole job, not just solving murders. I don't think you're interested in the rest of what I do."

"You mean making traffic stops and breaking up bar fights and all?"

She nodded.

"No, I'm not interested in that."

"You do like being a programmer, don't you?"

"Absolutely. It's fun in a geeky way I won't even try to explain."

"So why do you keep getting tangled up in murder?"

I could have told her that I only did it because people asked me to. But that wouldn't have been honest. My family wouldn't have kept asking me if I'd told them not to. Well, maybe Vasti would have, but even she would have given up eventually. There was more to it than that. "You know what I think it is, Junior? The fact is, I'm a good programmer, but I'll never be a great programmer. There are fourteen-year-olds who can write more elegant code than I can, and they can write it faster, too."

"Are you serious?"

"Absolutely. The great programmers seem to be born to it, just like with other artists. I met some real-life geniuses in college, and that's when I realized that I just wasn't that good. Don't get me wrong. I do solid work, and I make my deadlines, and I can supervise projects. That's all important. But I'm not ever going to be anything *special* at work. The only time I feel like I'm special, that I'm doing something other people can't do, is when I'm trying to solve a murder."

"But other people do solve murders. Other than cops, I mean. I was talking to cops from other parts of the state one time, and they told me there's an older lady in Asheville who's a peach of a crime solver, and a judge near Raleigh. Charlotte's got a realtor and an antiques dealer."

"There are people other than Larry Bird who play basketball, but I bet he still feels special."

"You've got a point," she admitted, then paused for a minute. "Laurie Anne, you know I'm not sentimental and I'm not good with words. Heck, if it weren't for Hallmark, I wouldn't be able to wish my own mama happy Mother's Day. But I want to tell you something. You are special. Not just because of finding killers or programming or anything like that—it's because of who you are. The way you dropped everything to come down here so Richard could direct this play, and the way you help out your family when they need you, and the way you put yourself out for your friends. I think that's mighty special."

My eyes teared up, and it wasn't the hormones that time. "I don't know what to say."

"Good," she said firmly. "Because I sure as heck don't want to hear that you've repeated this to anybody else." She swigged down the last of her Coke. "Now let's get back to work."

"Can I hug your neck?" I asked.

"Lord, no." Then she relented. "All right, but don't expect a Christmas present from me!"

Chapter Twenty

O nce Junior had endured my hug, I was ready and raring to go. All I needed was a direction. "Any suggestions?" I asked Junior.

"We've still got the Murdstone brothers to talk to."

"I've been avoiding them," I said, wrinkling my nose. "I've questioned bereaved parents, siblings, and spouses without blinking, but I have a problem with the recently orphaned. It's probably because I wonder how I'd have felt if somebody had bothered me right after my parents died."

"I understand, but if we're going to do this . . ."

"I know, we've got to talk to David and Jake. Wouldn't it be better for you to talk to them solo? Having the two of us approach them might make them suspicious."

"Laurie Anne, do you think there's anybody in this building who doesn't know what we're up to?"

"All right, which one first?"

"Since David's onstage, and I don't think your husband would appreciate our taking him away, let's try Jake."

We found Jake in the workshop backstage. There was a board laid across two sawhorses to use as a table, and around it were scattered bits of wood and cloth and a miscellany of tools. Jake was carefully painting a freestanding fake fireplace.

"Hey, Jake," I said cheerily.

He turned our way briefly and said, "Hey," before turning back to his work.

I asked, "Is that Scrooge's fireplace?"

"Yep," he said, not looking up.

"It's very convincing. If somebody didn't know better, he'd try to set a real fire in there." Then I remembered how his son had died, and hastily added, "All the sets look great."

"Thanks."

A minute passed. I said, "Can I help you any?"

"You could hand me that rag on the table."

"Sure," I said, and did so. "Anything else?"

"Not a thing."

Junior and I stood there while Jake continued to paint. When I started to feel my feet swelling, I nudged Junior. She was the professional. Let her interrogate the man's back.

"Jake, I imagine you know Laurie Anne and I have been asking questions about your father's death," she said.

"That's what I hear. Mark Pope said I don't have to talk to you if I didn't want to."

"No, I suppose you don't," Junior said, "but why wouldn't you want to?"

"You wouldn't want to talk about it either if you were in my place," he said, his voice catching. "But your daddy's alive."

"Mine's not," I said softly. "We can't bring Seth back no matter what we do, but if it were my father, I'd do everything I could to find out what happened to him."

He stopped painting—stopped moving at all for a few seconds. Then he put his brush down, wiped his hands on the rag, and turned around. "All right. What can I tell you?"

Junior said, "Do you know why somebody would have wanted to kill your father?"

"Everybody liked Daddy."

"What about in his business?"

"You mean the chairs?" Jake asked, and I thought I heard sarcasm. Of course he must have known that Junior had wanted to arrest Seth for moonshining.

"In any of his business dealings," Junior said evenly.

"Daddy wasn't the kind of man to make enemies."

"Is that right? I hear he and your brother didn't always see eye to eye."

Jake flushed angrily. "That doesn't mean David would kill him!"

"You know I had to ask," Junior said.

He took a deep breath and said, "I guess you did."

"What about Florence?"

"Daddy wasn't against the marriage, if that's what you're asking. Even if he had been, that wouldn't have stopped them two. Daddy's only regret was that at their age they weren't likely to give him any more grandchildren." He paused. "Anything else?"

Junior looked at me.

I said, "I heard that Big Bill Walters was interested in buying your house, but that your father didn't want to sell."

"That's right, but there wasn't enough money involved to kill over."

"Are you going to sell the house now?"

He flushed again but answered me. "I haven't decided yet. I haven't decided much of anything."

"What about your father's business? I assume you inherit it."

"I get the business and the house, and David gets Daddy's insurance," he said tersely, "which comes out about even."

"Are you going to keep the business going?"

Jake looked me in the eye, as if trying to decide how much I knew about his business. "I expect I will. I don't know anything else. Just making chairs."

I mentally ran through our other suspects, but I couldn't think of anybody Jake would be able to tell us about. Apparently, Junior couldn't either.

"I guess that's it, then," she said. "Thank you for talking to us."

He didn't answer—just went back to his painting. I wanted to say something comforting to him, but there wasn't anything I could say.

Junior and I came out from backstage and found ourselves in the middle of a three-way argument involving Vasti, Aunt Maggie, and Carlelle.

"Why haven't you been keeping up with it?" Vasti was asking.

"I only volunteered to be in charge of props, and it's not a prop," Aunt Maggie said. "Scrooge's cane is part of his costume."

Vasti turned to Carlelle. "Then you should be keeping up with it."

"Maybe I should be, but I haven't been," she retorted. "I didn't make it, so I didn't store it."

"Don't tell me somebody booby-trapped Scrooge's cane, too," I said.

"How would I know?" Vasti snapped. "We don't even know where the foolish thing is."

"When was the last time anybody saw it?" Junior asked sharply.

"Big Bill says he never saw it, so Seth must have—I mean, it must have gotten misplaced in all the confusion. I could ask Jake to make another one, but . . ." Even Vasti must have realized how awkward that would be.

Aunt Maggie said, "I think I've got one Big Bill can borrow for the show. It won't be authentic, but—"

"I'm sure it will be fine," Vasti said. "Just make sure this one doesn't get lost."

The three of them went in separate directions, and I noticed Junior was looking speculative.

"Junior?" I said. "What did I miss?"

"I was just wondering about that cane."

"It sounds like the practical joker struck again."

"Maybe. But don't you remember Seth carrying that thing around all the time, practicing with it?" Then she answered herself. "No, of course not. You and Richard weren't here when Jake made it for him."

"What's your point?"

"I'm just wondering if Seth had it in his hand when he went for that last cigarette break. Because now that I think of it, that cane was just about the right thickness to make that dent in his skull."

"Lord, I bet you're right." I thought about it. "Then the murder must have been a spur-of-the-moment thing. Otherwise the killer would have brought something along to do the job."

"Not necessarily. The killer might have had something else in mind, but when he saw the cane, he decided to use it instead." Before I could object, she said, "But I think you're right. I've thought all along that this killing felt unplanned, and the cane as murder weapon just reinforces that. I just wish we could find the thing so we'd know for sure."

Junior wanted to talk to David after that, but there was no chance of that. Since all three Murdstones were going to be missing rehearsal the next day to get ready for Seth's visitation and funeral, Richard was making the most of Florence's and David's time by working on their scenes. Even when David wasn't onstage, he was staying close by Florence, obviously making sure she came to no harm.

With opening night just two days away, everybody else was working at a fevered pitch, too, so we decided to call it quits for the day. Junior did lurk some more, both to defuse any other practical jokes and to search for Scrooge's cane, but I spent the evening hemming a black robe for the Spirit of Christmas Yet to Be.

It was far too late when Richard finally shut things down for the night. I tried to bounce our ideas off him, which might have worked had he not been trying to bounce ideas for blocking off me. We finally decided that we both needed distraction, and went to bed to provide the best distraction we knew. We fell asleep immediately afterward.

Chapter
Twenty-one

At least the next morning started out well. I think the Murd-stones' absence improved the mood. I always feel kind of guilty having a good time when there are people in mourning nearby, and maybe others felt the same, because up until mid-morning, people were more enthusiastic than they'd been since we got into town.

Then Vasti showed up and things went downhill quickly. She started out griping because the program page proofs weren't ready yet, and she was sure Sally Hendon was behind the delay. Since she couldn't do anything about that, she laid into the triplets for not having the costumes ready, refusing to remember that rearranging the cast had slowed them down. Then she went after Aunt Maggie, because we still needed a coal scuttle and an artificial turkey, but Aunt Maggie gave her a look that shut her up pretty quickly.

Before she could find another target, Vasti's in-laws showed up. They were supposed to be watching Bitsy, but she was coming down with a cold and was refusing to take a bottle. So Vasti had to take her, and though I felt sorry for both mother and daughter, their combined whining started to get on everybody's nerves.

"She's got good lungs, hasn't she?" Junior said, talking loudly to be heard over the caterwauling.

"Do you mean Bitsy or Vasti?"

"Both, now that you mention it," she said.

If all that weren't enough, Sally Hendon picked that moment to
sail in, immaculately clad in pink as always. Bitsy had spit up on
Vasti twice, had thoroughly wrinkled her blouse by hanging on to
her and crying into her shoulder, and had yanked on Vasti's hair so
much that every bit of curl had fallen out. It was not Vasti's proudest
moment; Sally smiled broadly when she saw her.

"Oh, bless your heart," she cooed. "Is the baby not feeling well?"

Vasti glared at her. "What do you want?"

"Vasti, don't you think you should take that little darling home?
She needs her rest, and it looks like you could use a little down time
yourself."

Bitsy picked that moment to sneeze, messily, on Sally, which improved Vasti's spirits. "Actually, Bitsy loves being around people,"
she said with a smile. "Don't you want to hold her?"

Bitsy sneezed again and Sally hastily stepped back.

"I better not," she said. "I was wondering if you'd received any
more packages from Morris Costumes."

"Why would we?" Vasti asked suspiciously. "We already got what
we ordered. In fact, I've been meaning to ask you about that—"

"Shoot!" Sally said, cutting Vasti off. "I was hoping they'd delivered them here by mistake. Let me call my stage manager again."
She pulled a cell phone—pink, of course—out of her pocketbook,
and dialed a number. "Lil? This is Sally."

Vasti glowered, both because Sally had ignored her question and
because Lil was another Junior League member who could have
helped vote Vasti in.

Sally said, "Has that box shown up? The one with the musicians'
costumes? . . . It has? All of them? . . . Are you sure they're going to
fit? You know what a big man Roger Bailey is. . . . Wonderful. I'll be
back over there in two shakes. Bye, now." She put the phone back
in her purse and said, "Silly me. The costumes were there all along.
I'm so sorry to have interrupted you when I know how far behind
y'all must be."

"Why do you have costumes for the Ramblers?" Vasti asked.

"Haven't you heard? They're going to be playing in the Follies."

Vasti's face turned bright red. Roger's Ramblers was Byerly's only group of professional musicians, and they were a big draw at any local event. Roger was also our uncle, so for him to be playing in Sally's show was adding insult to injury.

"Aunt Ruby Lee said they were booked all month!" Vasti said.

"I guess they had a cancelation," said Sally, smiling so much like the cat who ate the canary that I was surprised there weren't feathers between her teeth. "I've been meaning to ask you, Vasti. What kind of music are you having for your show?"

"It's a play, not a musical," Vasti snapped. "We don't need music."

"That's funny. The version of the script I looked at said there was supposed to be music before and after the show."

"What?" Vasti shot a look at Richard onstage.

Richard said, "Traditionally, there is music while the audience is seated, and sometimes Scrooge leads the audience in a carol at the end, but it's not necessary."

"I suppose you can use a tape," Sally said sweetly. "That would be almost as good as real music."

"We're having live music, too," Vasti declared.

"Really? If you like, maybe I can help you find somebody."

"I can find somebody myself. In fact, I've already got somebody in mind."

"Who?" Sally wanted to know.

Vasti assumed an air of mystery. "It's a surprise."

Sally hesitated, probably trying to decide if Vasti was bluffing, but finally said, "I can't wait to hear who you get."

"Buy a ticket," Vasti said ungraciously, "and you can find out."

"Oh, I'll be here, ready to help out with any last-minute problems you have come opening night."

"There won't be—" But I guess Vasti realized that she might be tempting fate. "You go tend to your own show." Then she looked around for a handy victim. "Odelle, would you walk Sally to her car? I don't want any more practical jokes."

"Whatever do you mean?" Sally said, but Vasti grabbed her cell phone and started dialing. Realizing she'd lost her audience, Sally let Odelle accompany her to her car.

As soon as she was gone, Vasti put down the phone and said, "All right, who around here can sing or play an instrument?"

"Vasti," Richard said, "the play really doesn't need music. Or maybe we can use a Victrola—that's what one version of the play calls for."

"I *said* we're having live music," Vasti said in a tone that brooked no argument.

"If that's what you want," Richard said, sounding exasperated, "but you'll have to handle that part yourself. I've got my hands full already."

"Fine," Vasti snapped. With Bitsy on one shoulder, she got out her address book and started thumbing through it furiously while Richard went back to his scene.

Junior came over, looking alarmed. "We better get out of here."

"What's the matter?"

"Your cousin is on a rampage. Five will get you ten that in a few minutes she'll be dragging people together to make them sing. I'm a terrible singer, Laurie Anne."

"You can't be that bad," I said.

"Have you ever heard someone run their nails down a blackboard?"

I nodded.

"I'm worse."

"Then don't worry. Vasti won't try to force you."

"Are you sure about that? She's got that same look Daddy gets on Christmas Eve when he hasn't found a present for Mama."

I looked at my cousin, and sure enough, she was already asking Mrs. Gamp if she knew the words to "God Rest Ye Merry, Gentlemen." "Where do you want to go?"

"Anywhere but here."

I grabbed my pocketbook and coat, waved to get Richard's attention, and mouthed the words *we're going out*. Vasti called my name as we headed for the door, but I pretended I hadn't heard. We didn't stop until we were out of the parking lot.

"We weren't doing any good in there, anyway," I said. "The one we really need to talk to is David."

"He's probably at home," Junior pointed out. "We could go pay him a visit."

"We can't just barge in and start questioning him. Especially not today. They're burying his father tomorrow."

"In this line of work, I can't always afford to be sensitive."

"You're a cop. Nobody expects you to be sensitive."

"Thanks."

"Sorry. What I mean is that people will forgive you if you bypass the niceties. If I do, I'll get grief for the next umpteen years." Five years earlier, I'd worn black to a wedding, and even though people did it all the time in Boston, it wasn't done in Byerly, and I still heard about it every time anybody planned a wedding. "Of course, it is acceptable to go calling if we bring food."

Junior looked at me sideways. "We don't have to cook it ourselves, do we? My cooking is as bad as my singing."

"I think we could get away with buying something." I wasn't a bad cook, but I wasn't interested in spending a lot of time in the kitchen. "They've always got nice fruit baskets at the grocery store this time of year. Let's go get one of them."

It was still early in the day, so the store wasn't crowded, and it didn't take us but a few minutes to find what we wanted.

As we walked back to the car, I saw a familiar face. "Looks like your deputy is on foot patrol," I said to Junior.

She looked over to where Mark Pope was leaned up against a car, drinking a cup of coffee. "The criminals of Byerly must be shaking in their boots," she said in disgust. "Not that we've done a whole lot of good ourselves."

"The day is young," I said, determined to be cheerful. "Come to think of it," I said, "the day's a bit young to go to David's house, don't you think?"

She checked her watch. "You're right. I don't think it would be polite to go over there until ten, eleven o'clock. Any suggestions?"

"Nothing to do with the case," I admitted, "but how would you like to go to the mall in Hickory?"

"Laurie Anne, please don't make me go to the mall during Christmas season."

"Come on, Junior, it'll be fun. How crowded can it be on a Wednesday morning?"

At least, that was what I thought. As we circled the parking lot at the Valley Hills Mall, trying to find a reasonably close spot, I admitted that I might have been overly optimistic. But I still needed to get some stocking stuffers for Richard, and unlike Junior, I enjoy Christmas shopping. So I sweet-talked her into continuing to look for a space, with promises of a treat from Charleston Cookie Company.

On the third or fourth circuit, I said, "Junior, look!"

"Is somebody pulling out?"

"No, but look over there. Isn't that Mark again? In that green Saturn."

She peered through parked cars. "Yes, it is. What's he doing here?"

"Shopping?"

She shook her head. "Trey has a dentist appointment today and won't be on duty until six. Mark's on his own, which means he shouldn't be outside the city limits, let alone in Hickory—and he's not even in the squad car."

It suddenly dawned on me. "Junior, he's following us."

"I think you're right."

"He's sure going to be disappointed when he figures out we're just shopping. Unless you want to borrow a camcorder so we can videotape him neglecting his duty and show it to the city council."

"It's tempting, but he'd come up with some excuse or another." Then she grinned. "Want to have some fun?"

"I'd love to."

The parking place gods must have approved, because just that second, a station wagon pulled out in front of us. Junior parked, but we stayed in the car long enough to plan, and to give Mark a chance to find a place to leave his car.

Then, with much ostentatious looking around and whispers, we headed inside the mall. Mark walked down the next row, hunched over as if that would keep us from seeing him over the roofs of the parked cars. The funny thing was, if he'd just walked normally, we probably wouldn't have noticed him, but walking like that made him painfully obvious.

Once inside, Junior and I led the poor fellow on the wildest goose chase we could manage. We synchronized our watches, shared significant looks, and exchanged hand signals. We'd stop suddenly at window displays, and just as suddenly take off again. I made a point of asking half a dozen people for the time, trying to make it seem as if something more meaningful were being said. Junior made two or three cell phone calls, then switched to pay phones, as if she were trying to avoid being traced. Then we split up, just to see which one he'd follow.

Mark looked terribly confused, but he finally decided to take off after Junior. That gave me time to do what I'd wanted to do in the first place, which was shop.

I quite enjoyed myself despite the crowds. The mall was festooned with garlands and lights, with a very credible Santa Claus holding court in the middle of the mall. I imagined Richard and me in another year, taking our baby to get a picture taken on Santa's lap, and had a hard time resisting the impulse to buy something made of velvet and ruffles to put on a baby that hadn't even been born yet.

It was also a relief to get my thoughts away from Seth's murder. What with the last-minute trip and the play, Richard and I hadn't had much time to savor the holiday season, and it did me good to remember the message the three Spirits had brought to Scrooge.

An hour and a half later, I went to meet Junior and found her in the food court, sipping a Coke and looking mighty satisfied.

"Didn't you buy anything?" I asked her.

"Just this Coke and a bottle of water for you. It looks like you bought enough for both of us." She took my shopping bags so I could sit down. "Is all of this for Richard?"

"Most of it," I said sheepishly.

She looked into one bag, pulled out my new pocketbook, and raised one eyebrow. "I didn't realize that the men in Boston were carrying pocketbooks."

"That's for me. Belk had a sale on them—it's a D'Arcy Designs. It cost less than half what it would in Boston."

"And this?" she said, pulling out a music CD.

"It's Christmas music," I said defensively. "Richard likes Kathé Ward's songs, too."

"I'm sure he does." She reached for the bag from Tamsin's Toy Chest, but I took it from her before she could open it. "That's a surprise. So where's our tail? Or did he give up?"

"Nope, he's over there by that planter. He looked so worn out, I sat down early so he could catch his breath."

"Where have the two of you been?" I asked.

"Where haven't we been?" she said. "I think we must have walked every foot of this mall, not to mention three rides on the merry-go-round."

"He followed you onto the merry-go-round?"

"He wanted to, but he settled for finding a column he could duck behind every time I came around." She shook her head. "I bet that now he thinks he should have followed you instead." She checked her watch. "Are you about ready to head back to Byerly? I think we've tormented him enough."

I finished up the bottle of water. "Just let me take a quick pit stop." Darned if Mark didn't follow me to the ladies' room. In fact, he was so busy watching me instead of looking where he was going, that he almost came inside.

Junior and a semi-hidden Mark were waiting when I came out, and we all headed for the door. There was a bench right next to it, and I nonchalantly dropped the bag from the toy store on it and kept going.

"I thought that was my Christmas present," Junior said.

"It is, in a way." As I'd expected, Mark saw me leave the bag and couldn't wait to grab it. I started snickering on the way back to the car.

"What's so funny?" Junior wanted to know. "What's in that bag?"

"An official junior detective kit," I said. "I figured Mark could use all the help he can get."

Junior burst out laughing, and then we drove by Mark's car. He was in the front seat with the detective kit in his hand, and the expression on his face started us laughing all over again.

"Laurie Anne," Junior said, "we have got to go shopping together more often."

Chapter
Twenty-two

Though we kept a sharp eye out on the drive back to Byerly, apparently Mark had quit following us, so we went to David and Florence's house.

I wasn't sure what David did, but whatever it was, it paid well. Or maybe Florence's law practice brought in the money. They had a large, white shingle house in the nicest part of town, just two doors down from the Walters estate, which was the benchmark for society in Byerly.

There were a couple of cars already in the circular driveway, but Junior thought the BMW was David's and the MG was Florence's—meaning that we'd caught them at home and alone, which was what we wanted.

After we rang the door chime, I looked doubtfully at the grocery store fruit basket I was carrying. "Are you sure this is nice enough, Junior?"

"Social niceties are your department, remember?"

Florence opened the door then, and her smile of delight reassured me. Though I didn't quite believe her when she said it was the prettiest fruit basket she'd ever seen, at least I could be sure that she hadn't been insulted by our offering.

"Y'all come right on in," she said, taking the basket from us. "David was just saying he could use a break, and I know he's going to dig right into one of these lovely tangerines."

"I hope we're not interrupting anything," I said.

"Not at all. We've just been checking e-mail and voice mail. I'm afraid we've been so distracted by all that's been going on, that we've neglected our businesses terribly."

"I'm sure everybody understands that."

"Of course they do, but one does like to live up to one's obligations."

As we spoke, Florence led us down the entry hall with its sparkling chandelier and mirror-polished black and white tiles, through a living room that was far too big to be as cozy as it was, and into a kitchen that was as large as the Todger family's but far more modern.

"You go ahead into the sun room and let me get y'all something to drink," Florence said. "Iced tea? Maybe a Coca-cola? Or would coffee be better on a cold day like this?"

"A Coke would be great," Junior said.

"I don't suppose your iced tea is decaffeinated, is it?" I asked wistfully.

"I've got both kinds. Y'all go have a seat and tell David to shut down his computer for a minute or two."

David must have heard his wife, because he was already rising to greet us when we came into what Florence had called the sun room. It was another spacious room, with two desks and accompanying office furniture in one half, and a wicker love seat and chairs in the other half. Both sides were lined with hanging baskets of plants and flowers, including poinsettias and a blooming Christmas cactus.

"Junior, Laurie Anne. How nice of you two to come by. Did I hear Florence say you'd brought us something?"

"Just a little fruit basket," I said. "So you'd have something to snack on."

"It was so kind of you to think of us. Please, come sit down and visit for a while."

The two of them were so gracious, I almost felt guilty. But my rational side reminded me that if either of them had killed Seth, I had nothing to feel guilty about. And if not, surely they'd want his murderer found, so I still had nothing to feel guilty about.

When Junior took one of the chairs, I sat in the other to leave the love seat for David and Florence. Sure enough, after Florence brought us our drinks, she promptly cuddled up next to him.

"How are things back at rehearsal?" Florence asked.

"A little rocky," I admitted, and explained how Vasti was trying to find somebody to play or sing as part of the play.

"Goodness," Florence said, "your cousin is so energetic."

"That's Vasti, all right," I said wryly. "She never gives up when she really wants something."

"That must be a family trait," Florence said, a twinkle in her eye. "I think we all know this isn't just a condolence call."

"No, it's not," I said. "I know y'all realize that Junior and I are looking into Seth's death."

"That's what Florence told me," David said, "but I have to admit that I'm not comfortable with the idea. I can understand your interest, Junior—it must be frustrating to be sidelined during an investigation. But Laurie Anne . . ." He shook his head, as if disappointed in me. "I can't say how much the thought of making my father's death into some sort of game pains me."

I flushed, half in anger and half in shame that he might be right, but before I could say anything in my own defense, Junior spoke.

"That's where you're wrong," she said. "Laurie Anne doesn't think Seth's death was anything other than what it was: murder. Now there are people in this world who could see a man drowning and not jump in to save him, or see an old lady fall and not stop to help her up. Not Laurie Anne. She knows that somebody killed your daddy, and that Mark might not be able to find out who it is. So she's not going to sit by and let a murderer go free. Here she is five months pregnant, but instead of knitting booties, she's spending every minute trying to get a murderer off the streets. Maybe you call that playing a game, but I don't!"

I don't know who was more astonished by Junior's outburst,

David or me. He stammered, "I had no idea that—I mean, I thought that—" Finally he gathered himself together. "I beg your pardon, Laurie Anne. Please forgive me."

"That's all right. I know my snooping around is kind of weird, but—"

"No, not at all. Now that I can appreciate what you're trying to do, please tell me what I can do to help."

"Me, too," Florence chimed in.

They gave me their full attention, and it made me downright nervous. After Junior's build-up, I was sure they expected a brilliant bunch of questions, and mine were bound to disappoint them. "My first question is the obvious one. Why would anybody have wanted to kill your father?"

"I just don't know," David said. "My father had no enemies. I can't even think of anybody who didn't like him."

"That fits in with what I've heard elsewhere, with only one exception." Actually, there were two, but I didn't think Junior would want me to bring Clara Todger into the conversation. "Tim Topper didn't care for him."

"Really?" David sounded sincerely surprised. "I didn't think Tim had ever met Dad before we started rehearsals, and they seemed to get along. They even went out together one night."

"Maybe I misunderstood," I said, though I didn't think so. Tim was one of those folks who let their feelings show, and the feelings he'd shown about Seth hadn't been friendly ones.

"In fact," David said, "I'd be a more likely candidate than Tim. Not that I wanted Dad dead," he quickly added, "but it's no secret that we didn't agree about everything."

Florence chuckled. "You didn't agree about anything."

"I'm afraid not. Even though we were both in town, we didn't see each other all that often. I regret it, but the best explanation I can give is that my father and I were very different men, and we wanted different things in life."

"Do you mean in terms of Seth's business?" I said carefully.

For the first time, David wouldn't meet my eyes. "That was an old argument. Dad had always assumed that once I finished school,

I'd go into business with him and Jake. Unfortunately, I had no interest in . . . in furniture."

"Or in moonshine," Florence said.

"Dear Lord!" David's face turned white. "How did you . . . ?" Then, "Not in front of—"

"Pish," Florence said, waving her hand airily. "Junior already knows, and I'd be very much surprised if Laurie Anne didn't, too. So why pussyfoot around?"

"But . . ." Words failed him.

"Poor darling, I didn't mean to spring it on you this way, but I've known for ages that your father wasn't supporting himself making lawn furniture. I've sat in his chairs. There's no way he could have raised a dog on them, let alone two boys. But don't worry. It's still a closely guarded secret. My source is completely discreet, and I'm sure these ladies are, too."

"You knew before the wedding?"

"Of course."

"And you married me anyway?"

"David Murdstone, I'd have married you if your father were General Sherman come back from the grave to burn down Byerly."

"Oh Florence . . . I'm so sorry I didn't tell you, but I was afraid. Not just because of your place in society—"

"Pish to that!" Florence said.

"But you're an officer of the court. I didn't want to compromise your position."

"I thought as much, which is why I don't blame you for keeping your secret." She waggled her finger. "As long as you don't keep any more secrets from me."

"Never," he said, catching her hand to bring it to his lips.

While still holding his wife's gaze, David said, "I'm sorry, Laurie Anne, but I don't think there's anything else I can tell you."

"I hear Big Bill Walters wanted to buy your father's land," I said.

"He did, but my father told him he wasn't interested in selling for a few years, and Big Bill was willing to wait."

"Didn't your father have an argument with Sid Honeywell?"

"That was years ago. Dad bought gas at Sid's station every week."

"What about Mrs. Gamp?"

"What about her?"

"Never mind." I looked at Junior, who shrugged. "I guess there's nothing else we need to ask you. Unless either of y'all know of anything."

"No," they said in unison.

"We'll let ourselves out," Junior said, and neither Florence nor David argued the point. They were still looking deeply into one another's eyes when we left the room, and we got out of the house as quickly as we could.

"I wonder if that love seat folds out into a bed," Junior said once we were back in the car. "Not that that would stop them."

"Junior Norton, you ought to be ashamed."

"Ashamed! Hell, I'm jealous. You might be, too, if you didn't have Richard."

"I didn't realize you were in the market for a husband."

"Do you think I want to stay single my whole life? I'm not in a hurry, but it'd be nice to have somebody to come home to."

"Kids, too?"

"Sure, why not?"

I couldn't help but picture a pregnant Junior with a gun belt stretched across her maternity smock. Then I thought about her under the sway of hormones, which was scary. My own mood swings were terrifying enough, and unlike Junior, I didn't carry a gun.

Junior must have misinterpreted my silence, because she said, "You're not going to start fixing me up, are you? My sisters keep dragging single men over to meet me, and it's worrying me to death."

"Of course not. Though I do know a guy—"

"Laurie Anne, you've got the right to be silent, and I advise you to take advantage of it."

I didn't push it any further. After all, Junior was well equipped to track down a man for herself. Instead I said, "I appreciate what you said in there."

"Daddy always told me to say whatever it takes to get a suspect talking."

"Oh," I said, disappointed. "Does that mean you don't—"

"Of course," Junior said, interrupting me, "this time all I had to say was God's honest truth."

"Thank you, Junior."

"You're welcome. But no hugs!"

Chapter
Twenty-three

Junior was still worried that Vasti was going to try to get her to sing, so instead of heading straight for the recreation center, she talked me into having lunch with her at Birmingham Bill's Burritos. Though Alabama isn't known for authentic Mexican food, the burritos were excellent and, unfortunately for Junior's anxiety, quite fast.

We needn't have worried. By the time we got back, Vasti had arranged for the First Baptist Church children's choir to sing at all three performances of the play. Not only were we going to have the live music, but this guaranteed that every one of those children's parents, grandparents, and other relations would buy a ticket to the play just to see their little ones singing in their holiday finest.

The cast and crew were eating lunch when we arrived, so I dragged Richard away long enough to tell him what Junior and I had been up to. He was as surprised as we'd been to find out that Florence knew about the moonshining, and he nearly fell off his chair when I told him what we'd done to Mark.

Once he caught his breath, he said, "Are you sure it was wise to make an enemy of him that way? As Dickens said, 'Never be mean in anything; never be false; never be cruel.' *David Copperfield*, Chapter Fifteen."

"Copperfield never had to deal with Mark Pope. Has he been around today?"

"I don't think so—at least, he hasn't interrupted anything."

"How's the rehearsal going?"

He looked pleased. "I probably shouldn't say this, but I think we're actually going to pull it off. We're still rough on a couple of scenes, and the blocking isn't quite right at Fezziwig's party, but we just might make it."

"Hey, what are you worrying about? You've got two more days."

"Easy for you to say. I'm the one stuck cracking the whip over these people. I doubt any of them will want to talk to me by the time this is done."

"I bet they're grateful you're making them look good." Oliver Jarndyce picked that moment to walk by, glaring at Richard. "Most of them, anyway. I'm sorry I haven't been here to lend support."

"That's all right. I just wish I'd been able to help you out. Though it looks as if you and Junior make a good team."

That last part sounded wistful. "It's okay," I said, "but not nearly as much fun as working with you. She doesn't quote anybody except her daddy, and she won't let me hug her, and—"

"Does this mean I get to play Doctor Watson next time?"

"Honey, you can play doctor with me anytime," I said, fluttering my eyelashes.

Once rehearsal started up again, Junior decided to have another lurk, just in case our practical joker had struck again. I wasn't convinced that the jokes had anything to do with Seth's murder, but I was sure I was tired of them. I still couldn't lurk, of course, so I wandered around.

With opening night coming closer, people had begun to overcome their reluctance to go down the hall where Seth had died, and the triplets were working in the dressing rooms. I saw Carlelle working furiously at her sewing machine in the women's dressing room while Idelle added flounces to a bonnet, so I decided not to disturb them. When I passed by the men's dressing room, Odelle saw me and said, "Hey, Laurie Anne, can you give me a hand?"

Odelle had Tim Topper in front of a makeup mirror and was applying a heavy coat of foundation. "What do you think of this color?" she asked me.

I took a look. "The color's fine, but isn't the makeup kind of thick?"

"It has to be," she explained. "Stage lights are so bright that he'll get washed out if I don't put it on like that."

"Right," I said, remembering how long it took Richard to clean up after a performance. "In that case, he looks good." I wasn't sure if Tim had already given his opinion, or if he even got to voice one. "How's it going, Tim?"

"Fine. Though after this, I've got a whole new appreciation for what you ladies go through with your makeup."

I looked at the table in front of him, which was covered with a rainbow of greasepaint, brushes of all sizes, triangle sponges, false eyelashes, spirit gum, crepe hair, and a big cake of powder. "Tim," I said, "I've never worn this much makeup in my entire life."

He started to smile, but Odelle said, "Don't move your face!"

"Sorry," he said, through unmoving lips.

Odelle smudged pinky-brown greasepaint under Tim's cheeks and then smoothed it into his skin. "How's that? Do you think it gives his face more shape?"

"Absolutely. It looks great."

"It does, doesn't it? I better change it."

"Why?"

"Because this makeup is for the first scene, when he's about to freeze to death while working in Scrooge's office. He shouldn't look this good. But I can use these colors for Bob's happy scenes, like during Christmas dinner and when Scrooge gives him a raise."

"I had no idea makeup was so complicated," I said, impressed by the level of detail.

"Oh, it's not that bad," she said modestly. "I love fooling around with makeup. If a woman really knows what she's doing, she'll never need a facelift."

"Really?" I looked at my own face in the mirror, wondering if Odelle would have time to give me a pointer or two once the play was over.

"Could you get me that notebook over there?"

"Sure." The notebook was a thick three-ring binder that was bristling with dividers. "What is it?"

"It's our makeup bible. We write down what colors each person takes for foundation and blush and all, so that we'll be able to do it in a hurry for the performance. Take a look."

I thumbed through it and was impressed again. Not only was every character's makeup described, but Odelle had even pasted in photos of each person before and after makeup, along with notes like "Add bags under the eyes," and "Bring out eyes." For the actors playing more than one role, like Florence and David, both sets of makeup were in the book. I said, "This must have taken forever to do."

"Not as much time as it would take to recreate everything later on. Could you write some notes down on Tim's page? My hands are covered in makeup, and I don't want to get the book dirty."

"Sure." I found the page for Tim and dutifully printed the color names Odelle read out to me. Then she told me how to use the instant camera so I could add a photo of Tim's "happy" makeup to the book.

While I took care of that, Odelle wiped Tim's face clean with healthy amounts of cold cream and started all over again with makeup designed to make him look miserable.

I hung around, both because I thought Odelle might need me to take more notes and because it really was interesting. I looked at the pictures in the notebook, amazed by how much difference a color choice or a drawn line could make in a person's appearance.

The actors were in order of appearance, naturally enough, so I looked at the page for Scrooge first. If Odelle had worked up makeup for Seth, she'd already taken it out of the book, because only Big Bill was included. I was amused to see that they hadn't had to do much to change his appearance.

Next was Tim, and then three pictures of David: as himself, as Scrooge's nephew Fred, and as the young Scrooge. At first glance, it looked like three different men. Of course, there were plenty of characteristics that couldn't be changed, so I had no doubt that it was all David.

It was while looking at Tim's and David's pictures that I noticed something. The two men looked a whole lot more alike than I'd realized before. Though Tim's face was fuller, probably from sampling his own barbecue, both men's cheekbones had that slant that usually means American Indian blood. Their noses were almost the same shape, and their eyes were the same shade of hazel. Even their eyebrows were shaped alike. The longer I looked at the pictures, the more I noticed how much the two men favored one another. In fact, if I hadn't known better, I'd have said . . .

I stopped the thought and went from just looking at the pictures to flat-out staring at Tim, mentally cataloging David's features. It was while I was comparing the shape of their earlobes that Tim caught my eye. Despite Odelle's complaints, he turned around in his seat until he could see the page of the notebook I was looking at, and I could tell that he knew exactly what I was thinking.

Odelle turned him back around long enough to add one more puff of powder and announced, "Tim, that's how we're going to do you for the first scene. All I need to do is take another picture and you're done."

I don't think Odelle noticed that Tim didn't say a word while she finished up with him, but she did look surprised when he said she didn't need to wash the makeup off. He left the room with it still on, and I excused myself to follow him.

He was walking away quickly, and I nearly had to run to catch up with him. "Tim, can we talk for a minute?"

"What about?" he said.

I just looked at him and he nodded. Nobody was in the room Aunt Maggie was using to store props, so we went in there.

Once the door was safely shut behind us, I said, "How long have you known?"

"Known what?"

"How long have you known that Seth Murdstone was your father?"

Chapter
Twenty-four

Tim leaned up against the Cratchits' dining room table and shook his head ruefully. "I should have known you'd figure it out."

"It took me long enough." In fact, I was embarrassed by how long it had taken. For years I'd bragged to Richard about how good I was at spotting family resemblances, but I'd missed it completely with those two, and I knew that if David hadn't been white and Tim black, I'd have caught it right off. Talk about being color-blind! "How did you find out?"

"He told me—Seth, I mean. You'll excuse me if I don't call him 'Daddy.' " He looked disgusted at the thought. "It was right after we started rehearsing the play. I was a little worried when Vasti gave me the part—a lot of people wouldn't want a black man playing a white role. But Seth was real nice and seemed interested in talking to me. Then he asked me out for a drink after the second night of rehearsal. I thought he'd bring his boys along—at least Jake—but it was just the two of us. We met over at Dusty's—you know Dusty's, don't you?"

I nodded. It was a hole in the wall, but since it was just outside the gates to the mill, it was the favorite place to get a beer after shift's end.

Tim said, "There weren't many people in there at that time of night, and Seth got us a booth in the back. He'd said he just wanted to talk about the play and relax, but I could tell he had something on his mind. He was kind of agitated, and drank down the first beer like it was water. He was working on his second when he started asking me questions about Mama and what it was like growing up without a father."

"Didn't you think that was kind of odd?"

"Naturally, and after I'd talked a little, I asked him if he'd known Mama."

"What did he say?"

Tim's mouth turned down as if he'd tasted a bad batch of barbecue sauce. "He said he'd known her real well, and that there was something he wanted to tell me. That's when he said it: 'I'm your father, Tim.' Like it was something to be proud of."

"What did you do? What did you say?"

"I didn't say anything. Hell, Laurie Anne, I didn't know what to say. He told me how he and Mama had done business together, and how one thing had led to another late one night. I think it was just the one time. He said he didn't even find out she'd gotten pregnant until after I was born."

"Did you believe him?"

"I wasn't sure."

"Did he ever try to see you? Or to do the right thing by you and your mother?"

"A white man marry a pregnant black girl? Back then?" He snorted. "Hell, I don't know many who'd do it now."

"I suppose not," I agreed sadly.

"Besides, he was married at the time and already had the two boys."

"Still, he could have done something. Sent y'all money, at least."

"He said he waited for Mama to contact him, and when she didn't, he figured she didn't want anything from him."

"Right," I said, rubbing my belly. I couldn't imagine Richard just waiting around for somebody to ask him to bear responsibility for his child. He'd do it no matter what. Nor could I imagine an unmarried black girl crossing over to the white side of town to beg for what was due her and her child. "What a weasel."

"He hinted that he wasn't sure he was the father, but I stopped that talk right then and there. I don't have any idea that Mama was a saint, but she wasn't a tramp, either."

"I've never heard one word against your mother," I said firmly. "He had no right to imply that."

"To give him credit, he did apologize. He said he'd been immature and that he'd been worried about what people would do if they found out. His wife was sick, and he was afraid of what knowing about me would do to her. Besides, he had his sons—his other sons—to think of. I could understand that."

"He's had plenty of time to come up with excuses," I said cynically.

"Maybe so. Anyway, he said that he wanted to make up for his mistake by us getting to know one another."

"Did you want that?"

"I wasn't sure, Laurie Anne. I've wanted a father my whole life. I had Uncle Eb, of course, but I always knew he wasn't my real daddy. Maybe Seth wasn't the kind of daddy I'd dreamed of, but I could look at him and see part of myself. He was blood, and I thought that meant something."

I nodded. Goodness knows, I'd put up with a lot from my own relatives for no better reason than our blood connection.

Tim said, "I told him I needed to think about it, and he said he understood. When I got up to leave, I think he wanted to hug me, but all I could manage was a handshake." He shook his head. "If I'd known the truth, I wouldn't even have done that."

"What do you mean?"

"The next morning, I talked to Uncle Eb and Aunt Fezzie. They'd always said that they didn't know who my father was, and even though I believed them, I've always felt like they knew more than they would say. So I didn't let up on them until they told me everything." He looked down. "Then I almost wished I hadn't asked."

I didn't know what to say to that, so I waited for him to go on.

"They had told me the truth, Laurie Anne. They didn't know who my father was. But they did know what happened to Mama."

"I don't understand."

"Part of what Seth told me was true. The night it happened, Mama told Uncle Ed and Aunt Fezzie that she was going to meet with somebody about buying something for the bar. They thought it was liquor, but once they knew it was Seth, they realized that he must have wanted to sell her some furniture."

Actually, they'd probably been right the first time, but I didn't say anything. Maybe I'd eventually tell Tim about Seth being a moonshiner, but it wasn't the right time yet.

"Mama and Seth met after the bar was closed," Tim said, "and had a few drinks. Then they had a few more. I always wondered why Mama was so down on drinking when she ran a bar, and now I know. She took one drink too many that night, and the next thing she remembered, she was waking up with her clothes all over the place while Seth got dressed."

"Did he rape her?" I asked softly.

"I don't know if you would call it rape or not. What Aunt Fezzie said was that he took advantage of her. Mama wasn't exactly sure herself how it happened. She might have gone along with it, her being drunk and all. I don't know for sure that he forced her."

"Still, the best you could say for him was that he was a married man who got a single woman drunk and seduced her."

Tim nodded. "Mama was pretty much sober by the time he left, and he kissed her goodbye and said he'd call her."

"Did he?"

"What do you think? The next time she heard anything out of him was the Fourth of July picnic a few weeks later. She saw him at the park and then went in his direction. By then she had a pretty good idea she was pregnant, and she wanted to tell him about it. But she felt funny going up to him, him being married and white, so she was hanging back, waiting for him to see her. But before he did, she heard him talking. About her."

"Oh, Lord," I said, sickened. Though I knew comparing notches in the belt was considered normal male behavior in some circles, I'd never understood it.

"Not by name," Tim said, "and in a way, that made it worse. Seth was talking about the 'brown sugar' he'd had, and how he was going to get himself some more that night if the 'bitch' hadn't gone off with somebody else."

"Your poor mother," I said. "What did she do?"

"What could she do? She couldn't confront a white man in public, not without everybody finding out what she'd done. So she went back home and cried it out of her system."

"Bless her heart."

"Aunt Fezzie said Mama promised herself she'd never let it happen again. I don't think it would have made much difference to her life if it hadn't been for me."

"She never told him about you?"

"After hearing him talk about her that way, the last thing she wanted was to have him as part of her life or mine. Besides, she figured he'd just deny that he was the father. She couldn't afford a lawyer, so she just decided to raise me on her own, and that's what she did."

"She must have been one strong woman. I can't imagine having a baby all alone." I patted my tummy absently. "I can just barely imagine doing it with Richard."

"You're going to be a fine mama, and I know Richard is going to be a good daddy," Tim assured me, "but Seth wasn't any kind of daddy, leastways, not to me. At the next rehearsal, he came looking for me, wanting to know if I'd thought about what he'd said. I told him I'd found out what really happened with Mama, and that I didn't want anything more to do with him. After that, I don't think I spoke another word to him other than the lines Dickens wrote."

"I'm surprised that you didn't quit the show."

"I thought about it, but I didn't want to let Seth take anything away from me." Then he half-smiled. "I was enjoying myself too much. I'd always wanted to try out for community theater, but with the restaurant and taking classes at night, I've never been able to. I wouldn't have done it this time if your cousin hadn't talked me into it. I sure didn't want to let her down by backing out at the last minute."

"I know Vasti appreciates it. And Richard has been raving about what a good job you've been doing."

"Is that a fact?" he said, smiling more broadly. "Now that Big Bill is playing Scrooge, I think we're going to have ourselves a pretty good show." Then, as if remembering why we'd gotten a new Scrooge, he got serious again. "Anyway, now you know why I didn't have any use for Seth Murdstone."

"I don't blame you, Tim, not one bit."

"I realize that this all sounds like a good reason for me to kill the man, so I've got to ask. Do you think I killed him? Because I didn't. I hated what he'd done to Mama, but Mama's been gone a long time. Killing him wouldn't have done her any good. Hell, Laurie Anne, he wasn't worth the trouble it would have taken to kill him. Even if I had wanted him dead, I'd never have done that to Jake and David."

"I didn't know you were friends with them."

"We're not exactly friends, but they are my brothers. Half-brothers, anyway."

"Do they know?"

"They haven't shown any signs of it. I guess that when I didn't welcome Seth with open arms, he decided not to tell them. Still, I've been trying to get to know them, and I like them both. At first I thought Jake was too much like his daddy, but he's not sneaky like Seth was. If he tells you something, you know it's true."

"Are you going to tell them?"

"I don't think so. Even if I could prove it, they'd probably think I was just after their inheritance."

"You are entitled to it."

"I don't want nothing that belonged to Seth Murdstone."

I wasn't about to argue with the tone in Tim's voice.

"Anyway, whatever else he was, Seth was David and Jake's father. I spent my whole life with no daddy—the last thing I'd have wanted to do was to take theirs away from them."

"It's hard losing a father," I said. I'd been through it when I was fifteen, and then again when my grandfather died. "No matter how old you are."

"Do you think I killed him, Laurie Anne?"

I didn't think Junior would have considered it proper procedure, but I said, "No, Tim, I don't. I just don't think you're a killer."

His smile came back in full force. "That means a lot to me." Then he asked, "Do you think this is going to have to come out? About Seth being my father?"

"I don't see why. Like Mark keeps reminding us, Junior and I have no official standing, so we don't have to file any reports. I will tell Richard, if that's all right, and probably Junior. But you know you can trust the two of them to keep quiet."

"That's fine," he said. Then Mrs. Gamp came looking for Tim to get him out on stage. I went back into the auditorium to get a bottle of water, then watched Tim and Florence run through the scene of the possible future where the Cratchits were mourning the loss of their son. I realized I was starting to cry.

It wasn't because of the play, though Tim and the others did a wonderful job. It just seemed so sad to me that Tim had waited his whole life to find his father, and when he found him he wasn't even worth killing, let alone keeping.

Chapter
Twenty-five

"You probably think I'm silly for believing him," I said to Junior after telling her Tim's story, "but—"

"Not really," Junior said. "You've known Tim Topper quite a while. Making a judgment call on somebody you've known that long isn't exactly jumping to conclusions."

"Really?"

"Still, going into a room alone with a suspect wasn't the brightest thing to do. Especially not in—"

"Don't you dare say, 'in your condition'!"

Junior went on as if I hadn't spoken. "What if he had been the killer?"

"Odelle saw us go off together," I said. "He'd have to have been nuts to try anything."

"Don't forget the killer attacked Seth in a hallway that anybody could have walked down at any time."

"Good point. I'll be more careful."

"I'd appreciate it. If I let you get hurt, the entire Burnette family would come after me."

"Then the Nortons would come after them. . . ."

"And we'd end up with a feud that would make the Hatfields and the McCoys look like best buddies."

I shuddered at the thought. "Anyway, even if Tim wasn't the killer, he could have provided a motive."

"How's that?"

"What if Tim's wrong, and David and Jake do know he's their half-brother? They might not want anybody else to find out." Though I'd never seen signs of either brother being particularly racist, it might not show when they were dealing with another white person. "Having a moonshiner in the family could be romantic, but having a black, illegitimate half-brother is something else. I know it's better in Byerly than it used to be, but racial stuff goes pretty deep."

"Especially with somebody like Florence Easterly in the family," Junior said. "She could have done it to keep her name unbesmirched."

"Or if David knew and she didn't, he could have done it to keep her from finding out. Jake might have done it because he was ashamed."

"Or either David or Jake could have done the math and realized that Seth cheated on their mama while she was dying of cancer."

"Right! Though the timing seems funny. Do we still agree that the killing looks unpremeditated?"

"We could be wrong about that, but I've got a hunch—"

"Say no more. I'm not arguing with one of your hunches. So if the killing wasn't premeditated, that implies that Seth had just told either David or Jake about Tim, and whichever brother it was reacted immediately by killing him." I shook my head. "I don't think that works."

"Go back to the scandal, then," Junior said.

"If they were trying to avoid scandal, killing Seth was the absolute wrong thing to do. There's nothing like a murder to get tongues wagging and people prying into secrets."

Junior nodded. "It would have made more sense to kill Tim than Seth. Considering how long Seth had kept the secret, I don't think he'd have come forward if Tim were dead."

"And there's no way to guarantee that Tim won't come forward now," I added. "Though with both Tim's mother and Seth gone, he couldn't prove it."

"Sure he could. DNA testing. They could exhume Seth's body, or even just compare Tim's DNA to Jake's or David's, the way they compared samples from Sally Hemmings' descendants to Thomas Jefferson's to find out they're related."

"Wouldn't they have to get permission?"

"That's right. If any of the Murdstones killed to avoid a scandal, they sure as heck wouldn't allow it."

Remembering something Tim had mentioned, I said, "What about the money? Tim said he didn't want Jake and David to think he was after Seth's inheritance. Maybe they didn't want him to get it, either. Jake said he and David are splitting everything, and half is a whole lot more than a third. Florence could be involved, too, because she'll have access to David's share." Then I had to add, "Of course, it doesn't sound as if Seth had a whole lot."

"We could find out. The will's probably gone into probate."

"This soon?"

"Florence is a lawyer," Junior reminded me. "With Jake living in the house, they'd want to get the title clear as quickly as possible."

"That makes sense. Though you realize that the will might not tell the whole story. I bet it doesn't include the money Seth made from moonshining."

"You may be right. Most moonshiners only deal in cash, and then hide it in a jar or under a mattress. Daddy and I have both taken peeks at Seth's finances, and we never saw anything that wasn't accounted for legitimately. Which is probably why he kept the furniture business going—to cover his tracks."

"So there might be a lot of money involved after all."

"Of course," Junior said, "all this hinges on whether or not Jake or David or Florence knows about Tim, which we have no way of knowing other than asking them."

"We can't do that without breaking my promise to Tim, and they wouldn't necessarily tell us the truth anyway." I thought some more. "Even if they didn't know about Tim, one of them might have been after the money. In fact, I feel like an idiot for not thinking about Seth's money before now. Isn't 'Who benefits?' one of the classic questions a real investigator asks?"

"Don't beat yourself up over it, Laurie Anne. I thought about the money even before I asked you to help."

"You don't think Seth's ill-gotten gains are involved?"

"Not really. When people kill for money, it's usually from greed or desperation. If either of the Murdstone brothers were that greedy, they'd have left Byerly years ago. There are a whole lot better places to make a living. I don't think either of them is desperate, either. Jake gets the house and the business, but he already lived in the house and made a decent living off the business, so he's not gained that much. David gets the insurance money, but from looking at his house, he's not exactly short on cash. And if either of them are in debt, I've never heard anything about it."

"What about Jake's son? The hospital bills must have been high."

"They were pretty steep, but Jake had insurance to cover part of it and the community has been helping with the rest. That's why we're doing this play, remember?"

"I almost forgot," I admitted.

"Anyway, I don't think money was the issue, but it's not a hunch, so you can argue with it if you want to."

"No thanks. What you said makes too much sense." I thought for a minute. "One other thing. Why did Seth pick now to tell Tim the truth?"

"Maybe because he was handy, what with the two of them working together. Does it matter?"

"It might. David said Seth had been diagnosed with a bad heart, and we know he was thinking about retiring. Those two combined could make a man start thinking about coming to the end of his life."

"Which he did," Junior said, "though a bit sooner than he expected."

"It reminds me of Richard's Uncle Claude. When he found out he had cancer, he started cleaning up all kinds of loose ends. He wrote his will, and gave away all the stuff he said he wouldn't need anymore, and made up with people he'd been feuding with. He wanted to die with a clear conscience."

"That must have been comforting at the end."

"Actually, he didn't die. The chemotherapy worked, and he's healthier than ever. The point is that maybe Seth was trying to clean up unfinished business. That's why he told Tim."

"I still don't know why it matters."

"What if he confessed to others, too? Maybe he finally told Mrs. Gamp that he's the one who caused her husband's death."

"Meaning that she has a motive after all?" she said.

"Right. I couldn't see her holding a grudge against Seth all these years, but if she'd just found out, that's another story. The timing would have been tight, but I think she had enough time to kill him. Remember how bad off she was when we got to her? Maybe that's when she realized what she'd done."

"Or maybe she'd just found an ex-lover dead. That would throw most people for a loop."

"So would killing somebody. It seems to me that a grown woman with an imaginary friend might not be the most stable person in the world."

"I don't know, Laurie Anne. She's never shown any sign of violence. Being eccentric doesn't make somebody a killer."

"But—"

"Do you want examples from your own family?"

"Never mind," I said. "I get your point. But I still think we should keep Mrs. Gamp on the list."

"Fair enough, but I sure as heck wish we could take *somebody* off of that list."

Right then, Richard announced that he was shutting down rehearsal so that people could get home in time to dress for Seth's visitation.

"Are you going, Junior?"

She shook her head. "Mama invited some of her cousins over for dinner. You?"

"I imagine so. Richard said he thought he should go."

"Then keep your eyes and ears open. Not that I've ever known a killer to break down and confess at one of these things, but you never know." She left to gather up her nieces and nephews, and I went to find Richard.

Chapter
Twenty-six

"**D**o these shoes look ridiculous?" I asked Richard as he helped me out of the car. I'd quit wearing high heels after having my feet swell during an early holiday party, and even my flats weren't comfortable anymore, so the only shoes I'd brought to Byerly were sneakers. I just didn't feel properly dressed.

"Don't worry," Richard said. "You look fine, and anybody should be able to figure out why a pregnant woman isn't in stilettos."

"I guess," I said doubtfully. At least the outfit I'd borrowed from Vasti was suitable. I'd been trying not to spend a lot of money on maternity clothes and didn't have anything appropriate with me, but my cousin had an entire wardrobe of maternity dresses, including the navy blue one I was wearing.

The sign inside the funeral home directed us to the Magnolia Room. "Florence must have set this up," I told Richard. "That's the nicest room in town. I've heard that deathly ill society types will hang on for just another week to make sure they get it."

"You're making this up."

"I am not," I insisted. "Byerly's Junior League set takes these things just as seriously as the Boston Brahmins would."

"If you say so."

Thinking about the rules of society led me to think about Florence marrying David Murdstone. As crazy as it sounded to me, women were frequently judged on their husband's lineage and bankbook. Of course, Florence was an Easterly, and the Easterlys were thoroughly entrenched in local society. So I didn't think anybody would dare snub Florence, especially not with David being so well dressed and such a successful businessman. But what if they found out what Seth had done for a living?

Admittedly, I'd considered bootleggers romantic figures, at least until I found out about Seth and Clara Todger, but the Junior League members might not have those same fantasies. I was willing to bet that they wouldn't accept a real, live bootlegger in their midst. Easterly or not, Florence would have been cut dead. The question was, would she have minded? She said she didn't care what people thought, but then again, she'd booked the Magnolia Room.

I was relieved to see that the Murdstones had opted for a closed casket. Though I can certainly understand wanting to see a loved one one last time, I've never felt comfortable making small talk with that loved one's face in sight. To me, the casket covered with flowers was more than enough of a reminder of why we were there.

David, Florence, and Jake were receiving people as they entered, and Richard and I joined the line to greet them. After Junior's and my earlier conversation with Florence and David, I felt a little awkward, so I relied on the standby line my mother had taught me. "I'm so sorry for your loss."

"Thank you, Laurie Anne," David said. "I appreciate your coming, and everything you're trying to do for us." To Richard, he said, "My father was so pleased to have a part in the play, and he'd be glad you were here."

Though David was holding up well, Jake looked terrible. His clothes were fine, probably thanks to David or Florence, but his hair was a mess and his hand must have been shaking like a leaf when he shaved to have left so many nicks.

"I'm sorry about your father," I said helplessly. Jake just nodded and swallowed hard.

Florence gave me a quick hug and, with a tiny grin, said, "Sorry we didn't see you out properly this afternoon."

"That's all right. I was a newlywed once myself."

"It's wonderful, isn't it?" she said. "Now don't stay on your feet too long. There are some comfortable chairs right over there."

Richard and I moved on to let the next group of people come through. I imagine that a real investigator wouldn't have hesitated to hang around the receiving line to eavesdrop, but I couldn't do it. Especially not with swelling feet. Instead, I found the chairs Florence had pointed out and took advantage of them.

"Are you feeling all right?" Richard said. "Do you want anything?"

"I'm fine," I said, trying to calculate how many more times I'd have to tell him that before the baby was born.

I saw Tim Topper going through the receiving line and wondered what he was feeling. He'd just found his father, and even though he'd had no reason to like him, surely the man's death had meant something to him. He shook hands with his two half-brothers just as Richard had, when by rights he should have been receiving guests with them.

Big Bill Walters came through the line next, dressed elegantly in a black pinstripe suit. He was widely known as a tough business-man, but I honestly couldn't imagine him killing Seth over a piece of land. Which was a relief, considering his obvious feelings for Aunt Maggie.

"Laura," Richard said, "do you mind if I go see Big Bill? I've got an idea for the last act I'd like to discuss with him."

"Go ahead," I said. "I'll keep on people-watching."

He gave me a quick peck on the cheek and joined Big Bill just as he made it through the receiving line.

It was actually an interesting group of folks to watch. There were some rough types who looked as if they didn't come to town often, and I suspected that some of them were Seth's moonshining col-leagues. Then there were society types, paying their respects to Florence. Or maybe, I thought cynically, scoping out the family she'd married into. And naturally, there were quite a few people from the play.

I hadn't been by myself long when Oliver Jarndyce came over.

"Hey there, Oliver," I said.

"How're you doing?" he asked.

"I'm doing all right. I think it's nice that so many of us from the play came. Or did you know Seth before then?" It wasn't the smoothest opening gambit, but since conversation at a visitation is always awkward, I figured Oliver wouldn't notice.

"I didn't know Seth well," he said, "but I had done some business with him. At least, I tried to."

"Is that right?"

"He and I went to see some land late last summer, but he decided it wasn't what he was looking for."

"Maybe he was thinking about moving," I said idly, "since Big Bill wanted to buy his property."

"Big Bill Walters is in the market?" Oliver said eagerly, his ears all but pricking up.

"I don't know that for sure," I said, not wanting to steer him the wrong way. "It's just something I heard."

"Still, it won't hurt to inquire. Now that I think about it, Jake will almost certainly want to move now. That house is far too big for just one man, especially considering the tragedy that happened there." He looked over at where the Murdstones were still greeting people, and straightened his tie. "If you'll excuse me, Laurie Anne, I should pay my respects to the family."

"Of course," I said. There's nothing quite so determined as a real estate agent who smells a commission, even if it did mean talking business at a visitation.

Then again, there were those for whom a visitation was business. Pete Fredericks wafted toward me, carrying a tray with a glass of ice water.

"Mrs. Murdstone was concerned that you might be overexerting yourself," he said, "and asked me to bring this to you."

"Thanks, Pete," I said, taking it from him. "Thank Florence for me, too." I lifted it to my lips and then hesitated ever so slightly. After all, Pete was still a murder suspect, and I didn't know for sure that Florence had asked him to bring me anything. Then I went ahead and sipped. It tasted fine, of course. Pete would have had to be a fool to try anything in public, in his own place of business. Besides, I didn't even have a motive for him. Not yet, anyway.

I said, "You've done an excellent job pulling this all together so quickly."

He nodded in acknowledgment and said, "Our services are usually performed expeditiously. Even with advanced planning, there are always last-minute details to attend to."

"I suppose so." He looked as if he was about to leave, so I quickly added, "Does it ever bother you, working with a client you know?"

Pete smiled as if he'd heard the question before. "In simpler times, the women of a family would prepare the departed for his final farewell. They saw it as their duty to tend to the remains with care and respect, all the more so because they'd known the person. I regard my work the same way."

I'd always thought of a mortician's job as fairly grisly, but Pete made it sound like a noble calling. Thinking of how hard it must be to deal constantly with bereaved families, I was glad there were some compensations for the job. "Were you and Seth good friends?" I asked.

"No, we only met in connection with the play, but I knew of him through David, who I met through the chamber of commerce. Since I left the mill, I've lost touch with many of my old friends and have had difficulty cultivating new ones. You may not realize this, but many people are reluctant to socialize with a man in my line of work."

"Is that right?" I said, trying to sound shocked even though I'd have been just as reluctant as anybody else.

"It's ironic, actually," he said. "David encouraged me to talk to Vasti about a part in the play because he thought it might help if people saw me in another aspect than as a funeral director. My assisting with Mr. Murdstone's final arrangements has only reminded the community of what it is I do."

"I hadn't thought of that," I said sympathetically. "Don't worry, Pete. People will figure it out eventually. Maybe you can try out for another play." Though if he really wanted to change people's assumptions about him, he might do better than playing Jacob Marley's ghost and the spectral Spirit of Christmas Yet to Come.

"I hope you're right. Now if you'll excuse me, I should check in with the Murdstones."

Richard came back then. "Hi, love. Are you all right?"

"I'm still fine, Richard," I said in exasperation.

"What's wrong?"

"Nothing. I'm just aggravated. Finding out who killed Seth should be simple. It *was* simple—somebody hit him upside the head, and there aren't that many people it could have been. Why can't Junior and I figure out which one? Maybe being pregnant kills brain cells."

He patted my leg. "Come on, Laura. It has nothing to do with being pregnant. You always come to a point where nothing makes any sense and you start grasping at straws."

"Thanks," I said sarcastically.

"Then you figure it all out. Just be patient."

"Patience is not my strong point."

"You'll forgive me if I don't respond to that."

I looked back over at Oliver, now deep in conversation with Jake. "Maybe Oliver killed Seth so he could play Scrooge."

"But he didn't get the part."

"I know, but he thought he was going to. Remember how shocked he was when you picked Big Bill instead of him? Maybe he'll go after Big Bill next."

"I told you not to joke about my cast."

"Sorry." I looked around the room and saw that the crowd was thinning. "Do you suppose we can get away with leaving now?"

"I'm sure we can," Richard replied. "Did you have another avenue to investigate?"

"All I'm interested in investigating is dinner. I've got a craving for a hamburger and french fries."

"Hardee's or McDonald's?"

"McDonald's," I said, my mouth watering. I knew I was supposed to be eating good, healthy meals, but ever since I'd been pregnant, nothing had satisfied me quite so much as junk food. "Wait a minute! Is it all right to eat at McDonald's?"

"Why wouldn't it be?"

"If it's bad luck to quote the Scottish play, it must be bad luck to eat at a Scottish restaurant."

"What Scottish restaurant?"

"Isn't McDonald's a Scottish restaurant?"

Chapter
Twenty-seven

I got up the next morning fully intending to go to Seth's funeral, both to pay my respects and to snoop. But it was drizzling, and my feet hurt from being on them so much the day before, and I was still sleepy. I knew the Murdstones had planned the funeral for early in the day to keep from interfering with rehearsal, but that didn't make it any easier for me to get moving.

Still, I managed to get into the shower, but when I pulled on the second loaner dress from Vasti, I looked at myself in the mirror and said loudly, "For pity's sake!"

"What's the matter?" asked Richard, who was already dressed.

"Look at this." I held my arms out so he could see how the dress fit, which was much the same way that a circus tent fits the center pole. "It's huge!"

"It is kind of loose, isn't it."

"Richard, there's enough room for you in here. I wouldn't fit in this if I was having quintuplets. Does Vasti think I look this big?"

"I'm sure she doesn't, but if she does, obviously she's wrong."

"I can't wear this!"

"Then wear the dress you wore last night."

"People have already seen me in it."

"Then wear a scarf or something—my mother says you can wear the same outfit a dozen times if you accessorize properly."

"I didn't bring any accessories with me. Besides which, I spilled ketchup down the front of it last night."

"Then keep your coat on. Or wear your regular clothes."

"I can't dress that way for a funeral."

"Then—" He stopped. "You don't want to go to the funeral, do you?"

"Not really," I admitted. "I know I should . . ."

"Why? You barely knew Seth."

"Then for the investigation."

"Laura, how often do people really say anything meaningful at a funeral? They're coming to bury him, not to confess to killing him."

That sounded suspiciously like Shakespeare, at least in para-phrase, but I didn't think it was *Macbeth* so I didn't point it out. "I know, but—"

"Junior is going to be there, and so am I. You go back to bed, and we'll tell you if you miss anything important."

I looked at the bed, cozy with the fluffy quilt my grandmother had made. "Are you sure?"

"Go to bed. I'll pick you up on the way to rehearsal."

"I'll go you one better. I'll get a ride to the recreation center and meet you over there."

"It's a deal." Then he got me a drink and put me to bed. I should have felt bad about it, but I didn't have enough time before I fell asleep.

An hour and a half later, I was much better rested. I called around to see who was available and caught Aunt Nora on her way out the door. She said she'd be glad to drop me off, and even brought me a hefty breakfast of eggs with fruit salad on the side. Being Aunt Nora, she also had fresh biscuits handy.

The funeral must have still been going on, because the parking lot was empty when we got to the recreation center. Vasti had made a production out of keeping the doors locked in a vain attempt to prevent practical jokes, so I couldn't go inside, but it was such a balmy day for December that I didn't mind. Aunt Nora volunteered to stay with me, but I knew she was meeting Aunt Edna so they could plan what we Burnettes were having for Christmas dinner. I had a vested interest in their doing a good job and didn't want to hold them up, so I sat down on the stone wall and pulled out the latest issue of the *Byerly Gazette*.

Byerly not being a hotbed of news activity, it didn't take me long to read the *Gazette* from cover to cover. I was surprised people hadn't shown up by then, but I figured the Murdstones must have laid out a good spread back at their house after the funeral. Or maybe the killer had confessed after all, I fantasized, and Junior was busy taking his or her statement.

It was about then that I heard something, a kind of rhythmic sound. More restless than curious, I wandered toward the building, trying to figure out what it was and where it was coming from. I got to the front door and decided it was definitely coming from inside. Now that I was closer, it sounded like someone sawing wood.

The front door was at the far end of the building, with the stage all the way at the other end. With the lights out I could just barely make out motion at the back of the stage. Somebody was sawing something.

My first thought was to knock on the door, so whoever it was would let me in, but I changed my mind. What was that person doing in there, anyway, and why hadn't he or she turned the lights on? I thought Vasti was the only one with a key. Besides which, almost everybody in the cast and crew was at the funeral.

There was only one reason I could think of for somebody to be inside. Our practical joker was setting up another prank.

My first thought was to run along the side of the building until I found a window closer to the stage so I could see who it was. I probably would have, too, but the baby started kicking, reminding me that I needed to look before I leaped. Though Junior and I didn't think the practical joker was Seth's murderer, I sure as heck didn't want to be proven wrong by making him come after me. Even if he wasn't the killer, he'd been working hard to hide his tracks. I didn't know how he would react if I caught him red-handed.

Before I could decide what to do, the sawing stopped. I ducked down and crept to the nearest bush that was big enough to hide behind. I was hoping the prankster would come out the front door so I could see him in the daylight, but eventually I heard the distant sound of a car door shutting and realized that he must have been parked in the back parking lot.

I quickly moved to the other side of the bush, where I couldn't be seen by the driver of the car that appeared and drove out the exit. It was moving too fast for me to read the license plate, but I didn't need to. I knew that car, and I knew who was driving it. But why would he be playing practical jokes? It didn't make sense, and I decided not to say anything until I was sure I'd seen what I thought I'd seen. There had to be another explanation, even if I couldn't begin to figure out what it could be.

Only when the car was long gone did I get out from behind the bush and go back to my seat on the fence. This time I was too nervous to read the newspaper or to do anything other than keep watch in all directions. I was mighty relieved when Vasti's red Cadillac pulled into the parking lot, followed closely by Richard in our rental car. The rest of the cast and crew were close behind.

"Hey, love," Richard said, giving me a hug. "I hope you haven't been waiting long."

"Not too long," I said. "How was the funeral?"

Richard shrugged. "Very nice. Tasteful. About what you'd expect a funeral to be."

"I hope you gave the Murdstones my regrets."

"They didn't mind your not coming, if that's what you mean. They'll be here later. In the meantime, Florence sent you a box of food from the post-funeral gathering."

"That's nice."

Vasti had the door open by then, and we followed her inside.

"Is anything wrong?" Richard said.

"Why do you ask?"

"You look pale, and you didn't ask what food Florence sent."

I managed a smile. "I'm fine, but—"

"Richard!" Vasti yelled. "Have you proofread the program yet? It's got to go to the printer right away or it won't be ready in time."

"Sorry," he said to me. "Do you mind?"

"Of course not," I said. I wanted to know more, even before I told Richard what I was thinking. "You go ahead."

He went to see what Vasti needed, and I stared at the stage, trying to remember where the prankster had been.

Everything was laid out for the scene where Scrooge spies on the Cratchits' Christmas dinner. There was a dining room table with chairs stage left, with the fireplace Jake had made in the center, and Tiny Tim's chair stage right. The scenery flats were painted to create the illusion of a plain house, just this side of poverty-stricken, with faded wallpaper and a framed needlepoint sampler.

I headed toward the stage, walking carefully to make sure I didn't set anything off. I decided that the prankster had been standing stage right, near the door into the set, and sure enough, there was sawdust on the floor all around there. But what had he been sawing?

Gingerly, I reached over and touched one of the flats. It wobbled, but just a little. Then I touched the one next to it, the one with the door through it. It wobbled a lot. I jumped back, watching it rock back and forth, and only breathed again when it stopped moving.

"Richard!" I called out, surprised at how shrill my voice sounded.

"Just a minute!" he called back.

"I need you now!"

He came at a dead run. "What's the matter?"

"Something's wrong with that flat," I said, pointing. "When I touched it, it nearly fell on top of me."

"Are you sure? I know Jake braced them." He reached out.

"Don't touch it!" I yelped. "I'm serious, Richard. I think it's about to fall."

"It's okay," he said soothingly, then yelled, "Can somebody flip on the spotlights?" A few seconds later, someone complied.

"There's sawdust on the floor," I offered, and though Richard looked confused, he realized the implication and started looking up and down the wooden frame of the flat. "Jesus!" he breathed.

"What is it?"

He stepped completely out of range, and in a tight voice said,

"Somebody sawed through the frame on both sides. One little push, and the damn thing would fall right over."

"But it's just boards and canvas, right?" I said. "It wouldn't hurt anybody, would it?"

"Most of them wouldn't, unless you got hit by the frame itself," he said, "but this one is heavier than the others so it can support the door. If it hit you, you could get a concussion, or a broken arm, or . . ." He didn't bother to finish. "Get off the stage."

"But—"

"Now. Please."

I got off the stage.

Richard looked around at the gathering cast and crew, who were watching us with more than a little curiosity. "Folks, our practical joker has been busy again, and this one is nasty. He's rigged one of the flats, and we've got to get it down before it falls down. Martin, Sid, and Big Bill, I could use a hand."

I suppose I should have been offended that he only called for the menfolk to do the heavy work, but I was too shaken to think about it. I just stepped out of the way while they carefully took hold of the flat and brought it down. Even though I was watching them, I jumped when they let it fall the final foot or so. As much noise as it made, I didn't want to think about what would have happened if it had hit one of the cast. Had the prankster recognized the set? Had he realized that Big Bill, Sid, Florence, and David would have been on stage, along with all of Junior's nieces and nephews? Or did he care who it was he could have hurt?

On stage, Richard and the others were checking the other flats and starting to talk about repairing the damaged one. Everybody else had gone back to their various jobs, and I was sure they didn't know how bad it could have been.

Except Junior. She was staring at the stage, and from the look on her face, I could tell she realized what might have happened.

"How did you catch it?" she asked.

"I saw him doing it."

"What? Who?"

"It was Mark Pope."

Chapter Twenty-eight

Junior swore fluently under her breath for a full minute, then said, "What did you see?"

I explained getting there early and hunting down the source of the noise I heard. "I recognized Mark's car when he drove off. It was the same one he was in at the mall yesterday."

"Did he see you?"

"I don't think so." Then, a little embarrassed, I said, "I was hiding."

"Good!"

"Has he been playing all of the jokes?"

"It's possible," she said in an odd tone of voice.

"Did you know Mark was setting these things up? Is that why you didn't want to spend any time tracking down the jokester?"

"I didn't know for sure," she said carefully.

"Junior! You've been holding out on me!"

She looked around quickly. "Keep your voice down."

"You knew!" I said angrily.

"I didn't *know* anything," she said. "I only suspected."

"Yeah, right."

"I mean it, Laurie Anne. It's just that I saw him outside not long before Florence slipped on the soap that day. And I thought it was interesting that there weren't any jokes set yesterday, the one day he didn't show up."

"I've told you everything I suspected," I reminded her. "I haven't held anything back."

"I know, and I'm sorry."

"Do you know why he's been doing it, or are you keeping that a secret, too?"

"The fact is, I've been watching Mark pretty closely ever since this started."

"Why?"

"Because of something he did the day Seth was killed."

"I don't understand. What did he do?"

"It was right after he got here that day. I'd expected him to be pissed that I was at the murder scene ahead of him, knowing that he wanted to make a big show for the city council. And I was willing to let him run the investigation as long as he didn't mess it up too badly. The way I figured it, if him solving one case was enough to make them want to replace me, they could go ahead and do it."

"But you love your job."

"Of course I do," she said, "but not enough to kiss anybody's butt to keep it. Anyway, I was planning to tell Mark that I'd stay out of his way, but he started throwing his weight around before I could. Reminding me I wasn't in charge, threatening to tell my mama I was working during my vacation. I'd known for a while that he was after my job, but he'd been fairly subtle up until then. All of a sudden it was out in the open, as if the stakes were higher than they'd been before."

"I can see where that might have gotten you thinking."

"There's more. Since Mark was being so high and mighty, I decided he could do all the scut work himself, and I let him think I hadn't done anything while waiting for him except stand over Seth's body. Then I watched him do all the looking around I'd already done; I was kind of hoping he'd miss something so I could rub it in."

"Did he?"

"Yes and no. His initial examination was fine. At least, he hit everything I would have. But when the medical examiner came,

Mark tried to get him to say that it could have been an accident, that maybe Seth fell and hit himself."

"On what?"

"Exactly. It took you two minutes to see it wasn't an accident. Mark should have seen it faster than that. Of course, the medical examiner set Mark straight, and I could have let that pass. But then I heard Mark and some of the state troopers talking about who was going to take statements from which witnesses. One of them was planning to talk to Jake, and she asked Mark if there was anything special about him she ought to know. That's when Mark should have told her about Seth and Jake being moonshiners. Criminal connections are *always* of interest in a murder investigation. But all Mark told her was family background: stuff about Jake's son recently dying and him being in the furniture business with Seth."

"Did you tell her about the moonshining?"

"I should have, but that's when Mark chased me off, and that didn't sit too well, so I thought I'd let him make a fool of himself. Then I could step in and solve the case, which would have ended any talk about Mark getting my job once and for all."

I must have looked disapproving, because Junior said, "I know, it wasn't a mature thing to do. Here I've been maligning Mark for playing politics instead of getting the job done, and I'd done the same thing myself. I don't think I'd have let it go on for much longer, but while I was waiting to be interviewed, I started thinking. How on earth had Mark made a mistake like that? Two mistakes, if you count him thinking that Seth could have died by accident."

"People do make mistakes."

"Laurie Anne, Mark has been my deputy ever since I've been chief of police, and I have never known him to make a mistake like that. Maybe he's not brilliant, but he's always been thorough and he's always been competent."

"Dead bodies tend to make people nervous."

"Mark's seen people shot, knifed, and so torn up by car accidents that you couldn't tell which parts belonged to which person. As bodies go, Seth's was darned mild."

"Still, he was in charge this time."

But Junior shook her head. "Mark's been in charge before. I do go on vacations sometimes, no matter what my mama thinks, and so did Daddy."

"Then what did you think?"

"Nothing specific, but I knew something was going on. First he didn't want it to be a murder at all, and when that didn't work, he withheld information that could have led to the murderer. So I decided to let him run things his way so I could see what he'd do."

"Giving him enough rope to hang himself?"

"Which he did by the way he handled the investigation. Everybody knows that the first place you look for a killer is the family, but he didn't do much with any of the Murdstones. Failing that, he should have done something with the moonshining connection, but instead he came up with that fairy tale about a thief sneaking into the building. Then he dreamed up the idea that the practical joker was the killer, only now we find out he was setting up those pranks himself. It's been like he's been working as hard as he can to keep from catching the killer. Which is why I wanted to work with you, so I could keep an eye on him."

I nodded, remembering all the things Mark had been doing that I had thought were just bone stupid. Of course, I was feeling pretty darned stupid myself because of how Junior had been using me. I didn't need any hormones to make me furious. "Junior, I thought we were working together. If all you want to do is play games, you can do it by yourself."

"Hey, I didn't mean to get you mad."

"What *did* you mean to do? Make a fool out of me?"

"Come on, now, Laurie Anne. Give me a chance to explain."

I might have walked out on her, but I could see where Richard and the others were still trying to fix up the damaged flat, and I remembered that what we were doing was more important than my ego. Still, I wasn't happy with Junior. "You could have told me what you were really up to. After all we've gone through together, I'd think you'd trust me."

"I do trust you."

"Then why did you tell me all that stuff about wanting to see how I work?"

"I really did want to see how you work. I'm learning a lot."

"Sure," I said, not believing her.

"I mean it."

"Thanks, but that doesn't make up for not telling me the truth."

"I'm sorry, Laurie Anne, I really am, but I had my reasons."

"I'm listening."

She took a deep breath. "Look, I was hoping I was wrong about Mark, and I didn't want to ruin his reputation without knowing for sure what's going on." She held up one hand to stop me before I could object. "I know you wouldn't have told anybody but Richard, but I didn't want even y'all distrusting Mark without a good reason."

"I can understand that," I said.

"And I wasn't all that sure of my own motives, what with the way he's been treating me. I was afraid I was making something out of nothing."

"You wouldn't do that, not with something this serious."

"I'm glad you think so, but other folks might not see it that way."

I nodded, knowing that there were people in town who'd think that she'd framed Mark to protect her job.

"One other thing," she said. "I felt like I owed Mark a chance to do the right thing. I thought that once he knew I was working with you, he'd come clean because he'd know I wasn't going to just go away. The fact that he hasn't—that he's following us and setting up pranks to distract us—that worries me, Laurie Anne. But I've still got to know exactly what's going on before I make a move."

"You don't think he . . ."

"Go ahead and say it," she said wearily.

"You think he may have killed Seth himself."

Chapter
Twenty-nine

Neither of us said anything for a long time after that. I don't know about Junior, but I was picturing a murderer riding around with a gun and a badge. It wasn't the first time I'd heard of police corruption, of course—the *Boston Globe* was filled with articles about cops stealing valuable evidence, and FBI agents letting informants get away with terrible crimes—but it wasn't something I'd ever expected to see in Byerly.

The front door opened, and I said, "Speak of the devil. Mark just walked in."

"Remember, Laurie Anne, I don't want him to know we suspect anything."

"I'll do my best," I said, but I wasn't feeling confident. Not only am I a lousy liar, but I've got an awful poker face.

Mark came right to us. "Junior, Mrs. Fleming."

"Deputy Pope," I said.

He looked at all the frantic activity on the stage. "What's the problem now?"

"The practical joker rigged one of the flats to fall over," I said, watching his face for some sign of guilt or remorse.

"Was anybody hurt?"

Before Junior or I could answer, Aunt Maggie stomped over. "It's about time you showed up. When are you going to do something about all the foolishness going on around here? You see that piece of scenery? Somebody could have gotten hurt if that thing had fallen!"

"I thought it did fall," Mark said.

"Lucky for us, Laurie Anne found it before it went down."

"Is that right?" Mark said, looking at me.

"Don't even think it," Aunt Maggie snapped. "Laurie Anne didn't do it, even if she was here before the rest of us. She was waiting for us outside the whole time. Right, Laurie Anne?"

"Yes, ma'am," I said, trying not to sound as nervous as I felt. Though I appreciated Aunt Maggie leaping to my defense, I sure wished she hadn't given Mark so much information.

"You've got a job to do, deputy," Aunt Maggie said, "and I expect you to get off your duff and do it. Is that understood?" It didn't really call for an answer, which was just as well, because Aunt Maggie was gone before he could say anything.

"Then you weren't at the funeral?" Mark said to me.

"Nope, I was too tired from running around the mall," I said, trying to sound nonchalant. "So, did you get much shopping done yesterday?"

Mark didn't answer, but his face turned bright red, and he marched off.

"Laurie Anne . . ." Junior started to say.

"I wasn't teasing him just for the sake of teasing him, Junior. I just wanted to make him mad enough to leave before I gave anything away."

"You made him mad, all right."

"Better mad than suspicious, but he's probably both now, thanks to Aunt Maggie." Just knowing that was an uncomfortable feeling, and I resolved not to spend any time alone until this thing was finished. "Do you know why Mark would have killed Seth?"

"I've got an idea."

"Do I get to hear it?"

"I've already apologized once."

"You're right. I'll behave."

"Anyway, I was trying to figure out why Mark was avoiding the moonshine angle. After all, it would have been quite a coup if he'd been able to prove Seth was a moonshiner when neither Daddy nor I ever could. It might even have helped him convince more council members that he ought to be chief of police. Then I wondered if maybe that's what he was after all along."

"You lost me."

"What if Mark decided to go after Seth while I was out of the picture? Even though he doesn't know Clara Todger, he could have heard from other sources that Seth was thinking about retiring. If that happened, Mark would never have had another chance at him. Daddy and I have never been big on harassing suspects, but suppose Mark decided that was the only thing left to try. Suppose he confronted Seth that day, trying to get him to admit he was making moonshine. When Seth wouldn't, Mark lost his temper and hit him. His night stick would have been just about right for that dent in Seth's head. But he hit Seth harder than he meant to and killed him. So he hightailed it and waited for the call to come through."

"That's not bad," I said, "but was Mark even here that day? And did he know about that door?"

"I don't know for sure, but I do know he'd been here other days. Vasti got him over here at least once so she could complain about the first batch of practical jokes. As for the door, I saw him go out that way to talk with Big Bill when Big Bill was smoking one of his cigars."

"Then it really could be him," I said. "How do we prove it?"

"Hold your horses," Junior said, holding up one hand. "We've still got other suspects."

"I didn't see any of them setting a flat to fall."

"Oh, Mark's up to something, but it may not be murder."

"Then what?"

"He could be trying to distract us from the murder so he'll be able to solve it himself."

"If he's been setting up all the pranks, he hasn't had time to solve a murder."

"Then maybe he already knows who it is and is covering for him."

"Who? Why would he do that?"

"I don't know, Laurie Anne!" she snapped. "Maybe he thinks it was Florence, but he's got a secret passion for her and doesn't want to see her in jail. Maybe he hated Seth so much he thinks the killer should get a medal instead of a jail term. Maybe he really thinks it was an accident. All I know is that we've got other suspects." She took a deep breath. "Sure, Mark is still on the list. Maybe he's even at the top of the list. But he's not the entire list."

I opened my mouth to argue but closed it when I realized what Junior's problem was. I'd been in a similar position myself the summer before, when my cousin Linwood was the main suspect in a series of arson fires.[9] Even though I wasn't all that fond of Linwood, and even though I wasn't sure he was innocent, I'd defended him because he was family. Though Mark wasn't exactly a member of Junior's family, they'd worked together a long time, and before that, he'd worked with her father. On top of that, they were both cops, which was another powerful bond. So even though he wasn't related by blood, in a way Mark was part of Junior's family. Even though I would have loved to pin it on him, if for no other reason than to keep Junior's job safe, I couldn't push her on it.

I said, "Okay, who's after Mark?"

"David, for one," Junior said.

"To hide the moonshining and/or Tim from his society wife," I said.

"Florence."

"To hide the moonshining and/or Tim from her society friends."

"Jake."

"To keep the moonshine flowing, or to keep Tim away from Seth's money."

"Mrs. Gamp."

"If she found out that Seth was the one to kill her husband."

"Tim Topper."

"Revenge for his mother, or to get an inheritance."

"On the not-very-likely end of the list, we've got Oliver, Sid, and the Todger family."

[9] *Death of a Damn Yankee*

"Don't forget the Mafia," I added.

"I hadn't forgotten. They're smack dab at the bottom of the list."

I started to count them up but then decided I didn't want to. "That's scary. Everybody liked Seth, but here there are this many people with reasons to kill him."

"If everybody had liked him," Junior pointed out, "he wouldn't be dead."

"It still doesn't seem right. Of course, I didn't really know Seth."

"Me neither. Under the circumstances, it would have been difficult for me to socialize with him. I wish I had known him better. It's easier for me to work a case when I know the victim."

"I almost always know the people involved, myself," I said. "How do you get a feel for a victim you didn't know?"

"I talk to the spouses and family and friends—just like we've been doing. And at some point, I check out the victim's house."

"Does that help?" I asked.

"Sometimes. Most murders don't come out of the blue, you know, and there's usually something in a person's house to show that trouble has been brewing. Angry letters from an ex-wife, or new locks on the door if the person's been running scared, or all kinds of things. I never know what I'm going to find."

"Has Mark searched Seth's place?"

Junior looked irritated, so I left that alone.

"There must be a way to get inside that house," I said. "Maybe Jake left a window or a door unlocked."

"No breaking and entering," Junior said sternly. "I am still chief of police, you know. Besides, we wouldn't be able to use anything we found in court."

"How's this? We went to see David and Florence, but we haven't paid a condolence call on Jake. We can take him a fruit basket, and while you keep him busy, I'll tell him I have to go to the bathroom and go snooping instead."

"You wouldn't have enough time to find anything. What if you pretended to go into labor on Jake's front lawn, and when he carried you in, you sent him off to boil hot water while you tossed the place."

"Hey, you're the one who wanted a look around Seth's house."

"Sorry," she said, unable to hide a grin. "Any other ideas?"

"Just one." I don't know if Junior thought it was a good idea or not, but at least she kept a straight face when I told her about it and made the phone calls necessary to set it up.

Chapter Thirty

It took a while to get the ball rolling, but that was just as well. We had to wait for Jake to get to rehearsal anyway, which he didn't do until after lunch. A little while after that, Aunt Nora showed up with Aunt Edna and Aunt Nellie in tow.

They looked in my direction just long enough to make sure I saw them, then went to where Jake was repairing the damaged flat. "Jake, have you got a minute?" I heard Aunt Nora say, and they spent a little while talking before he handed her a set of keys. I'd expected him to be reluctant, but he seemed grateful, which made me feel guilty about what I had in mind.

Aunt Nora came my way next, saying brightly, "Hey there, Laurie Anne. Are you busy this afternoon?"

"Nope, just taking up space," I said, trying to sound natural. "Why do you ask?"

"Are you up for some housecleaning?"

"Housecleaning?" I repeated, thinking that it was a good thing I wasn't in the play, because my performance would have given Richard conniptions.

"I was talking to Edna," Aunt Nora said, "and we realized that the church hadn't done a thing to help poor Jake during his troubles, so we volunteered to go clean his house. If you're not busy, we could use another set of hands."

"Sure," I said. "Just let me get my coat."

Junior was watching us play-act, and Aunt Nora said, "What about you, Junior?"

"I can't," she said. "I'm keeping up with the kids." Actually, she refused because we'd decided that her being directly involved would taint anything I found. Besides, she hated housecleaning nearly as much as I did.

We kept our fake smiles in place until we were in Aunt Nora's car. Then Aunt Nora excitedly asked, "Did we fool everybody?"

"I think so," I said, watching the recreation center door until we pulled out of the parking lot. "Nobody is following us."

"Thank goodness. I was so nervous I was afraid I'd forget what I was supposed to say."

"You did fine, Nora," Aunt Nellie assured her. "Laurie Anne, do you really think there's anything important in Seth's house?"

"I don't know, but there might be." I hadn't told them who Junior and I suspected, only that we hoped to find something that would point us in the right direction.

The Murdstone house was an old farmhouse, painted brick red with dark-gray shutters. It was surrounded by a couple of acres of land, most of it wooded, and the place was a good distance off the road, with no neighbors in sight. It reminded me of the Todger compound, and I figured Seth had liked his privacy for the same reason they did. Though he hadn't run his still out of his home, he still wouldn't have wanted people to know about his comings and goings.

Aunt Nora unlocked the front door with Jake's keys and waved me inside. "You go ahead. We'll get the cleaning things out of the car and get to work."

"Thanks, Aunt Nora. I really appreciate this."

"Don't be silly. We're all glad to pitch in for your last time."

I resented the "last time" part, but decided it was no time to be picky. After one look inside the front door, I was glad I hadn't argued with her. My aunts were getting more than they'd bargained for.

The place was a pigsty. The hardwood floor was muddy, there were newspapers and empty bottles scattered around, and every ash tray was filled with cigarette butts. Of course, I reminded myself, Jake had lost his son and then his father in the space of a few months. I didn't think my place would be any cleaner under those circumstances.

The triplets had told me that Seth lived on the second floor, while Jake and his son had lived on the first, so I headed up the stairs, turning on lights as I went.

It wasn't as bad up there. A bit dusty, and since Seth had been a smoker, the smell lingered, but I didn't think anybody had done much in there since Seth died. That was all the better as far as I was concerned.

Knowing the age of the house and the usual layout for places like it, I could tell that there'd been a lot of modifications made to the place. I'd have expected a bathroom and three or four bedrooms. Instead, there was a den, a compact kitchen, a larger than usual bathroom, and a roomy bedroom. I wondered if Seth and Jake had done the work themselves, because if they were that good, they should have gotten out of moonshining and into construction.

There were a desk and a filing cabinet in one corner of Seth's bedroom, and I started there. I found a ledger book right off, and I went through it first, hoping that I'd find some solid evidence of Seth's moonshining. Unfortunately, it only had records of the household expenses, and listings for buying supplies and selling furniture. The rest of the desk drawers held the usual stuff people accumulate: unpaid bills and giveaway pens and tape and a postcard reminding Seth to make a dentist's appointment. The filing cabinet looked promising at first with its neatly labeled folders, but though I glanced through every folder, I didn't find any threatening letters or panic-stricken journal entries.

It didn't take long to search the rest of the bedroom, but unless I counted the three well-thumbed copies of *Penthouse*, there was nothing suspicious. Then I hit the living room, then the kitchen, and even the bathroom. Nothing. At least, nothing that pointed to Seth's murderer.

There were a few paperback men's adventure novels scattered about and a couple of woodworking magazines, but apparently Seth hadn't been a big reader. There were some videos on the shelf under the TV and VCR, but all store-bought ones. Seth had liked *Top Gun* and *Benny Hill*. Plus, there were photo albums, and the memorabilia any parent or grandparent collects: graduation programs, homemade cards of construction paper, school book reports, and crayon drawings. But I didn't find anything out of the ordinary.

Knowing that Seth and Jake were carpenters, I tapped around on the walls and furniture, looking for secret compartments. All I got were sore knuckles.

I even tried to get mystical. I sat down on the end of the couch that showed the most wear, figuring it must have been where Seth liked to sit, and closed my eyes, trying to sense what the dead man had been like. Why had he spent his life breaking the law, and what had he done when he wasn't making moonshine? Why had he slept with Tim's mother and only admitted it recently? Why had he never remarried after his wife died? Who in the heck was Seth Murdstone?

I opened my eyes. Maybe the strangest thing I found was nothing. Despite the obvious signs that Seth had lived there and kept his belongings there, there was almost no personality in those rooms. It was as if Seth had hidden himself as carefully as he'd hidden his still. Maybe Junior or a psychologist could have gotten to know Seth Murdstone by looking at his home, but I couldn't.

I finally decided I might as well go help my aunts, but halfway down the stairs, I stopped and stared in amazement. If I hadn't known better, I'd have thought I was in a different house. Every surface either shone or gleamed, as appropriate, and every newspaper, cigarette butt, and beer bottle was gone. I wouldn't have to worry about leaving fingerprints while searching that house—my aunts would polish them right off again.

"Hello?" I called out.

"We're in the kitchen," one of them replied, and I followed the voice through the newly immaculate living room. They'd just gotten started in the kitchen, so I could see what a mess the room had been, but the smell of Pine-Sol promised that any germs were on their way out. Aunt Nellie had her head in the refrigerator and was pitching styrofoam containers into a green garbage bag while Aunt Edna sprayed glass cleaner and Aunt Nora loaded plates into the dishwasher.

"Did you find anything?" Aunt Edna asked eagerly.

"Not a thing," I said. "I thought I'd look around down here."

Aunt Nora said, "Go right ahead. We've got plenty to keep us busy."

In fact, they had enough to keep me busy for a month, but I suspected they would be done in an hour or two.

The downstairs part of the house was bigger than the upper floor because of a long room along one side that had probably started out life as a porch. There was the living room and kitchen I'd already seen, a half bathroom off the front hall, and a full bathroom with doors to both bedrooms. The former porch had been set up as a combination den and playroom, although from the number of toys scattered around, I suspected the playroom function had taken over.

Even though my aunts hadn't cleaned in there yet, and despite the toys, it was probably the neatest room downstairs, and I wondered why. Then I saw the scorched patch of carpet and realized that was where Barnaby must have gotten burned. I was surprised it wasn't worse, considering how badly Barnaby had been hurt. Even thinking about the boy's injuries made my stomach roll, and though it was the wrong time of the day for morning sickness, I decided I needed some fresh air.

There was a door leading outside from the playroom, and I called out, "I'm going out back," before stepping through.

The yard wasn't much to see. The grass had been mowed and the weeds kept under control, but it didn't look as if Jake or Seth had spent any time planting flowers or bushes. There was a large-ish wooden building out there, too big for a playhouse, and when I checked the door, it was unlocked.

Inside was a home handyman's dream, with all the woodworking tools anybody could want. Not that I knew what most of them were, but they looked impressive. There was also plenty of lumber waiting to be made into furniture, and a few completed pieces. Even though their real business lay elsewhere, clearly Seth and Jake had spent a lot of time in the workshop. There was a little refrigerator, a coffeemaker, and even a telephone.

One of Seth's signature chairs was sitting in the middle of the room, and after making sure the varnish had dried, I took a seat. Florence was right; it wasn't as comfortable as the average church pew. While sitting there, I saw a mangled pile of metal on one of the worktables. It took a closer look and some imagination to picture what it must have been, but once I did, my stomach turned again. It was the remains of a space heater.

I nearly ran out of the little building, and went back inside the house. My aunts had finished up in the kitchen, and I offered to tackle Jake's bedroom. Then I looked inside and started to regret it. It was strewn with the same kinds of trash as in the rest of the house, but with dirty clothes thrown in for good measure.

"Aunt Nora," I called out, "did y'all bring any spare rubber gloves?"

Once my hands were protected, I brought myself to start searching, but other than learning that Jake was a briefs man, I didn't know a bit more than I had before. Aunt Nora came in while I was gingerly picking my way through. She said, "Throw the dirties into the hall, and I'll put them in the washer later."

"You're a braver man than I, Gunga Din," I said.

"Lord, Laurie Anne, after washing up after Buddy, Augustus, Thaddeous, and Willis all these years, this is nothing!"

"Do kids make that big a mess?" I said, worried for the future.

"Not until they start walking," she said cheerfully. "Unless they spit up a lot, of course."

"Maybe I should hire a cleaning service."

She just laughed. "You start over there, and I'll start over here, and we'll meet in the middle."

Actually, we met when I was only one-third done, and she'd already gotten two-thirds of the way through. She might have gotten farther along than that if she hadn't stopped at Jake's chest of drawers. A minute later, I realized she was crying.

"Aunt Nora?" I said. "What's wrong?"

She waved a piece of paper at me. "Oh, Laurie Anne, this breaks my heart."

"What?"

"Read it," she said, handing it to me as she looked for a tissue to blow her nose.

It was a letter, hand printed on notebook paper and dated December 1.

Dear Santa,

How are you? I am fine. Only I'm in the hospital, but the doctor says I might get to go home for Christmas. If not, you can find me here.

I have tried to be a good boy this year. I did lie once, but Grandpaw says it's okay to lie if it's for a good reason. So I hope it doesn't count.

I would really like the new PlayStation if you can get one. Daddy says they are hard to find, but I figure you can make one yourself. And games for it, too.

I would also like you to bring my Daddy a CD player for his car. I broke the old one, and have been trying to earn money to buy a new one, but I got hurt before I got enough. If you'll bring him one, I promise to spend the money I have saved on CDs for him. Or on PlayStation games so you don't have to bring me so many.

I hope Mrs. Claus is good, and that the reindeer are, too. Especially Rudolph, if he's real.

Love,

Barnaby Murdstone

PS: If you can't find a PlayStation, that's OK, but don't forget the CD player for Daddy.

I started crying, too, and Aunt Nora handed me the box of tissues she'd found. Aunt Nellie and Aunt Edna must have heard us, because they showed up, wondering what was going on. Both of them read the letter and reached for the tissues.

"I've never read anything so sad in my whole life," Aunt Nora sniffed. "Asking for a present for his daddy when he was in the hospital dying. Can you imagine?"

I shook my head. I'd never been that sweet in my Christmas letters. After a perfunctory inquiry into Santa's health, I'd methodically listed a page's worth of stuff I wanted.

"He had such pretty handwriting, too," Aunt Nellie said.

"He didn't write that," Aunt Edna said. "Mrs. Gamp told me she did it for him. He died not long after he wrote this, and she never got around to mailing it, so when she found it in her pocketbook the other day, she gave it to Jake. It must have torn the poor man up. She should have just thrown it out."

Aunt Nora said, "No, she did the right thing. Now Jake knows what a wonderful boy he had."

That made us start crying all over again, and we had to stop working long enough for Aunt Nora to brew some iced tea for us to drink. For once I didn't pay attention to the caffeine or the amount of sugar she added. I had to have something to loosen my throat.

After we pulled ourselves together, we started cleaning as if our lives depended on it. There was no way we could comfort Jake for the loss of that little boy—we couldn't even admit we'd read such a private letter. What we could do was get that house so spic and span that you could have eaten off any floor in the place.

I knew I was going to have to tell Junior that I hadn't seen anything that would lead us to Seth's killer, but I didn't regret having spent the time out there. Making Jake's house fit to live in was the least we could do for him.

Chapter
Thirty-one

It didn't take long to report to Junior what I'd found at Seth's house, once Aunt Nora dropped me off at rehearsal, because there wasn't much to tell. So we hashed over what we knew, and we rehashed it, and then we made goulash out of it. None of it did any good. All it did was make me hungry.

Richard kept everybody but the kids late that night, trying to make up for the time lost because of Seth's services. But finally he admitted that we'd accomplished as much as we were going to. The next day was the technical rehearsal and the dress rehearsal, with our first performance the night after that, so he warned everybody to get plenty of sleep because come tomorrow, he wasn't going to let anybody go until everything was perfect. People were out of there in record time.

As soon as we got into the car, I said, "Richard, I can tell you're worn out, but we've got to talk."

"Are you feeling all right?"

"I'm fine; the baby's fine. It's about Seth's murderer." I launched into a report of everything Junior and I had done over the past couple of days, which lasted through the ride home and into our preparations for the night. Only when we were in bed, with Richard's arm around me, did I tell him about what I'd seen Mark doing.

"Jesus, Laura!" Richard said. "Why didn't you say something before?"

"I didn't get a chance," I said, "and I was so horrified, I didn't want to. It was like when I was a little kid. If something bad happened, I thought that if I didn't say anything, nobody would find out, and it wouldn't be real. Telling somebody would have made it true. I know that doesn't make much sense—"

"No, I think I understand."

"Once we saw the flat was broken, you were busy trying to make sure nobody got hurt. I told Junior because he's her deputy. She and I decided not to tell anybody else."

"Why not?"

"There's no proof. It would be his word against mine."

"Don't you think people would believe you over him?"

"I don't know. The point is that it wouldn't do any good to tell people now. We need to find out what's going on, and we can do that better if he doesn't know we're onto him."

"Are you sure he doesn't already know?"

I thought about how he'd acted after talking to Aunt Maggie. "He might suspect, but he can't know for sure."

"Laura, if this is true, Mark's got to be getting desperate, and he's got a gun. I'm worried." He gently rubbed my tummy. "About both of you."

"I'm worried, too," I said, "but I'm going to be careful. I won't go anywhere without somebody with me—preferably you or Junior—and I'm going to stay as far away from Mark as humanly possible."

"Good," he said firmly. "Otherwise I'd be tempted to get us onto the next plane out of here."

"We can't do that! The play is the day after tomorrow, and everybody is depending on you. And Junior is depending on me."

"Do you think any of that would make a difference to me if I thought you were in danger? Would it mean anything to you if I were in danger?"

"No, I guess not. But I don't think I'm in danger."

"Then we'll stick around. But if there's the first sign that Mark, or anybody else, might hurt you—"

"We head for the airport. Got it."

"Good. You get some rest," he said. "I love you."

"I love you, too."

Despite everything, Richard was asleep in minutes. It took me a little longer. I was thinking about what Richard had said about Mark getting desperate. He was right, and that explained why the so-called practical jokes had been getting nastier. The question was, how much more desperate was Mark going to get?

Chapter
Thirty-two

Thanks to my taking so long to get to sleep, Richard and I were late getting to rehearsal the next day, and when we arrived, people were milling around and looking a lot more upset than they should have been over missing five minutes of rehearsal. I snagged Mrs. Gamp as she rushed by, and said, "What's going on?"

"Haven't you heard?" she asked. "The most terrible thing happened last night. At least, it almost happened. Though of course it would have been much more terrible if it had happened. But like Mrs. Harris always says, to have something almost happen is nearly as bad as it actually happening. Don't you think?"

I just blinked at her, wishing mightily that there really was a Mrs. Harris, because surely she'd be able to explain things better than Mrs. Gamp did.

Fortunately, Junior came over then. "It's about time y'all got here. People are kind of stirred up."

"So we see," Richard said. "What has Mar—" Junior looked at him sharply, and he changed it to, "What has our practical joker done now?"

"No joke. Jake Murdstone nearly died last night from gas fumes."

Mrs. Gamp said, "He's going to be fine, but if he'd been in there much longer . . ." She wagged her head. "Thank goodness for his brother. Because poor Jake was feeling no pain, if you know what I mean."

Actually, I had no idea what Mrs. Gamp meant, so I looked to Junior for a more coherent explanation.

"David went over to the Murdstone house last night," Junior said obligingly. "Jake's car was there, but Jake didn't answer the door, and when David went inside, he smelled gas. Jake was passed out at the kitchen table, so David dragged him outside and called for help. By the time the ambulance showed up, Jake was already coming round. He was sick as a dog, but he's going to be all right."

"Good Lord," I breathed. "How did it happen?"

"These things do happen," Mrs. Gamp intoned. "Especially when liquor is involved. Mr. Gamp went that way. Only he was driving a truck, not using a stove, and of course he would never have taken a drop when he was driving, but it happened just the same. You just never know."

"Mrs. Gamp," Junior said, "did Vasti find you? I think she wanted you to help her fold programs."

"Did she? I better get right over there." She trotted away.

"Did Vasti really ask for her help?" I asked Junior.

"No, but I knew I'd never get the whole story out if we didn't get her out of here. Anyway, when the fire department got there, they found one of the eyes of the stove had been turned on full blast and the pilot light was out. Jake is just lucky his brother picked last night to bring him something to eat."

" 'Accidents will occur in the best-regulated families,' " Richard said. *"David Copperfield,* Chapter Twenty-eight."

"How did that eye get turned on?" I wanted to know.

"Ask Jake yourself. He just came in the door."

Pretty much everybody in the room looked in Jake's direction as he walked past. Jake's face colored and he refused to meet anybody's eyes.

David stepped toward him. "Jake, what are you doing here? The doctor said you need to take it easy for a few days."

"I feel fine," Jake said, but I don't imagine anybody believed him. Other than the angry flush on his cheeks, he looked as pale as could be. "I've got things to do before the play opens."

Richard said, "Jake, nobody appreciates your devotion more than I do, but there's no reason to make yourself sick."

"I'm fine," Jake insisted. "I had a little accident, that's all. Just let me get back to work."

"Jake, be reasonable," David said. "Go back to the house and lay down."

"I'm not going to sit out there all day!" Jake snapped.

David looked at his brother for a long time, then nodded. "All right, if you think you can handle it—"

Jake laughed, but it was a bitter sound, not a happy one. "This isn't the part I'm having problems handling." He walked past David and went backstage.

Richard, Junior, and I went over to David. "Is he really fit to work?" Richard asked.

"You heard what he said," David said helplessly. "It probably is better for him than sitting around the house by himself. I'll keep an eye on him."

"Okay, but let me know if you need me to order him out of here." Then, to me Richard said, "Are you going to be sticking around here today?"

"As far as I know. I'll let you know if anything changes."

"Good." He gave me a kiss on the cheek and headed for the stage.

"What happened?" I asked David. "Was it really an accident?"

"Of course it was an accident! What else would it have been?" He glared at me briefly before stalking off.

"Sounds as if you hit a nerve," Junior said.

"Apparently so. Look, I don't know about you, but I need to sit down."

"Lead the way."

Finding a quiet corner was getting harder to do the closer we got to opening night, but we finally settled in the back of the auditorium.

"What I want to know," I said, "is whether or not it was really an accident."

"That's what Jake says. In fact, I was talking to a friend of mine at the hospital, and she says that when he was being treated, Jake put the blame on your aunts."

"What?"

"He thinks one of them accidentally turned on the eye when y'all were out there cleaning."

"They did no such thing!" I said heatedly. "Besides which, if they had, it would have stunk up the house. If we hadn't smelled it when we left, Jake would have noticed as soon as he came in the door."

"He claims all he could smell was Pine-Sol."

"They did use a lot of it, but—"

"You don't have to convince me. I don't have any idea that that's what happened."

"Well, I don't see how Jake could have done it himself. If the kind of mess left around is any indication, he hasn't cooked anything in a while. All I saw were takeout bags and the trays from some microwave meals. Nothing that would require him firing up the stove."

"He was drunk," Junior pointed out.

"I'm not surprised. I can't tell you how many empties we carted out of there." I thought about it. "Do you think Jake tried to kill himself?"

"David says he didn't find a suicide note."

"Do all suicides leave notes?" I asked.

"Nope, plenty of them don't. Some don't want people knowing it was suicide, so they try to make it look like an accident."

"Goodness knows Jake has had more excuses than most to want to give up. His son dying, and now his father being murdered." I paused. "Maybe guilt, too."

"You mean over killing his father?" Junior said. "I thought about that, but I've never known a killer to commit suicide because of remorse. At least, not one who's gotten away with it. Once they get caught, sometimes they'll take the easy way out, but not before. I'm not saying it never happens, but if I ever ran across a case that looked like it, I'd be mighty suspicious.

"So it could have been an accident, but it doesn't seem likely, or it could have been attempted suicide, but we don't have any proof of that, or . . ."

She finished for me. "Or somebody tried to kill Jake. Probably the person who killed his father."

"Jesus, Junior, Jake could have been murdered while we run around playing cops and robbers."

"I *am* a cop! How do you think I feel?"

"Sorry. This just throws me for a loop."

"Do you want to bow out? I'd understand if you did."

"You know me better than that!" I said. "If that so-and-so thinks he can get away with killing more people, he's got another think coming!"

"That's what I wanted to hear," Junior said.

"Let me put this together. If it really was an accident, then it doesn't mean anything to our investigation."

"Right. If it was attempted suicide, it might mean that Jake is off our list because murderers almost never kill themselves. So if he did try, then he wasn't the killer."

"This is starting to sound like one of those logic puzzles," I said. "If somebody tried to kill him, it should also get him off our list. Unless there are two killers running around."

"Possible," Junior admitted, "but I'd rather assume that Seth's killer went after Jake. So why did somebody want Jake dead?"

"Maybe Jake knows who killed Seth," I suggested. Then I had to add, "But if he did, why wouldn't he have come forward?"

"What if he's protecting the killer?"

"Then it would have to be David, because I can't imagine who else Jake would protect, when it's his own father who was killed. Since David is the one who saved him from the gas last night, he can't be the one who tried to kill him."

"Right. What other motive have we got?" Junior said.

"What if Seth was killed to shut down the still, and once the killer realized that Jake was going to keep it going, he went after him, too?"

"Why? We ruled out the idea of anybody in organized crime caring about the still, and all that leaves is David trying to keep Florence from finding out about it. But she already knows, and he knows that."

I thought for a minute. "Let's go back to the two-killer theory. What if Jake killed Seth, and somebody found out and tried to kill him for revenge?"

"That gets us back to David," Junior said. "Those two are the only kin Seth had."

"Could David have intended to kill Jake and then changed his mind? After all, David is the most reasonable choice for being able to get in the house and set it up. How do we know he really just wanted to bring Jake something to eat? Did anybody actually see any food?"

"That's a point."

"Come to think of it, could Jake have faked the attempt to draw attention away from himself?"

"Nice idea, but my friend at the hospital saw how sick Jake was last night—he wasn't faking that. Not to mention the fact that he was lucky that the gas didn't ignite. More people die from gas fires than gas poisoning. All it would have taken was one little spark and the place would have gone up. Jake's not the sharpest knife in the drawer, but I don't think he's that dumb."

"You're probably right," I had to agree. "Maybe the killer is going after all the Murdstones. Seth was just the first, and Jake was supposed to be next. Heck, even Florence slipping in the bathroom could have been part of his plan—she's a Murdstone by marriage."

"Except that anybody could have slipped in the soap. Any female, at least."

"Then ignore the soap spill. Somebody could still be trying to take out the Murdstones."

"Why?"

"Maybe Seth really does have moonshining money hidden away,

and some relative is planning to step forward and inherit once all the Murdstones are gone."

"Who?" Junior said skeptically. "I told you, they didn't have any other family. Unless you think Seth had a secret twin living out in the woods somewhere."

"Don't make fun unless you have a better idea."

"Sorry. It's just that I'm used to dealing with likely solutions. That one was getting pretty far out there."

"If there were a likely solution, don't you think we'd have been able to figure it out by now?"

"All right, keep speculating," Junior said.

"Thank you. You know, there might be a reason somebody would want all the Murdstones dead. Aunt Nora said Big Bill wanted to buy their house but Seth wouldn't sell."

"Laurie Anne, please don't make me interrogate Big Bill Walters."

"I'm not saying it was Big Bill. I'm just wondering why he wanted it. Is there going to be a factory built there or something that would make the land worth a lot?"

"Sorry to burst your bubble. Big Bill wants the land because it's next to a piece he already owns, but he doesn't have any specific plans for it that I've heard of."

"Then I guess that leaves us with . . . Shoot, Junior, what does that leave us with?"

"Heck if I know," she said in disgust. "Other than the fact that somebody killed Seth and maybe that same somebody tried to kill Jake, and damned if he hasn't gotten away with it."

"Not yet he hasn't," I said firmly. "We are going to catch this killer if it takes us until next Christmas!"

Chapter
Thirty-three

I'd thought regular rehearsals were boring, but that was before I watched a technical rehearsal. As Richard explained it, we had to go through every lighting cue and special effect and make sure they were perfect. Unfortunately, we didn't actually have anybody in charge of lighting and effects, thanks to Sally Hendon making off with all the experienced people. Instead, everybody pitched in between other jobs and their lines on stage, meaning that it was darned confusing and provided endless opportunities for mistakes. Every time somebody messed up, Richard would make them go through things over and over again until they got it right.

As Junior whispered to me, the worst part of it was that Richard was keeping his temper through all of it, so we didn't even have a good tantrum to break the monotony.

Junior and I would gladly have gone somewhere—anywhere—to try to make sense of Seth's death and the attack on Jake, but neither of us could come up with anyplace useful to go. Junior indulged me by listening to my most whimsical flights of fancy, but even that didn't lead to anything that we could actually do. So we sat and brooded.

Richard didn't want to interrupt the tech rehearsal, which meant he wouldn't even let us break for lunch until it was done. By the time he was satisfied, we had an auditorium filled with cranky, hungry people. Including me.

Fortunately, Richard ordered in pizzas for lunch and announced that we'd have an extra long lunch break so that everybody could rest. Otherwise we might have had another murder.

Since Richard was too agitated to eat and I didn't want to sit with Junior and her ravening horde of nieces and nephews, I ended up at a table with the three Spirits of Christmas.

"Are you three about ready for tomorrow night?" I asked them over a bite of pepperoni pizza.

Sid and Pete only nodded, but Oliver said, "I can't wait! Of course, having two roles is particularly challenging, but I assure you that I'm up to it."

I caught the other two men rolling their eyes, and hid a grin.

Just to make conversation, I said, "I hope all these rehearsals haven't kept you too long from your work, not to mention getting ready for Christmas. Richard's so used to college vacations that he forgets everybody isn't so lucky."

"I don't mind," Sid said. "I like to take time off at the holidays, anyway. I've got a college boy who's tickled to death to earn some extra money for Christmas shopping, and he's taking good care of the station."

"My uncle has been handling everything for me," Pete said. "I only stepped in to assist with Mr. Murdstone's arrangements as a favor to the family, and they really took very little of my time."

"Then they sure don't take after Seth," Oliver said with a little laugh. "He made a habit of taking up people's time."

"Oh?" I said.

"Laurie Anne, do you remember how I told you I'd shown Seth some land a while back, but that he'd decided not to buy it?"

I nodded.

"Well, when I was at the realty board's Christmas party last night, I found out I was only the last in a long string of realtors that he'd gone to. He's been looking at land for years. We couldn't even count all the parcels he's looked at, let alone the amount of time the realtors around here have wasted sending him listings and taking him out to see plots."

"I know a woman like that," I said. "She goes to every open

house she sees, even though she's not in the market for a new house. She says it's for decorating ideas, but I think she just likes snooping around houses."

"I've seen that, too," Oliver said, "and those people are easy to pick out, but Seth only looked at undeveloped property."

"Why would he do that?" Sid asked. "Was he planning to build a new house?"

Oliver said, "Beats me. I'm just glad I found out before he wasted too much of my time." Then he looked abashed and added, "May he rest in peace."

The conversation wandered elsewhere after that, but I wasn't really paying attention. I was mulling over an idea, and as soon as I could do so politely, I excused myself and headed for Junior. Fortunately, the kids were fast eaters and had already run off to play with their Gameboys, so I could explain what Oliver had told me without interruption.

When I was done, she said, "You think looking at real estate had something to do with Seth's murder? Maybe the realtors got together and decided to do away with him to keep him from bothering them?"

"No," I said, exasperated. "What I think is that now we know where Seth's still is."

"You lost me."

"You said that Seth never put a still on his own land, and that he kept moving it places where neither you or your father could find it. So how did he find places that were safe? I bet he kept going to realtors so he could find out which places were empty. Once the land sold, or if he decided things were getting hot, he'd go to another realtor and find out another piece of land to use. Rent free, I might add."

"Slick," Junior said admiringly.

"Seth or me?"

"Both."

"Thank you," I said, but I had to add, "Of course, it's too late to catch Seth now."

"But not Jake. When did you say Oliver showed Seth that piece of land?"

"Late in the summer. Why?"

"I bet that's the last time Seth relocated. It's a pain to move a still, because you have to set up another place and get everything moved without being seen in either spot, so I don't see how Jake could have had time to move it since Seth died. Richard's been keeping everybody at rehearsal every waking moment."

"Then all we have to do is find out from Oliver where the land is."

"There's no time like the present. Where is the Spirit of Christmas Present anyway?"

"Why the hurry? Do you think there's some evidence about Seth's murder out there?"

"Who cares? Laurie Anne, I have been hunting for Seth Murdstone's still ever since I became chief of police. Do you really think I'm going to pass up a chance to finally find it?"

"Not to mention how badly you want to beat Mark to the punch."

"That, too. And maybe there will be something related to the murder out there."

"Then let's go get Oliver."

We found him reading his script, mumbling his lines out loud. "Oliver," I said, "can we talk to you for a minute?"

"Certainly. What can I do for you two ladies?"

Junior said, "We want to talk to you about the land you showed to Seth Murdstone."

"Why is that?"

I left the explanation to Junior. Since we weren't planning to mention Seth's moonshine operation, I wanted to see just how she was going to finesse the information out of Oliver. I should have realized that Junior doesn't need finesse.

"It's police business, Oliver," she said bluntly. "I need to know the location of the plot you showed to Seth, and I don't have time to mess around."

He blinked but didn't argue. "I've got the listing in my car."

"Then fetch it in here."

Darned if he didn't rush to do as he was told.

While he was gone, I said, "Do you think you can teach me how to do that? It sure would come in handy with the baby."

"Sorry, Laurie Anne, I think you have to be born with it."

By then, Oliver was back, leather portfolio in hand. He unzipped the case, licked one finger, and started turning pages. "It's been several months, so I'm not sure what it could have to do with the murder investigation."

"Who said it had anything to do with a murder investigation?" Junior said.

"I thought—or rather, I assumed—"

"Just show it to us."

He pulled out a page. "Here we go. A three-acre site on the north side of town."

"Three acres," I said, thinking about how long it would take to search that big an area.

"It's a lovely piece," Oliver said, "though a bit isolated. The nearest paved road is a ways off, though there is a well-cleared dirt track."

"Where's the track?" Junior demanded.

He pointed to a plot plan. "Here, in red."

That would help. Surely Seth and Jake wouldn't have wanted to lug their equipment and product too far over ground. Unfortunately the track went right through the middle of the plot, and the still could have been anywhere along it. We'd be able to find it eventually, but not without an extended search.

"What's this here?" I said, pointing to a blue blotch on the plan. "Water?"

"There's a small pond," Oliver said. "Seth was particularly interested in that because the plot isn't on the water system."

"Mud!" I nearly shouted. "Junior, there were muddy tracks on Jake's floor, and it hasn't rained the entire time I've been here. His clothes were muddy, too."

"And the pond isn't far from the track," she said.

We looked at each other and smiled. Maybe it wasn't an engraved invitation to the still, but it was close enough.

"Can we borrow this?" Junior said, taking the piece of paper away from Oliver.

"Of course, but—"

"Thank you, you've been a big help. Now I want you to forget we've had this conversation."

"But—"

She just looked at him.

"It's forgotten," he said.

"Good. I owe you one."

He brightened at that. Having Junior owe you a favor was no small thing in Byerly. "I'll just go practice my lines."

"You do that," Junior said. Once he was far enough away, she said, "Are you in the mood for a walk in the woods?"

"I might be." Then I saw the front door open. "Rats! Look who just came in."

"Tell me it's not Mark."

"I would if I could." He looked our way, and though he headed for the stage, I could see he was still looking. "He'll know something's up if we leave in the middle of dress rehearsal."

"He'll probably try to follow us, too. We need a distraction."

I thought for a minute. "I've got an idea. You go wait by the door."

She did so, and I went and found Richard, who was settling up front in preparation for the start of dress rehearsal.

"How's that blocking during Fezziwigg's ball working out?" I said for the benefit of Mark, who was listening.

Richard lifted one eyebrow, then saw Mark. "Much better," he said heartily. "I think that if we get people to move in a counter-clockwise reel pattern rather than in a waltz configuration, that should solve the line-of-sight problems and give more weight to the motion as a metaphor for the change in Scrooge in the past and in the present."

I didn't have the slightest idea what he was talking about, and I wasn't sure Richard did either. The important thing was that Mark walked away.

I leaned in closer and whispered, "Thanks. You scared him off."

"What's the problem?"

I quickly explained what was going on and added, "Junior and I need a distraction to make sure Mark doesn't see us leave. It won't take time away from the rehearsal. Not more than a few minutes, anyway."

"What do you have in mind?"

"Could you throw a tantrum?"

"Hey, I haven't lost my temper in days."

"I know, but if you throw one now, nobody will notice us sneaking out."

"You'll be careful? And you'll stay with Junior?"

"Yes on both counts."

"Now that you mention it, Bob Cratchit has been a bit distracted today. Maybe a tantrum would do him good. When do you need it?"

"In ten minutes. No, make that twenty. I've got to go to the bathroom."

"Good hunting!"

"Thanks, love. Break a leg, or whatever it is I'm supposed to say." I quickly smooched him, and took a bathroom break. By the time I got out, Richard had started rehearsing, and as unobtrusively as possible, I ambled toward Junior. She and I were pretending to talk when I heard Richard yell, "Stop, stop, *Stop!*"

"Right on time," I said.

We watched for a minute or so as Richard blasted poor Tim for not looking cold enough. Then I nudged Junior. Mark had his back to us and was watching Richard stomp in front of the stage and wave his arms around.

Junior said, "I hate to miss this. He's got a real head of steam up this time."

"If you like, he can throw you a tantrum for your very own for Christmas. Let's go."

We got out the door as quickly as possible, and I kept watch while Junior drove out of the parking lot. Then I announced, "We're clear!"

Chapter Thirty-four

Just to be sure Mark hadn't seen us leaving, Junior drove around aimlessly for ten minutes or so, but once we were sure he wasn't following us, she drove to the piece of land Oliver had told us about. I was glad we were in Byerly instead of Boston. At three in the afternoon, it would have already been starting to get dark in Boston, but we still had plenty of daylight left.

"According to this map, the dirt track should be coming up soon," I said.

"There it is." Junior turned down the road.

"I think the phrase *well-cleared track* means something different to realtors," I grumbled as we bumped along. "If I were any further along, this would bounce the baby clean out of me."

"Please, no labor jokes," Junior said. "My nerves can't take it."

"It would help if you weren't going so fast."

"Fair enough," she said as she slowed to a crawl. "Keep an eye out. Seth may have left a marker of some kind."

We had gone maybe five minutes farther, well out of view of the main road, when I saw something flapping on a tree. "What's that?" I said.

A red plastic strip was tied around an outstretched limb.

"That might be it," Junior said. "If we're reading the map right,

the pond is on that side and this is the closest the road comes to it."
She stopped the car, then reached past me to unlock her glove compartment and pull out a shoulder holster and gun.

"Do you think we'll need that?" I said.

"If I thought we'd need it, I wouldn't have let you come along,"
she said, "but there's no reason not to be careful."

I let Junior lead the way, though she was kind enough to slow
down so I could keep up. It was surprisingly quiet in the woods.
Years' worth of pine needles covered the ground, soaking up most of
the noise we were making, and at that time of year, there weren't
many bird sounds.

"It should be somewhere around here," I said, consulting the
map. "What exactly are we looking for, anyway? I've never seen a
still."

"I've seen plenty, but no two look alike. Just look for a good-sized
clearing. I expect that's where we'll find it."

A few yards farther on, we found the pond Oliver had told us
about, and we traced the edge until we stepped into a clearing
maybe twenty or thirty feet around. In the center was a metal contraption.

"Is that it?" I asked Junior.

"That's it."

It wasn't what I'd expected. I'm not sure what I had expected—
maybe something out of Willy Wonka—but this wasn't it. Junior explained the workings. The part that was the cooking chamber was a
stainless steel drum that had been painted mud brown to make it
harder to see. It was set up over a fire pit, a hole lined with rocks.
Condensing coils on top of the drum were attached to a funnel on
top of a metal bucket; that's what the moonshine would drip into.
Nearby was a stack of firewood.

Junior touched the side of the still and peered into the fire pit. "It
doesn't look like it's been used for a few days. I guess Jake's been
too busy with the play."

Off to one side of the clearing, placed where the trees would hide
it from anybody flying overhead, was a small storage building, the
kind Sears sells for people to put their lawnmowers in.

"I don't see a lock," I said.

"I guess they figured they didn't need to bother," Junior said. "If somebody found it, they were screwed anyway." She drew her gun. "Why don't you step back?"

I obeyed, making sure a nice, thick tree was between me and the door to the storage building. Only then did Junior push the door open with one foot. She waited, but when there was no reaction, she peeked inside without exposing much of herself. Finally she straightened up and reholstered her gun. "All clear."

We searched the shed together, but it was a disappointment. While there were plenty of supplies like sugar, yeast, cornmeal, malt, and empty jugs, there was nothing that pointed to Seth Murdstone or his killer.

I did get excited when I found a box of shotgun shells, but Junior said, "That's probably just to sweeten the moonshine."

"To do what?"

"Don't ask me why, but unless shine has a little lead in it, it won't sell. Supposedly it makes it sweeter. Some folks use lead apparatus, but I guess Seth added shot so a little lead would leech in."

"Isn't that dangerous?"

"Of course it's dangerous; people get poisoned all the time. But moonshiners still add lead to increase the market value."

When we gave up on the shed, we poked at the woodpile to see if anything was hidden there.

"Nothing," Junior said in disgust. "Not a damned thing."

"They must have left fingerprints," I said. "Or something!"

"Maybe they smeared some DNA on the equipment," Junior said sarcastically.

"Junior, we are *not* giving up. There has to be something here!"

"I didn't say we were giving up," she said. "I'm just . . . Never mind. Let's keep looking. You circle around that way, and I'll circle around this way."

We moved away from each other, looking at the ground, in the trees, anywhere there might have been some trace of Seth or Jake. I went faster because I couldn't come up with as many places to look as Junior, and I ended up back at the still first. So I had time to notice that there was a blackened circle on one side of the fire pit, as if something had burned there.

"Looks like they had an accident," I said.

Junior came over. "Somebody must have spilled some moonshine into the fire. Seth must have made some potent stuff for it to go up like that. Look at the scorch pattern."

"They're lucky nobody got hurt out here in the middle of nowhere." Then my eyes widened as a couple of things came together. "Junior, maybe somebody did get hurt out here. Maybe this was where Barnaby had his accident."

"What are you talking about?"

"You remember when I was out at the Murdstone house? I saw where Barnaby supposedly burned himself. The carpet was burned, but there wasn't nearly as much damage as I'd have expected, considering how badly hurt he was."

"Are you sure? The report said the carpet was ruined and soot all over the walls and ceiling."

"Who wrote the report?"

Junior's face turned grim. "Mark. Lord knows how many other things he's lied about."

Mark's perfidy was the last thing on my mind. "Jesus, Junior! That's what Barnaby meant in his letter to Santa when he said he was trying to earn enough money to buy Jake a Christmas present. Seth must have been paying him to work out here." I was suddenly furious. "A nine-year-old boy messing with a still! That's why Seth didn't call an ambulance for him."

I thought about the bumpy road Junior and I had driven down to get there, then imagined the pain driving over it must have caused that poor burned boy. If Seth had been standing in front of me right then, I think I would have hit him myself. "Could this be why Seth was killed?"

"I don't see how," Junior said. "That would mean Jake did it, but Jake knew that Seth was in charge when Barnaby was hurt, and I never saw any sign that he blamed him. Why would he suddenly decide to take it out on him?"

"We're still missing something, Junior. I just don't know what."

"We'll get there," she said, patting my back. "Now that I know where this place is, I can come back with a fingerprint kit and everything else I need to prove it's Seth's."

I realized she was smiling. Heck, she was beaming. "You're looking mighty pleased with yourself."

"I'm feeling pretty pleased with myself. Finding this place has taken a long time."

I was feeling pretty smug, too. Maybe we didn't know who'd killed Seth or why, but finding his still felt like a step forward.

Junior said, "I can't wait to tell Daddy. Maybe I'll bring him out here for a Christmas present."

"Beats the heck out of a tie."

"Cheaper, too," Junior said. "We better get going. It's getting late, and I don't think Richard would appreciate it if we get lost."

I followed her back to the Jeep, but just as we reached the dirt track where it was parked, the baby started kicking in an extremely inconvenient place. "Junior? I have to go to the bathroom."

"We'll stop at the first place we see," she said, unlocking the car.

"I can't wait that long," I said.

It must have been an effort for her to resist snickering, but she managed. "I'll wait while you head for the bushes. Be sure to go on the other side of the track from the still. Jake will probably be able to tell we were here, but let's not make it worse than it is."

"Just let me get my pocketbook from the car."

"Why?"

"Kleenex."

"Of course."

Despite my days as a Girl Scout, I absolutely hated going to the bathroom outside. I liked my privacy, especially since I was as big and as graceful as a beached whale. So I went a ways into the woods before I found just the right spot: hidden, with a nearby stump I could hold on to when I squatted.

Even so, I wasn't so far away that I couldn't hear Junior's voice. I had just pulled my pants up and was making a hole in the ground with my sneaker to hide the used Kleenex when she spoke. I froze instantly.

"What the hell are you doing here?" she said.

There was an answer I couldn't quite make out, but the voice sounded familiar.

"Are you crazy?" Junior said.

There was another mumble, and then quite clearly I heard Mark Pope say, "I said, drop it! Don't think I won't shoot you, Junior."

I stayed where I was, trying desperately to figure out what I should do. I didn't want to go toward where Mark had the drop on Junior, because with him armed there was nothing I could do. I didn't want to run the other direction either, because I was sure Mark would see me if I moved, and he'd shoot. The sheer frustration of knowing he had Junior made me sick to my stomach.

"Where's your friend?" Mark asked.

"She's not here."

"You're lying. Stay there while I take a look."

I heard the car door open. I thanked the powers that be for reminding me to take my pocketbook, because if I hadn't grabbed it, it would have been on the front seat, letting Mark know I was nearby.

"You think I'd bring a pregnant woman out to the woods?" Junior said. "I dropped her off before I came, but she knows where I am, and if I'm not back there in half an hour, she's going to call for help."

"Who's she going to call?" Mark said, and I could almost hear the sneer. "I'm the law, remember?"

"She'll call her family," Junior said calmly. "And mine. That's an awful lot of men to come looking for you, Mark. Are you ready for that?"

"Shut up!" he snapped. There was a pause, and then he said, "Put these on." I heard metallic clicks and guessed he'd made Junior put on handcuffs. "Now get in." There were rattlings and the slam of a car door. A minute later the car drove off, leaving me crouched in the woods alone.

Chapter
Thirty-five

Only when Mark and Junior had been gone at least five minutes did I stand up, nervous as a cat that a shot would ring out. There was nothing, so Mark must have really driven off. But where had he taken Junior, and what was he planning to do with her? As I started back toward the dirt track, I realized the more important question was, what was I going to do about it?

Junior's car was gone, and I decided that Mark must have parked his own somewhere else and walked in. Unfortunately, I didn't have any idea of where to look for it, and even if I'd found it instead of getting hopelessly lost in the woods, I wouldn't have been able to drive it without a key.

"Baby," I said to my tummy, "when Mama gets back home, the first thing she's going to do is learn how to hot-wire a car."

It was getting dark and colder, and for once I was glad that being pregnant kept me so warm. "All I've got to do is follow the track back to the main road," I told myself. "Then I can find a phone and call for help." I started walking, my feet already sore and swollen. "On second thought, the first thing I'll do is get a cell phone. Then I'll be able to call somebody to hot-wire a car for me."

I didn't remember coming more than five or ten minutes away from the main road, but that had been in a car. On foot, in the dark, it seemed to take forever, and the bushes and tree limbs looked like something out of *Snow White* as they pulled at my arms and hair.

My mind was moving much faster than the rest of me. Obviously, Junior had been right about Mark. He must have killed Seth and tried to kill Jake. Why else would he risk kidnapping her and . . . I didn't want to think about what else he might risk. There was nothing I could do to stop it if I didn't reach civilization soon. I walked as fast as I could without falling.

An eternity later, I saw headlights, and at first I thought I'd reached the main road. Then I realized the headlights were coming toward me, along the dirt track. Had Mark realized I was out there after all? I bolted into the woods, diving behind a bush as full and round as I was.

The headlights came closer, and I saw it was a pickup truck, not Junior's Jeep or Mark's squad car. The driver was going slowly, even more so than the rough going called for. As the truck got closer, I saw that the driver's window was open, and I heard a voice call out, "Laurie Anne! Are you out there? It's me. Jake Murdstone."

More relieved than I could have said, I stood up and started waving. "Jake! Over here." I stumbled toward the truck.

"Are you all right?" he asked anxiously.

"I'm fine," I said, though I must have looked pretty bad.

He reached over to open the passenger door for me. "Climb in and we'll get you out of here."

I gratefully clambered aboard and tried to catch my breath while he turned the truck around.

"Is Junior all right?" I asked.

"Junior?"

"She sent you after me, didn't she?"

He shook his head. "Nope, it wasn't Junior."

I reached for the door handle, wondering what my chances of survival—and, more important, my baby's chances—would be if I jumped from a moving truck. "Did Mark send you?"

But he shook his head again. "I got a call from a friend of mine. She said you were out in the woods all by your lonesome and could use a ride." He eyed me sideways. "I didn't know you knew Clara Todger."

"Clara?" I blinked. Junior had said the Todgers kept a close watch around the area, but I hadn't realized how close. For a moment I wondered if they'd seen me squatting to do my business, but I shook it off. "What else did she say? Was there anything about Junior?"

"No, just that you needed help, and I should come right away. You ought to get yourself a cell phone before you go traipsing off alone, in your condition and all." Then, all too casually, he asked, "What were you doing out in this neck of the woods anyway?"

"We found a still," I said carefully.

"Is that right?" he said, and I thought he was gripping the steering wheel more tightly.

Just because Mark hadn't sent him didn't mean that he'd be happy about my knowing how he made his money, so I said, "Of course, there's no telling who's been running it, out here in the middle of nowhere. I've heard that hunters run into them all the time and never do find out who they belong to."

"I've heard that too," he said, and his hands relaxed.

I went back to the important part. "Didn't Clara say anything about Junior?"

"What's the matter with Junior? Is she out in the woods, too?"

"Mark's got her!"

"Mark Pope?"

I took a deep breath, not wanting to waste the time to explain, but knowing that I had to. "There's no way to break this to you gently, Jake. Mark killed your father."

"That's impossible."

"I know it sounds crazy, but hear me out." I explained why Junior had become suspicious, and how Mark's actions had only made him look more and more like a killer. "We weren't sure, but he must think we know more than we do or he wouldn't have kidnapped Junior. We've got to find her before it's too late."

"You really think he's going to hurt her?"

"He took her gun and handcuffed her, Jake. What do you think he's going to do?"

He shook his head slowly, but I could understand why he was having problems taking it all in.

I said, "I'm sorry I had to spring it all on you this way, but we've got to figure out where he's taken her."

Jake was quiet for a long time, and by the time he spoke, he'd turned onto the main road. "I think he's heading for my house."

"You might be right," I said. "He's already tried to kill you once. Maybe he's planning to take care of you and Junior at the same time."

"Tried to kill me? What are you talking about?"

"Last night, with the gas."

"That was an accident."

"Mark wanted it to look like an accident—or even suicide." I half laughed. "The funny part is that until that happened, Junior and I thought you might have killed Seth yourself."

"I did," he said quietly.

I think my heart must have skipped a beat, and I put my hand on the door handle again. "What did you say?"

"I did kill Daddy. Mark's been trying to help me hide it, but I'm the one who killed Daddy."

I don't know how many questions ran through my head, but the one that came out was, "Why?"

"Haven't you figured it out? Mark must have thought you had."

I went over all we'd heard and the facts we'd learned, thinking so hard it almost hurt. "Did it have something to do with your son's death?"

"That's right."

"But that was an accident, wasn't it?"

"Yeah, it was an accident, but it should never have happened. Barnaby shouldn't have been at the still."

"Hadn't he been there before?"

"Never," he said, shaking his head vigorously. "Barnaby didn't know what I did for a living, and I didn't want him to know. Moonshining's caused me nothing but trouble. I know worrying about it is part of the reason my mama got so sick when she was so young, and it messed up my marriage, too. I decided it was going to be different for Barnaby. I was stuck with it, because I didn't know how to do anything else, but I wanted Barnaby to take after my brother. To go to school, and get a good job, and make something of himself— maybe even marry a good woman like Florence. That meant he wasn't ever to know anything about the moonshining. Daddy knew how I felt, but he took him out to the still anyway."

Jake was watching the road in front of us, but I wasn't at all sure that was what he was seeing. "It shouldn't have happened, Laurie Anne. Barnaby shouldn't have been there. I might have been able to forgive Daddy for that, and even for the accident, but I couldn't forgive him for lying to me. He looked me right in the eye and told me that Barnaby got hurt at the house—even made me think it was that space heater I bought that did it to him. Those days and nights I spent with Barnaby at the hospital, wishing I could make it quit hurting, and thinking I'd done it to him myself . . ." He took a sobbing breath. "Then to find out that Daddy had lied . . ."

"How did you find out? Was it Barnaby's letter to Santa Claus?"

"Mrs. Gamp gave it to me that day at rehearsal. She thought it was so sweet that Barnaby had been working to get me a present, but I realized that Barnaby had been working for Daddy. I wanted to believe that it was with the chairs, but I had to know for sure. I saw Daddy going to take a cigarette break, and I went with him. Before I got a chance to say anything, Daddy handed me the cane he was using for Scrooge and asked if I could sand it down because it was rough on his hands." He snorted, as if amazed that anybody would care about anything like that. "I asked him about Barnaby, and that's when he told me how my boy really got hurt."

He looked at me, but I was too appalled to speak.

Jake took a ragged breath. "You know he even got Barnaby to lie for him? Daddy told him that if he told anybody the truth, the police would put Daddy and me in jail, and Barnaby would have to go to an orphanage. They don't even have orphanages anymore, but Barnaby believed him, just like I always did. So he lied, even though he was afraid Santa Claus would hold it against him. Daddy said he was sorry, like that was enough. He expected me to forgive him, right then and there. Can you imagine that?"

"So you . . ." I couldn't bring myself to actually say it.

"So I took that cane and I hit him. As hard as I could."

"Did you mean for him to die?"

"I don't know, Laurie Anne, I swear I don't. But I didn't call for help afterward. I just left him there. So I don't guess it matters what I meant to do, does it?"

I wasn't sure of the answer to that one myself.

"I should have gone ahead and told Junior what happened, but I couldn't."

"Because you were afraid?" I said.

"Afraid? What did I have to be afraid of? My boy was gone. My daddy was gone. What else could anybody do to me that would matter? I wasn't afraid. I was ashamed?"

"Of what you'd done?" I said, not quite understanding.

"No, not of what I'd done. I was ashamed of what Daddy had done." He made a sound that might have been a laugh if it hadn't been so sad. "David was always ashamed of Daddy's moonshining. He tried not to be, but I know he was. Not me. I was proud of the way he pulled the wool over everybody's eyes. I knew we had to keep it quiet because of the law, but if it hadn't been for that, I'd have shouted it from the housetops. But I couldn't stand the thought of people knowing how Daddy had let his only grandchild get hurt. How when Barnaby was in all that pain, all Daddy could think of was covering his tracks so nobody would find the still." He looked at me. "Would you want folks knowing that about your daddy?"

I couldn't even imagine being in that situation, but I said, "I guess I wouldn't."

He was quiet then, as if he'd explained everything, but I still had questions. "How did Mark get involved?"

"Didn't y'all figure that out? Mark said you would if we weren't careful."

"Figure out what?"

"That Mark was part of it. Of the moonshining, I mean."

"What?"

"He didn't do any of the work himself. He just told us when to lay low and when it was safe to deliver. When Andy Norton took a notion to watch us, he'd tell us that, too."

"Why?"

He looked at me as if I was crazy. "For the money, of course. Daddy paid him the first of every month."

"Mark's been taking bribes?" I leaned back in my seat, both aghast that he would do such a thing, and aggravated that Junior and I had suspected Mark of the wrong crime. "How much did he want for helping you cover up your father's murder?"

Jake looked shocked. "That didn't have anything to do with money. After I saw Daddy's—after I saw what I'd done, I meant to come clean. So as soon as I could, I told Mark what had happened. He said he didn't blame me, that no court in the country would convict me. The thing was, if it went to court everybody would find out about Daddy's moonshining."

"Not to mention finding out about Mark being on the take," I added. That would have quashed his hopes of being police chief forever, in Byerly or anywhere else.

"That wasn't it. We were worried about David and Florence. How would it be for them if everybody found out?"

"Mark cared about that?" I asked suspiciously.

"Of course he did. He said that there were some things people didn't need to know."

I wriggled uncomfortably at that. I'd held on to more than one secret myself—things I'd decided people didn't need to know. Was I any better than Mark and Jake?

"Mark said we were lucky that Junior was on vacation, because she wouldn't understand. He figured he'd pretend to investigate until things died down, and nobody would be hurt. He even hid the cane where nobody would find it."

"It didn't bother him that a murderer would be walking around?" Then, remembering that I was sitting next to the murderer in question, I said, "I mean . . ."

"I know I'm a murderer," Jake said. "I killed my own daddy—there ain't nothing on earth lower than me."

"Then you did try to kill yourself last night."

"I keep telling you," he said, irritated, "that was an accident."

"But . . ." I couldn't understand why he'd admit to murder but not suicide. "How could it have been an accident, Jake? My aunts didn't leave the stove on. I saw Aunt Nora use it to make a pitcher of iced tea, and I was there when she turned it off. Unless you did it yourself when fixing dinner . . ."

"I didn't exactly eat dinner," he said sheepishly. "I meant to, but I got to drinking and fell asleep."

Passed out, in other words. "Then how did the stove get turned on, and how did the pilot light go out? I'm telling you, it was Mark. He must have decided that killing you was the only way to cover his tracks. Once you were dead, he'd have produced evidence proving you killed Seth. Didn't you say he's got the cane you used? It's bound to have your fingerprints and bloodstains from Seth. All he'd have to do is plant it nearby. He'd probably have claimed to have found out about your moonshining, too. What would that have done to David and Florence?"

"Mark wouldn't do that," he said, shaking his head over and over.

I couldn't really blame Jake for being taken in by Mark. How many years had he been fooling everybody in Byerly? "What now?" I asked. "Are you going to kill me, too?"

The car swerved sharply, then he pulled back into the lane. "Jesus, of course not. What do you think I am?"

I couldn't think of an answer other than the obvious one, and saying that might change his mind. "Then what are we going to do? Where are we going?"

"We're going to talk to Mark. I can't let him do anything to Junior, not on my account. He's done enough to keep me out of trouble."

I spent the rest of the drive trying to talk Jake into stopping so I could call somebody else for help, but he wouldn't do it. He kept saying that he'd handle it himself, and when I pointed out that Mark was probably waiting for him and had likely set a trap, all he would say was that Mark had no reason to hurt him. It didn't matter how much logic I spouted, how convincing my arguments were, or how fast I talked. He just kept shaking his head. I even tried pretending that there was something wrong with the baby. Maybe a visitation from Marley's ghost would have convinced him, but nothing less than that would.

If we'd passed close enough to one single car, I'd have pounded on the car horn or waved for help through the window, but the roads leading to the Murdstone house were empty that night.

Finally we turned into the long, dark driveway to the house. I'd expected Jake to drive all the way down, but he stopped about halfway, where a slight bend in the road blocked anybody in the house from seeing us.

"You better wait here," he said. "Just in case."

"You're starting to realize what Mark's been up to, aren't you? That's why you don't want me to come with you."

"No, it's just that—I figure we can't be too careful, not with you in the family way." Darned if he didn't reach over to pat my tummy. "You don't ever want to lose a child, Laurie Anne." He started to get out.

"Can't you leave me the keys so I can keep the heater running?" I said plaintively. It was lame, but I figured it wouldn't hurt to try.

Jake shook his head. "You wait here. If I'm not back soon . . ." He paused, and I think he couldn't stand to consider why he wouldn't come back. "Just wait until I get back."

He pushed the door closed and silently picked his way down the gravel driveway toward the house.

Chapter
Thirty-six

Needless to say, I had no intention of waiting for Jake. The question was, what could I do to help Junior? Even if I hadn't been waddling, I wouldn't have known what to do against an armed police officer. Mark might be crooked, but even Junior had said he was competent.

What I really needed were reinforcements, but the Murdstone house was so isolated that I might as well have been back in the woods. The Todgers had played guardian angel once already; I couldn't count on them doing it again. I still didn't have a cell phone and I still hadn't learned how to hot-wire a car.

Maybe I didn't have to, I thought. Surely Jake had a spare key somewhere. I climbed out of the truck and wasted five minutes searching both bumpers to see if he'd hidden a spare set before I gave it up as a lost cause.

So I couldn't drive anywhere, and in my current condition, I wasn't likely to get to the nearest neighbor fast enough to do any good. What did that leave?

I looked speculatively down the driveway. There was a phone I could reach—if I was lucky. Though I wasn't about to try to sneak into the house, I remembered seeing a phone in Seth's workshop. The door had been unlocked the previous day. Dared I hope that it was still unlocked? And that Mark hadn't cut the phone lines? And that . . . ?

I stopped myself. There was no point in imagining all the things that could go wrong, because there was nothing I could do about any of them anyway. So, just as I had known I would, I followed Jake to the house. Later on, I wondered if Jake hadn't also known that I would eventually come after him.

I did make a quick stop. I was trying to decide whether my pocketbook would be a hinderance or a help when I thought of something. Richard had joked for years that my bag was so heavy it must be full of rocks. Though I hated to do it to a brand-new D'Arcy bag, a bag of rocks could make a formidable weapon. I upended the bag on the seat of Jake's truck and then filled it up with gravel from the driveway. It was a testimonial to the designer's workmanship that the shoulder strap held.

Carrying it didn't slow me down much, because if I'd gone any slower, I'd have been going backward. As much as my nerves wanted me to hurry, I knew that I couldn't afford to be heard. That meant taking my time.

Once I got within sight of the house, I glued myself to the shadows, thankful that Seth had never felt the need to knock down trees and create a featureless lawn where I would have stuck out like a sore thumb. Junior's Jeep was parked in front of the door, and there were lights on in the house, but with the curtains drawn I couldn't tell where anybody was—or, more important, what condition they were in. I was tempted to creep closer just to see if I could peek in a window, but I resisted. There would be plenty of time to peek once I had a brace of my cousins and Junior's brothers-in-law at my side.

Instead, I kept going toward the workshop in the backyard, wincing each time I stepped on a twig or rustled a fallen leaf. Only when I made it to the door without being discovered did I relax. I reached for the knob. The only thing that saved me from walking right in was a loud thump from inside. I'd read about people's hearts jumping into their throats, but that was the first time I knew what it meant. I inched away from the door and to the side of the building farthest from the house. I don't think I even breathed until I was around the corner, where I couldn't be seen.

There was a small window on that side, and since it was only a workshop, Seth hadn't bothered to put up curtains or blinds. He had stacked half-finished chairs in front of it—not enough to keep me from looking in, but enough that I felt somewhat concealed from whoever was inside.

It wasn't just curiosity, though I had enough of that to burn. I needed to see who was inside so I would know if there was anybody left in the house.

The first thing I saw was an oddly familiar assortment of tubing and pots set up in the center of the room. It was the camp stove underneath it that helped me recognize it as a still. Before I could even begin to guess why it was there, I saw Mark dragging Junior across the floor. She was so limp that, for one horrible second, I thought she was dead. Then I heard her moan as Mark dropped her like a sack of potatoes.

Jake was in there, too, watching Mark lean down to unfasten the handcuffs from around Junior's wrists.

"You shouldn't have hit her like that, Mark," Jake said.

"I had to," Mark said matter-of-factly. "We can't let her body be found wearing handcuffs, and I couldn't take them off with her awake. It's got to look like she got caught in her own trap, which is exactly what she deserves for trying to plant a still on your property. If I hadn't followed her out here and caught her, she'd have put you in jail for moonshining, and then it would only have been a matter of time until she sweated the rest of it out of you. Then you'd have a murder rap on top of everything else."

What was he talking about? Mark hadn't followed Junior to the Murdstone house. He'd kidnapped her. And Junior hadn't planted that still. The man was laying down lies in layers, like Richard's lasagna. Surely Jake didn't believe him, not after what I'd told him.

"I can't go through with this, Mark," he said. "There's got to be another way."

"I'm telling you, this is the only thing that's going to save us. Not to mention your brother. Isn't David worth more to you than her?"

"What about Laurie Anne?" Jake said. I tensed, afraid he was about to tell Mark that he'd left me in the truck. But all he said was, "She'll never believe this, even if everybody else does."

"Then we'll take care of her, too," Mark said, sounding pleased at the idea.

"Mark, the woman's carrying an innocent baby."

"So what? What's one Burnette brat more or less?" Then he must have realized that hadn't been the best thing to say to a man who'd recently lost his son. "We probably won't have to worry about her anyway," he added quickly. "She and her husband will be back in Boston in another week or two."

"But Junior—"

"Forget Junior!" Mark boomed. "It's her or us. With her gone I'll be police chief, just like I should have been all along, and I'll make sure the record shows she accidentally ignited the still she was setting up and burned to death. Nothing could be simpler. We won't even have to fake the evidence this time."

Mark went to fiddle with the still, so he didn't see the look on Jake's face. If he had, he would never have turned his back on the man.

"Mark," Jake said softly, "did you know Daddy lied about where Barnaby got hurt?"

"Of course not," Mark said, still not realizing his slip of the tongue. "I told you that."

"You say a lot of things, Mark, but I'm not sure I believe you anymore. What did you mean, 'this time'?"

"What are you talking about?"

"You said we won't have to fake the evidence *this time.* Did you fake it before? Was it you who made it look like Barnaby hurt himself here, instead of at the still?"

Mark finally turned to face the other man. "You know I wouldn't have done that, Jake. It was Seth."

"That's what I thought, but when did he have a chance? Daddy was wrong to take Barnaby out to the still, and wrong to lie about it, but at least he got Barnaby up to the hospital as fast as he could. He stayed there with him until I got there, and then he stayed with me. When did he have time to burn that hole in the playroom floor?"

Mark's eyes widened for a second, then I could almost see what he'd decided to do. "The pressure is really getting to you," he said. "Tell you what, Junior's not going anywhere. Let's go to the house and work this out. Okay, buddy?"

Jake nodded, and this time he was the one to turn his back on the wrong man. Mark yanked his nightstick from his belt and whacked Jake across the back of his head. Jake dropped like a rock.

Mark looked down at the man as he replaced the nightstick, not looking apologetic or sorry, just irritated. Then he went back to messing with the still and the camp stove underneath.

Every muscle in my body was screaming for me to do something—anything—to save Junior and Jake, but I couldn't think of what I should do. Maybe I could make it to the phone in the house without Mark catching me, but what then? Nobody would be able to get there in time to do any good. The only one who could do anything to help was me, and I'd never felt so helpless in my life.

Mark had pulled out a jug and was splashing the contents around the workshop, taking particular care to slosh some on both Junior and Jake. Next he pulled a gun that had to be Junior's out of his waistband and placed it in her holster. Presumably he knew it would look suspicious for her body to be found without it. Then he glanced around the room, with the same expression Richard always had when blocking an act on stage. Clearly, he was making sure the scene was set properly. Then he picked up an open can of Sterno from the camp stove, walked toward the door, and pulled a lighter from his pocket.

Without really thinking, I ran toward the workshop door, carrying my rock-filled pocketbook. Mark must have seen the movement out of the corner of his eye, because he started to turn my way, but I'd already swung the bag, and it hit him across the shoulder blades. The breath rushed out of his mouth, and he stumbled forward, dropping the Sterno and his lighter.

Unfortunately, he was still standing, and he fumbled at his holster. I hefted the pocketbook to take another swing, but he drew his gun first, and I froze as he aimed the barrel right at my midsection.

"I should have known," he gasped. "The bitch lied to me, and—"

I never found out what he was going to say or do next, because Jake erupted out of the workshop and slammed into Mark. The gun fired, but the shot went wild as the men rolled around on the ground. Mark still had the gun, but Jake had a grip on his wrist, keeping him from aiming it.

I headed toward them, ready to use my pocketbook again. I knew I had just as good a chance of hitting Jake as Mark, but I didn't care if I had to knock both of them out to make sure Mark was out of commission.

Then I smelled something burning. I saw flames erupting from the workshop, and I realized that Mark's stray gunshot must have gone inside and set the fire he'd intended all along. I dropped the pocketbook, raced into the workshop to where Junior was, and wasted precious seconds trying to rouse her. As the air grew hotter, I gave up and grabbed her under her arms to drag her from the building. I didn't know what was going on outside, but anywhere had to be safer than in that firetrap.

Junior started coughing as we went, but though I had to pat out a burning cinder that landed on her side, we made it out all right. Between the coughing and the cold air hitting her, she started to come to.

Jake and Mark were still grappling, but it looked like Mark was winning. Jake must have been weakened from the blow to the head, and my pocketbook hadn't done nearly as much damage to Mark as I'd wanted it to. Once I was sure Junior was safe for the moment, I looked around for another weapon.

But then Junior croaked, "Laurie Anne, get out of the way!"

She had her gun in her hand—I'd forgotten Mark had given it back to her. I obeyed instantly, and Junior fired into the air above Mark's and Jake's heads.

They both jerked, and Jake's grip on Mark's arm slipped. Mark pushed him off and twisted around toward Junior. A shot cut through the night, but for an endless second I didn't know who'd been shot. Then Mark fell to the dirt while Junior stood motionless.

My knees gave way and I sank to the ground, my arms wrapped around my belly. Junior waited until she was sure Mark was no longer moving. Then she walked toward him, not letting her aim waver as she kicked the gun away from his hand. Only when she'd reached down to pick it up did she look back at me.

"Laurie Anne, are you hurt?"

"No, just—I'm fine."

"Is the baby all right?"

"Kicking up a storm."

She nodded and turned her attention toward Jake. "Are you all right?" she said.

"Junior, I didn't mean for—" he said. "I didn't know what Mark had—"

"Jake, I don't know what all happened in there or what's been going on between you and Mark. With him gone, I might never find out for sure. What happens next is up to you."

She and he looked at each other for a long moment, their faces transformed into angles and shadows by the light of the burning building behind us.

Finally Jake spoke. "I always told my boy to tell the truth, and now it's time for me to act the way I taught him to."

She held up one finger, and said, "Let me say something first. Jake Murdstone, you have the right to remain silent. If you give up that right . . ." She went through the rest of the Miranda warning. "Now go ahead, if you still want to."

He took a deep breath. "Chief Norton, I'd like to confess to the murder of my father, Seth Murdstone."

Chapter
Thirty-seven

If anybody had been watching the Murdstone house from above that night, it would have looked like nothing so much as an ant hill that's been stirred up with a stick. Junior held off on arresting Jake until she could take a hose to the still burning workshop while she used her cell phone to call the fire department. Then she called her brother Trey, and since it would have been awkward for either of them to be in charge of the crime scene, he brought along the county police.

Meanwhile, I went inside to use the phone to call Richard at the recreation center, where dress rehearsal had just ended. He high-tailed it over to the house, pushed past the county police, who were trying their best to secure the scene, and grabbed hold of me. He kept asking if I was all right, if the baby was all right, and though I insisted that we were, he said he wanted a doctor to look at me immediately.

Dr. Connelly, the medical examiner, had just arrived, so he postponed examining Mark Pope's body in order to check me out. Since Dr. Connelly had a general practice in addition to his duties as medical examiner, it wasn't as grim as it sounded. He confirmed what I'd told Richard, though he sternly ordered me to eat a hot dinner and get a good night's sleep, and suggested that I avoid attacking armed men with my pocketbook.

I guess the rumors started when Richard tore out of the recreation center, because it wasn't long before David and Florence showed up. I wasn't there when David found out what really happened to his father. Nobody was, other than David and Jake. Junior put them into a room alone and let them work it out for themselves. Whatever was said, when they came out, David had his arm around his little brother's shoulders, as if to protect him from the world. Florence took one look and announced that she would be representing her brother-in-law.

One of the county officers took my statement, and once that was done, Junior came over long enough to give me the abandoned contents of my pocketbook, and to tell Richard and me to leave. I wanted to hug her, but I figured she wouldn't want anybody to see. Darned if she didn't hug me instead.

Richard and I drove slowly out of the Murdstone's driveway, partly because of all the police cars and such parked along it, and partly because Richard wanted to hold my hand. Otherwise, we wouldn't have noticed the man sitting in a car in the back of the line.

We pulled up alongside, and I rolled down my window while the driver of the other car did the same.

"Tim? Is that you?"

"Laurie Anne, are you all right?"

"I'm fine."

"I heard somebody was shot."

"Mark Pope. He's dead."

"Jake?"

"He's fine." I hesitated, but knew it was better for him to know. "Jake killed your father, Tim." I quickly explained what I knew. "I'm sorry."

"Me, too. I just wish . . . I guess it doesn't matter now. Thanks for telling me."

"You take care," I said.

We left him sitting there alone.

I talked Richard into going through the drive-through at Hardee's on the way back to Aunt Maggie's, which was silly. Half the Burnette family was waiting for us, and of course Aunt Nora had brought more food than even I could eat. She plucked the Hardee's bag out of my hand and made me sit down to a real meal.

Richard wanted to put me to bed as soon as I'd swallowed the last bite of apple pie, but I stayed awake long enough to tell everybody what had happened. Then I went to sleep, knowing that they'd spread the word to any family members who weren't there—not to mention the rest of the town.

Richard wanted me to stay in bed the next day and even volunteered to stay with me, but I promised to take it easy and shooed him off so he could go to the recreation center. Otherwise, he probably would have exploded. He was so excited, he was nearly vibrating. Though there was no rehearsal, he had plenty of things to do to get ready.

To Richard's immense relief, David and Florence were still going to play their roles, and everybody pitched in to take over Jake's job. Though Oliver tried not to show it, he was clearly delighted that he was going to get to say the charity collector's lines.

Come curtain time, I'd expected Richard to stay backstage where he could issue last-minute instructions, but instead he was sitting next to me in the front row. Admittedly, he was holding my hand a little too tightly for the first few minutes, but eventually he relaxed, and I think he honestly enjoyed the show. I know I did, and I cried at the end when the audience gave a standing ovation. Richard nearly cried, too, when the cast and crew presented him with a copy of *The Annotated Christmas Carol*, inscribed by everybody.

The play was a huge success. There were so many curtain calls over the three-night run that, assuming one night out a week, Aunt Maggie was going to be eating dinners with Big Bill Walters for the next two months.

Vasti was ecstatic, both because of adding another feather to her cap and because Sally's Holiday Follies turned out to be all too appropriately named. Apparently, Sally had caught Bitsy's cold the day she came over to torment Vasti, and had managed to give it to half the people in her show, meaning that she had to cancel some of the best acts at the last minute. Dorcas Walters caught it, too, but refused to stay home, and her voice gave out in the middle of her dramatic reading of *A Visit from St. Nicholas*. She blamed Sally for the humiliation, which was hardly fair, but Vasti didn't mind.

Especially when it came out that Sally really had been playing practical jokes. Not the dangerous ones, but she had set up the merely annoying pranks, and she'd been the one to leave the boxes of costumes outside the recreation center after all. When she saw Mark Pope as she was driving away, she thought he'd seen her, but since nothing ever happened, she decided she'd gotten lucky. Still, it had scared her enough to make her stop playing pranks.

It turned out that Mark had seen her. He told Jake he was going to start playing jokes himself, and that was when they turned nasty. He'd gotten a skeleton key for the building and set up some of the pranks at night, and arranged others while supposedly investigating Seth's murder. As Vasti had suspected, the tricks really were intended to stop the show or, failing that, to distract Junior and me.

But Vasti wouldn't cancel the show, and Junior and I wouldn't stop investigating. Mark was afraid we were getting close, which was why he'd followed us to the mall that day. Then he realized that I might have seen him when he rigged the scenery flat to fall. He'd been afraid all along that Junior was suspicious, so he decided the only way to protect himself was to kill Jake. At some point in his dealings with Seth, he'd gotten a key to their house, and he knew that Jake had been drinking heavily since his father's death. All he had to do was wait for Jake to pass out, and then sneak in to turn the gas on.

When that didn't work, he planned to booby-trap the Murdstone still, but he ran into Junior on his way there. It wasn't until a week or so later that his car was found nearby, hidden in some bushes. Scrooge's cane, the one Jake used to kill Seth, was in the trunk. Junior might never have found it had it not been for an anonymous phone call. I guessed Clara Todger was practicing her peculiar brand of civic-mindedness again.

At any rate, it's hard to know exactly what Mark meant to do that night at the Murdstone house. Junior, who'd still been conscious at the time, said he'd been mighty surprised when Jake arrived, so he'd probably planned to set a trap that would kill both of them.

Thinking on his feet, he'd convinced Jake that Junior was his only target, but when Jake balked, he went back to the original plan. At least, until my pocketbook and I interfered.

As Vasti had hoped, Tim Topper invited the cast to Pigwick's for a party following the last performance. After I happily ate a heaping plate of pulled pork and hush puppies, Richard and I called Tim over to talk.

First, of course, Richard and Tim had to congratulate themselves.

"Richard, I don't think I've ever had as much fun in my life as doing that play. I don't mean to downplay the bad parts, but as soon as that curtain went up, all of that went away."

"You did a terrific job," Richard said.

"I couldn't have done it without you."

"No, you had the part down cold, and the stage presence is yours alone."

"Thanks, but you—"

"You were both great," I interjected. "Awesome, wonderful, incredible, amazing, whatever adjectives y'all want to use."

"Sorry," Richard said. " 'He that is proud eats up himself; pride is his own glass, his own trumpet, his own chronicle.' "

"*Great Expectations?*" Tim asked.

"*Troilus and Cressida*. Act Two, Scene Three." With the play over, Richard had happily gone back to his usual source of quotes.

"I wouldn't mind trying out some Shakespeare, too, if you'll come back to direct," Tim said. "Maybe *Othello*. I think I've got greasepaint in my blood."

Before they could start patting each other on the back again, I said, "Actually, it's your blood I wanted to ask about. Have you told the Murdstones yet?"

"I didn't think it was the right time, Laurie Anne—not with Jake's situation and all the talk about Seth. The last thing they need is to have an illegitimate brother showing up."

"Then again," I said, "it might do them good to have more family around right about now. You can't have too many shoulders to lean on."

"You think?"

"Yes, I do. Besides," I said with a grin, "at this point, you're the white sheep in the family."

Everybody in the room turned to see what had made Tim laugh so loudly, but we wouldn't explain. A few days later, I heard through the grapevine that the Murdstones had welcomed Tim with open arms. I was glad. Maybe Tim hadn't gotten the father he wanted, but at least he had two brothers and a sister-in-law who wanted him. That made a pretty good Christmas present.

What with the play wrap-up, the finishing touches on our Christmas preparations, and then the big day itself, it wasn't until the day after Christmas that I had a chance to go see Junior. She was back on duty, of course, and I found her at the police station. She was sitting behind her desk, and though there were papers in front of her, I suspected she was really just enjoying being back where she belonged.

"Hey there, Laurie Anne," she said. "Did you get everything you wanted for Christmas?"

"Pretty much. Richard even got me another D'Arcy pocketbook. How about you?"

"No complaints. Though I could have used a new deputy in my stocking."

"I am sorry about Mark. How it all turned out, I mean." Though I didn't think him much of a loss, I knew that shooting him hadn't come easily to her.

"I'm sorry I never realized who he really was. Daddy's feeling even more got away with, after having hired and trained Mark himself. Here Mark had been on the take all these years, and we never had the first clue." She shook her head. "You remember how Seth told the Todgers he left Mr. Gamp's body because he thought he heard sirens? According to Jake, he really did hear a siren. Mark was there that night and offered to forget what he'd seen. That's how far back it went."

"I take it that Jake's cooperating."

"Oh, yeah. Florence is making a case for temporary insanity or diminished capacity, because of what happened to Barnaby. So the more Jake cooperates, the better that's going to look to the judge and D.A."

"You realize that he could have turned me over to Mark, and Mark only hit him because Jake wouldn't let him kill you."

"I know. Maybe I won't add him to my Christmas card list, but I can't blame him for what my own deputy did. You can bet I'm going to be more careful about who I hire next time." She looked at me. "I don't suppose you're interested in law enforcement, are you?"

"Me?" I laughed. "Thanks anyway, but I'd never be able to keep up with all the rules you've got."

"Just a thought," she said. "If you ever do decide to turn professional, I'd be proud to have you work with me."

"Junior, that's the nicest thing you've ever said to me."

She looked alarmed. "You're not going to hug me again, are you?"

"Hey, it was you who hugged me last time."

"So it was," she said. "I never thanked you for what you did that night."

"You don't have to. In fact, I ought to apologize for not helping when Mark kidnapped you."

"Laurie Anne, don't you ever think that," she said firmly. "There was nothing you could have done to stop Mark. He was armed, he was trained, and he was desperate. The only reason I was talking so loud was to warn you. I wanted you to stay where you were."

"I know, but if Clara Todger hadn't sent Jake to come get me—"

"But she did. By the way, when I spoke to her the other day, she asked after you. And she says she loves your pocketbook."

I laughed. "Maybe I'll get her one as a thank-you."

Junior's face turned serious. "Laurie Anne, even though I appreciate your saving me more than I can say, I don't want you ever to put my welfare ahead of your baby's again. The day I let anything happen to a Burnette baby is the day I'd have to leave town. Because if your family didn't get a hold of me, my own mama would."

"I'll make a New Year's resolution to be more careful." Then I asked, "Do you think I should stop these investigations? For the baby's sake?"

"I don't know, Laurie Anne. It wouldn't hurt for you to be more careful, but that's true of anybody. Having a baby changes you, but it's not supposed to change you into somebody else."

"You lost me."

"Would I still be myself if I quit being a cop?"

"Lord, Junior, I can't imagine you doing anything else."

"Then what you have to ask yourself is this: can you imagine yourself not getting into these situations?"

I tried to picture myself no longer asking questions and tracking down answers, all the while knowing that solving problems made me feel special in a way nothing else did. I felt as if I was really helping people, making a difference, and other Peace Corps slogans. It wasn't that I *looked* for dead bodies, but I couldn't seem to ignore any that came my way. "I don't think I can, Junior."

"That's what I thought."

I got another hug out of her before I left, and as I walked out to the car, I rubbed my tummy and said, "Baby, we're going to have some interesting times together."